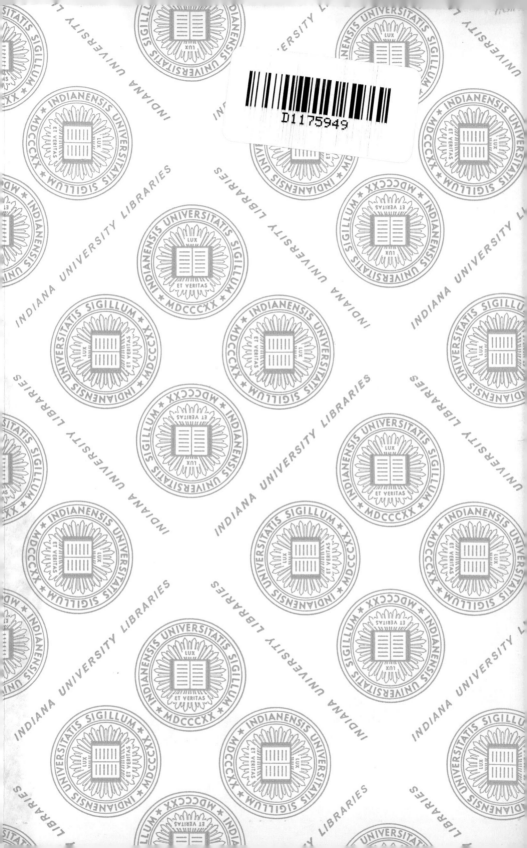

EXISTENTIAL THINKING

EXISTENTIAL THINKING

A Philosophical Orientation

by BERNARD J. BOELEN Ph.D.

ERDER AND HERDER

1971
HERDER AND HERDER NEW YORK
232 Madison Avenue, New York 10016

First published in 1968 by Duquesne University Press

Library of Congress Catalog Card Number: 68–57483
© 1971 by Herder and Herder, Inc.
Manufactured in the United States

TABLE OF CONTENTS

A FOREWORD is usually a postscript of the author placed at the beginning of the book for the benefit of the reader. The original objective of this study was to provide the uninitiated reader with a "Philosophical Orientation" that could serve as an introductory chapter for our projected book: *Mature Existence*. However, both the primordiality of our point of departure, and the actual thinking within this originative perspective proved to be so illuminating that we allowed ourselves to be guided by the intrinsic development of its content rather than by the mere motivation of any extrinsic objectives. The outcome is the present volume which, as the title indicates, is a comprehensive study on *Existential Thinking*. The original objective still stands, but the format has changed.

The intrinsic purpose of this book is also its original contribution. It is an attempt to systematically re-think philosophy out of its original beginning and most fundamental perspective: *the primordial phenomenon of wonder*. The insight that wonder does not merely "precede" philosophy, but remains its lasting source and guiding inspiration is the leitmotiv and focal point throughout the present study. It is this insight that places this book in its own original perspective. For although the idea that philosophy begins in wonder has become a commonplace in the history of philosophy, it has been a common practice *not* to begin philosophy in wonder. Wonder has been regarded as a trigger which sets the dynamism of philosophy in action without playing an intrinsic role in this dynamism. The present volume is an endeavor to show how philosophy itself is the progressive articulation of the very phenomenon of primordial wonder. Consequently, as this book begins, so too it ends, in wonder.

From the very outset, however, the reader should be reminded that there are two sets of possible obstacles that may prevent him from grasping the true meaning and significance of our discussion. The first set of possible impediments is due to the situation in which the reader may find himself, the second is inherent in the very nature of primordial wonder and existential thinking.

On the basis of possible prejudices, preconceived ideas or uncritically accepted opinions the reader may easily mistake primordial wonder for what it is not. He may decide that "of course" we are speaking of a "merely subjective" or "personal" experience, or of a "purely psychological" phenomenon. He may take it for granted that wonder is a being startled by something sensational. He may identify wonder with the frivolous curiosity of the sight-seer, or with the psychological reaction of a man who is confronted with unexplainable contradictions. Yet, *primordial wonder* as it is used in this book is none of these. Misconceptions such as these will naturally induce the reader to regard any philosophy rooted in this phenomenon as "unscientific," and will make him relegate all its basic insights to the realm of myths and dreams. We, therefore, invite the reader to follow the development of this study with an open mind and not to allow any previous approaches to our subject, or to philosophy in general, to intervene. Any preconceived systematization or classification of the author's intentions will prevent the reader from grasping the true meaning of this book and will lead to serious misunderstandings.

In addition, there are major obstacles, especially for the first beginner, inherent in the very nature of existential thinking. In the first place, the primordial phenomenon of wonder is an all-encompassing experience which entails that "the truth is in the whole" (Hegel), and that every step in philosophy involves the whole of philosophy. Every line implies the entire text. Consequently, it is unavoidable that the initial pages come into sharp focus only in retrospect. The reader, therefore, is asked to be patient with provisional obscurities, and to be content if only he can comprehend the whole.

Moreover, existential thinking as the progressive articulation of primordial wonder *is* the articulated self-questioning of its actual beginning. It is the progressive self-foundation, the ever renewed and enriched self-beginning of its primary data. This implies that a philosopher is essentially a "beginner": either a "first beginner," or an "advanced beginner." A philosopher is always "caught in the act," his thinking is "thinking thought" *(pensée pensante),* and never "finished thought" *(pensée pensée).* Philosophy cannot "result" in a static body of knowledge that can be "learned" and handed over from generation to generation. Everything would be much simpler, indeed, if this were the case, if we had to deal only with static concepts, abstract definitions, straight thinking and finished systems. It would be much simpler, but it would be unphilosophical. For fundamental thinking, as the book will demonstrate, is circular, experiential, open, dynamic and multi-dimensional. It goes without saying that all this cannot be "justified" in a foreword. Philosophy is self-justifying, and a book on philosophy cannot be verified by anything other than itself. A book on philosophy that does not "speak for itself" does not speak at all.

Rather than presenting the reader with the empty husks of a monolithic system, which would be as repulsive as it is unphilosophical, we make an attempt to be a guide for the reader that helps him to enter into the act of personal thinking out of his own questioning-being-in-the-world. This book hopes to encourage the reader to philosophize for himself, and to fulfill his self-questioning thinking in a personal dialogue with the great philosophers in general, and with the existential thinkers of today in particular. The author has not directed his book to any particular audience. It is hoped that it will prove illuminating to "first beginners," readers with no previous experience in the field, and to "advanced beginners," those who already have a comprehensive background in the subject.

We would like to acknowledge our indebtedness to Duquesne University for lightening our academic duties during a period of several years. We wish to express our special gratitude to the Kavir Institute of Paris for its generous Grant-in-Aid. And, finally, we owe special thanks to the undergraduate and graduate students in our courses at Duquesne University who through their genuine interest and creative participation have contributed so much to the inspiration of this study.

FOR MIA,
JOSEPHINE, LOUIS AND MIRIAM

CHAPTER 1

THE QUESTION OF
THE BEGINNING

A "Philosophical Orientation," it goes without saying, should begin with the beginning of philosophy. The first question, therefore, that calls for an answer is the question, "How should we begin philosophy?" This question is quite simple, indeed. But a brief reflection on the question leads up to an unsolvable antinomy which makes us sceptical about the very possibility of philosophy.

The question, "How should we begin philosophy?" presupposes in the first place that we know what philosophy is. How, otherwise, could we know *what* to begin? Consequently, the beginning of philosophy presupposes a knowledge of philosophy, but a knowledge of philosophy presupposes a knowledge of the beginning of philosophy. Does not this antinomy clearly demonstrate the impossibility of philosophy and the redundancy of our question? For if we do not know what philosophy is, we do not know what we are asking. But if we know what philosophy is, we have already begun, and the question, "How should we begin philosophy?" becomes superfluous.

THE IRRELEVANCE OF LOGIC FOR THE BEGINNING OF PHILOSOPHY

This, indeed, is the logical outcome of our question. For many people this would mean the last word which closes the debate. For is not "logic" the fundamental discipline that provides all thinking with its eternal rules? Is it not unscientific to begin or to think illogically? And how could philosophy maintain its alleged objectivity, if its thinking is unscientific?

With these claims, however, even the logician has become illogical. For by making statements about the *non-logical* the logician transcends his own domain instead of keeping a respectful silence. To be sure, the rules of logic are universally valid. This means that they apply wherever and whenever we think logically. But is logic the only valid way of thinking? To decide whether or not *de facto* there are other valid forms of thinking lies outside the competence of logic. The assertion that logic is the *only* legitimate way of thinking presupposes an understanding of what logic fundamentally is and of the ultimate "why" of its rules. Now, logic is as much incapable of this kind of reflection and self-questioning as a child is of studying child psychology. We want to make it clear from the very outset, that we do not intend to disparage logic itself, but the illogical arrogation to logic of being the final authority in *all* possible forms of thinking.

In addition, logic is very intolerant of anything mysterious. And this is only logical. For has not the Western philosophy, ever since its early Greek beginnings, defined man as *to zoon logicon,* as the logical or rational animal? It is precisely by the use of his logical reason that man assures himself of a progressive mastery of the universe, and, consequently, of his own privileged position in it. And it is only by de-mystifying the mysteries of the universe, by solving its riddles and by subduing its reality to the rigorous rules of rational thinking that man can predict and control the natural events. Logic, therefore, bases itself on self-evident principles, clear-cut concepts and precise definitions. Whatever refuses to yield to the force of logical mechanisms, whatever remains unintelligible, obscure and mysterious *in principle* is of no concern to logic. Of course, logic has to solve many problems. But these are questions that merely elude our understanding for a time; in principle they are perfectly soluble and intelligible. That which is basically mysterious, however, cannot be defined, classified and conceptualized, and is logically irrelevant. Once more, this is only logical.

It is logical to regard that which is basically mysterious and undefinable as logically irrelevant. But it is highly illogical to claim that such phenomena are *absolutely* irrelevant, that whatever is non-rational is *ipso facto* irrational, that whatever transcends reason offends reason. This claim mistakes the contradictory for the contrary. What is not beautiful is not *eo ipso* ugly. Moreover, this claim does not follow from any of the primary premises of logic. These principles, as we will demonstrate later on, presuppose extensive universality rather than comprehensive universality, determinism rather than freedom, and underlie our dealings with the material universe rather than our understanding of the totality of all that is. This, by the way, is the reason why modern symbolic or mathematical logic is able to successfully apply the mathematical method to formal logic. Now, it is logically correct to call *faulty* logic *illogical* and that which offends reason irrational. But it is logically incorrect, and therefore irrational to mistake that which transcends the logical reason for irrationalism. This attitude on the part of either formal or symbolic logic implies the assumption that any possible kind of thinking other than logic is *ipso facto faulty*. And this means, of course, that logic is the only legitimate way of thinking. But since such a claim, as we just have indicated, cannot be validated by logic itself, it must be based on an irrational dogma. The assertion that whatever transcends logic is irrational is based on *rationalism* or the dogma of the ultimacy of correct deductive and inductive thinking.

The rationalist asks himself only logical questions. Yet, any question *about* logic contradicts his dogmatic fixation. He becomes aggressive and calls us naïve and unscientific when we ask the question what logic ultimately is. He feels that we try to disparage logic by merely asking questions about its scope, its validity and limitations. Nevertheless, these questions should be asked, and we were compelled to ask them as a result of the logical outcome of our question, "How should we begin philosophy?" Although we are not yet ready to answer these questions, we at least know that we should not hesitate to continue our questioning for fear of being illogical. The fact that our question brought us into a logical impasse merely indicates the inadequacy of logic as an instrument to begin philosophy, but not the impossibility of the beginning of philosophy. The beginning of philosophy may be basically mysterious, and may require an expanded kind of reason, which differs from logic, which is broader and deeper in scope and leaves room for paradox and mystery. Such a reason, however, would transcend logic, but not offend it. And it would not be illogical to begin with mystery.

QUESTIONS RAISED BY THE RADICAL MYSTERIOUSNESS OF REALITY

In fact, *all beginnings* are fundamentally mysterious. We say that all beginnings are difficult. But in our rationalistic age we seldom realize that all beginnings are mysterious too! To begin means: to come into being, or to bring into being. Beginning, therefore, implies the emergence of something that has not yet existed, or has not yet existed in this way. Every true beginning, therefore, has a creative moment, for it brings something new into birth. There is novelty, spontaneity, originality and creativity in every real beginning. The reality of beginning is a phenomenon of profound mysteriousness and baffles the mind which is still open to experience and capable of wondering. The mysteriousness of this phenomenon, however, is a disturbing factor for the rationalist thinker who dogmatically asserts that all knowledge must start from rigidly defined concepts. He, consequently, tries to belittle this phenomenon by denying its relevancy, and to explain away its mysteriousness by calling it self-explanatory. But the rationalist cannot possibly disparage the fact and the significance of mystery without contradicting the basic data of our human consciousness.

For phenomena such as coming into being and passing away, birth, growth and death, causation and creativity have startled the mind ever since the early Greek philosophy and will continue to do so as long as there are thinking men on earth. These phenomena are encountered everywhere in the universe, but most fundamentally in the mysterious center of our immediately lived experience *(Lebenswelt)*. In the face of these phenomena we are compelled to admit that not a single being is obvious or self-explanatory as being, that not a single being in the universe has the ground of its existence in itself, and that we, human beings, are questionable to ourselves at the very core of our existence. Fundamentally *everything* discloses itself as groundless, unsettled and contingent. A full realization of the fundamental mysteriousness of reality disturbs our everyday security, keeps us in suspense, and arouses in us a profound sense of wonder. We experience an inner need to transcend the solid ground of everyday life and logic, and to probe into the significance of the ultimate mysteriousness of all that is. How are phenomena such as beginning and becoming possible? What is the ultimate meaning of my existence? Why is there anything at all and not rather nothing?

By asking such fundamental questions we have become involved in a truly philosophical situation. For *philosophy* (Gr. *philosophia*—love for wisdom) has always been regarded as the search for the rational explanation, for the ultimate causes or the fundamental "why" of all that is insofar as it is. Now, such a search, as we have seen, was prompted by our discovery of the fundamental mysteriousness of all that is. Philosophy, therefore, is our probing into the significance of the ultimate mysteriousness of reality. And philosophy originates in our existential discovery of this fundamental mysteriousness. In other words, the beginning of philosophy is *wonder*. This finding provides us with a first answer to our beginning question, "How should we begin philosophy?" This question first led us into a logical antinomy seemingly impairing the possibility of beginning anything at all. Yet, experience reveals to us that things do begin. The phenomenon of beginning lost its self-evidence and became a sudden challenge. A deeper realization of basic phenomena such as beginning, becoming and creativity disintegrated our everyday and logical security. We plunged headlong into the non-logical (but not illogical) discovery that everything is fundamentally mysterious. And in this primordial experience of wonder we felt an urgent inner need to probe into the significance of this mysteriousness and to ask ourselves fundamental questions. In other words, our urge to philosophize began in wonder.

Very well! But how does the fact that wonder is the beginning of philosophy answer our preliminary question, "How should we begin philosophy?" Since wonder transcends logic, it also transcends the controlling attitude of man. Wonder, therefore, is an overwhelming and inspirational experience rather than an object to be controlled. But if wonder escapes human control, we cannot evoke wonder at will any more than the artist can evoke his inspiration at will. No human effort can originate the beginning of philosophy. We can only bide our time in hopeful anticipation of a "gifted" moment. Strictly speaking, therefore, *we* cannot begin philosophy at all. But does not this clearly demonstrate the impossibility of philosophy? Is not all thinking by necessity human thinking? How can philosophy as human thinking originate from something superhuman? Moreover, does not our reliance upon a subjective experience such as wonder necessarily result in some sort of sham-philosophical subjectivism? How can wonder ever produce true objectivity and real universality? How can we possibly define, describe and demonstrate an inspirational experience which eludes the logical reason? A progressive exploration of these questions in the first few chapters of this book will demonstrate that it is not subjectivistic to begin philosophy in wonder. On the contrary, he who asks these questions is imbued with subjectivism. Instead of discouraging us these questions will greatly help us with elucidating the real significance of wonder and the fundamental structure of philosophy.

THE RATIONALISTIC "EXPLANATION"

But let us first go back to the rationalistic dogma which tries to silence philosophical questions even before they get a chance to make themselves heard. As we have seen, neither wonder nor questions rooted in wonder have any logical significance. Logic, therefore, can neither raise, *nor silence* philosophical questions. It is not the logician but the rationalist who is disturbed by such questions and tries to nip them in the bud. In order to do this, however, the confirmed rationalist has to overstep the limits of his competence and to close his eyes to his own fundamental experience. To accept the relevancy of wonder or fundamentally mysterious questions would invalidate his dogma of the monopoly of the logical reason. He, therefore, categorically denies that mystery as such has any significance, any real meaning or truth-value. Mystery merely is a problem that has not been solved yet, but that is perfectly solvable. In principle everything can become fully transparent and completely intelligible for the logical reason. Whoever takes mystery as such seriously becomes guilty of "mysticism." The term "mysticism," of course, is used by the rationalist in the derogatory sense of "obscurantism." Whoever takes mystery seriously *impairs* scientific progress and enlightenment, obscures the real issues, and is both unscientific and irrational. Whoever transcends the logical reason offends the logical reason. But we have already exposed this claim as an irrational prejudice of the rationalistic dogma. It is precisely this dogma which obscures the issues by bringing our thinking out of focus. For it is not irrational to allow oneself to be challenged by mystery. It is not illogical to transcend logic or not to believe in its alleged monopoly. And no rationalistic dogma can ever relieve us from the task of probing into the significance of the ultimate mysteriousness of reality.

The dogmatic denial, however, of the fundamental mysteriousness of reality rests on the rationalistic assumption that man can arrive at an ultimate understanding of all that is. Nothing is unintelligible in principle, the universe harbors no secrets that cannot be disclosed, and what we do not understand today, we will understand tomorrow. Ultimately there is a "rational explanation" for everything. Every unintelligible phenomenon, every kind of beginning, becoming or change, every motion or activity in the universe becomes explicable in terms of causality. In short, every effect can exhaustively be explained by its cause. The rationalistic world-view, however, presupposes "determinism" and allows only for one kind of causality, namely the "mechanistic" or billiard ball kind of causality. Causality is reduced to a force capable of producing a change in the motion of a material body. Now, classical mechanics states that force is equal to the product of mass and acceleration. And this law of motion finds its perfect intelligibility in the mathematical formula: $F = ma$. This mathematical intelligibility is indeed a characteristic perfection of our "abstractive" thinking. But the modern rationalist mistakes mathematical intelligibility for the prototype of *all* intelligibility. Thus he not only explains away the fundamental mysteriousness of phenomena such as beginning, becoming and causation, but he even explains away the very reality of these phenomena. All beginning, becoming and causation are regarded as mere change of place or locomotion.

ANGUISHED EXISTENCE

To be sure, the logical reason rightly bases itself on self-evident principles, clear-cut concepts and exact definitions. For logical thinking aims at a perfect control of the universe as a whole and of all its parts. But we cannot control that which remains unpredictable, and we cannot predict that which remains unforeseeable, and we cannot foresee that which is novel, original and not fully determined by its cause. Logic, therefore, presupposes "determinism" or the theory that all effects are exhaustively determined by their causes, and, consequently, fully explicable and predictable in the light of these causes. Logic as "calculative" thinking fragmentizes reality into fixities that can be classified, predicted and controlled. This requires an abstractive attitude on the part of logic. Logic as "abstractive" thinking progressively quantifies qualitative data, and tends to reduce all causation to "mechanical" causation. All beginning, becoming and change is explained on the basis of matter in motion, or locomotion. The conception of real causality becomes superfluous and is replaced by the notion of "predictability" of successive events. In other words, logic has an inner tendency towards mathematical thinking, and mathematical exactness is the prototype of logical intelligibility. It is, therefore, not to be wondered at that today we witness a great interest in mathematical logic. This merely demonstrates our growing awareness of the fact that mathematics underlies our logical thinking.

But to mistake mathematical intelligibility for the prototype of *all* intelligibility is rationalism or the dogmatic belief in the ultimacy of logical thinking. Logic is supposed to answer not only logical questions but all questions including ultimate or fundamental questions. We have already shown, however, that the rationalist with this dogmatic assumption contradicts the basic phenomena of human experience and oversteps the limits of his own competence. The mechanistic world-view of the rationalist, therefore, is a construct of the mind which does not coincide with the real dimensions of reality. The universe of the rationalist is a deterministic interplay of independent forces. It is a universe in which nothing is ever created and nothing ever passes away, in which real beginning, becoming and change are reduced to mere locomotion, and in which causality is nothing but predictability. The rationalistic universe is a universe which leaves no room for personal freedom and responsibility, which contains man as a mechanical part of the cosmic machine, and which has no meaning or value besides being a huge system of logical and mathematical relationships. Much of our modern uneasiness and anxiety is due to the fact that we are invited to adjust ourselves to a scheme of things in which man has lost his sense of wonder, his self-identity and the very meaning of his existence. Modern man feels existentially frustrated in a mechanized world in which he has been degraded to a replaceable function, to a mere product of biological, psychological and sociological driving forces, or to an anonymous part of the cosmic machine. Modern man has been reduced to a robot (*l'homme machine*—de Lamettrie) and is promised "perfect" happiness for his "perfect" adjustment to a "perfect" network of mathematical and logical relationships. Yet, modern man feels "perfectly" empty, despairs over the meaning of life, and wonders if his life is not ultimately "a tale told by an idiot." "This uneasiness," says Gabriel Marcel, "is enough to show that there is in all this some appalling mistake, some ghastly misinterpretation, implanted in defenseless minds by an . . . inhuman philosophy."[1]

Now, this modern uneasiness, this anguished experience of a depersonalized existence, this despair over the meaning of life is not merely a sentiment, or an indication of modern morbidity. On the contrary, this experiential uneasiness is a healthy indication that nature has an ascendancy over logic, that fundamental reality resists the quantifying analysis by the logical reason, and that fundamental questions *cannot* be silenced and *should not* be silenced. The inhuman philosophy that brings us into despair over the meaning of life is precisely the rationalistic persuasion of today that only that is meaningful which can be measured, which can be reduced to numbers and expressed in terms of mathematical relationships. We have already shown how rationalism is self-contradictory, how it contains a *contradictio in terminis* or a contradiction in terms. For rationalism is the illogical assumption of the monopoly of logical thinking. But, here, we find that rationalism also contains a *contradictio in actu exercito* or a contradiction between a proposed theory and the experience of the actual realization of this theory in one's concrete life.[2] To teach that the universe is mechanistic is one thing; but to *live* in a mechanistic universe is a different thing altogether. Man feels ill at ease when compelled to live in a universe where everything is self-explanatory in terms of matter in motion, where all beginning, becoming and creativity is reduced to the mere rearrangement of pre-existing elements, and where mathematical intelligibility is regarded as the prototype of all intelligibility. Such a universe may satisfy the logical reason, but it does not satisfy man; it may solve particular problems, but it dissolves the meaning of life; it may answer logical questions, but it confronts us with the urgent need to raise more fundamental questions such as, "Is life worth living?" and "Why is there anything at all rather than nothing?" Rationalism remains unsuccessful in its attempt to reject the mysteriousness of fundamental phenomena and to silence the questions they raise.

A BEGINNING "BEGINS"

Now, phenomena such as beginning and becoming are radically mysterious. And the rationalist can only give a "rational explanation" of these phenomena by explaining them away, by reducing them to a mere rearrangement in space, to a change in terms of matter and motion. And we are not supposed to ask the question what space, what matter and motion, or for that matter, what logic and science "really" are. But despite rationalistic theories, phenomena such as beginning and becoming continue to be mysterious and to baffle the minds of those that are still capable of wondering. The most remarkable thing about a beginning is *that it begins,* that something new comes into being, that something emerges that has not yet existed, or has not yet existed in this way. In other words, there is something original and spontaneous, something unpredictable and unforeseeable in every real beginning. This is why, strictly speaking, a beginning cannot be learned. We do not learn a beginning, we begin a beginning. At the heart of our educational activities is always something nonteachable. "This is why it is thought impossible," said Aristotle, "to be a harper if one has never played the harp; for he who learns to play the harp learns to play it by playing it, and all other learners do similarly."[3] We learn to swim only by swimming; we learn to philosophize only by philosophizing. And it is not until we can understand the instructions *in the light of the actual beginning* that they become truly meaningful.

And the same holds true for *questions,* since questions are actually beginnings; they are beginning answers. A question intrinsically refers to its answer, it *is* the answer in a beginning way. A historical question cannot be answered by mathematics. Only a historical answer, and in fact only this particular historical answer can satisfy this particular historical question. Questions are neither made nor learned, they are asked. A question is only found in the actual asking of the question. "Questions and particularly fundamental questions do not just occur like stones and water. Questions are not found ready-made like shoes and clothes and books. Questions *are,* and are only as they are actually asked."[4] Questions *about* a question become meaningful only in the light of the actual asking of that question. Our beginning question, "How should we begin philosophy?" was merely a question *about* philosophy and remained philosophically meaningless. The word "philosophy" in this question was not used in the light of actual philosophical questioning, remained extrinsic to philosophy and meant something like "that which philosophers have been interested in." This is the reason why our beginning question, "How should we begin philosophy?" cannot possibly be the beginning question of philosophy.

But this brings us to another question. Our beginning question, "How should we begin philosophy?" presupposed the very existence of philosophy. And if this is so, why should *we* begin philosophy? Did not we ask our question as if it were not prompted by the fact that we want to know what philosophers have been interested in, as if philosophy had not begun long ago, as if such a thing as philosophy had not been with us for more than twenty-five centuries? Throughout the long history of philosophy numerous philosophers have left us an abiding legacy by embodying their thoughts in multifarious writings. Moreover, in order to help us in the arduous task of probing into the depth of these thoughts, of unraveling the complexity of various systems and of organizing an overview of the great dialogues between these historical systems a vast ocean of "textbooks" has come to our assistance. They present us with a body of systematized information on what philosophers have been interested in, on what they have taught and written. From all these books we are able to learn what philosophy is as part of our general education. We do not have to begin philosophy ourselves.

All this, however, is based on a common misconception. To be sure, we can learn much *about* philosophy, and especially about its technique and its teachable aspects by consulting the great books and even by studying the textbooks. But we will never begin philosophy, learn to philosophize or even know what philosophy is or what is ultimately meant by these books, unless we are actually asking these philosophical questions *ourselves*. In the light of our foregoing remarks it is clear that our study of the history of philosophy remains meaningless except in a dialogue with our own philosophical questioning. "For it is owing to their wonder," says Aristotle, "that men both now begin and at first began to philosophize."[5] The weakness of many textbooks is that they do not attempt to awaken the student's personal questioning, and that they are characterized by oversimplification and problemless finality. The "learned" questions never become "asked" questions. The questions *about* philosophy never become philosophical questions. The student may have "successfully completed" his courses in philosophy without ever having philosophized. His study of philosophy gave him facts rather than vision, systems and names rather than insight, "academic" questions rather than vital questions, and worst of all the idea that he "knows" philosophy which in fact he has not even begun yet.

THE BEGINNING QUESTION OF PHILOSOPHY

By now one thing should be clear, namely that our beginning question, "How should we begin philosophy?" is not the beginning question of philosophy. In the first place, it is merely a question *about* philosophy. And secondly it is not the *most fundamental* question. Pedagogically and from the viewpoint of time it may have been the first question of our orientation. But our question is definitely not the first in rank. For, as we have seen, our question presupposes more fundamental questions such as, "What is philosophy?", "What is logic?", "What is man?", "What is a beginning?", "Why is there anything at all and not rather nothing?", etc. The observant reader, however, will have noticed that underlying these fundamental questions is a still more fundamental question, namely, "What is is?", or "What is to be?" In other words, the *primordial* question implicit in all fundamental questions, and, for that matter, underlying any question at all is *the primordial question of Being*.[6]

The primordial question of Being, therefore, is the most fundamental, the most encompassing and the most original of all questions. We cannot ask any fundamental question or any other question, including our question, "How should we begin philosophy?", without implicitly asking the primordial question of Being. As the most fundamental and the most original question of all fundamental questions the primordial question of Being is the origin or beginning and foundation of our asking of the fundamental "why" of all that is insofar as it is. In other words, the primordial question of Being is the beginning of philosophy.

Here we are confronted with another antinomy. Experientially we found that the beginning of philosophy is *wonder* or our discovery of the radical mysteriousness of all that is. Now the beginning of philosophy reveals itself as *the primordial question of Being* or the ultimate presupposition of all fundamental questions. Consequently, wonder and the primordial question of Being should be one and the same thing. But is not wonder a rich and most concrete experience, and Being an empty and most abstract concept? How, then, can wonder and the primordial question of Being constitute one and the same beginning of philosophy? Once again we are involved in an antinomy because we have come in contact with the primordial question of Being *outside* the actual asking of the question itself. We merely discover the question of Being as the necessary and ultimate *presupposition of all fundamental questions*. We have not even begun to ask the primordial question itself. And only in the actual asking of this question does the seeming opposition between wonder and primordial Being disappear. It is about time to begin our search for this primordial question of Being. What should we do to arrive at an actual asking of this question? In what situation does this question arise? What do we have to look for in order to encounter primordial Being?

Our exploration of the answers to these questions, and a discussion of various other questions concerning the primordial question of Being will constitute the content of the following chapter.

CHAPTER II

IN SEARCH OF
THE PRIMORDIAL QUESTION

We are trying to arrive at an actual asking of the primordial question of Being. But at this point of our philosophical orientation the reader may have become impatient. We seem to be drifting into vague generalizations. The highly abstract question of Being apparently does not give us any useful information. We certainly want to have information, but this information should be about real things, about concrete beings and their particular characteristics. Now *Being* does not even seem to be *a being,* and that which is not a being does not exist. For don't we call a tree a being precisely insofar as it is a real thing, insofar as it is not nothing and exists independently of the knowing mind? If this is so then there is no question of Being, for our point in question is *self-evident.* "Everyone" knows what we mean when we say that a thing is real, i.e., *not nothing.* If, however, we mean by Being something different from beings, then there is no question of Being, for our point in question is *nonexistent.* At any rate, there is no such thing as the question of Being. Whoever wants to begin philosophy with this alleged question turns philosophy into an empty, unreal and useless speculation. Philosophy simply becomes a sophisticated way of wasting one's time. Nowadays we have more important things to do.

THE PSEUDO-PHILOSOPHICAL DENIAL OF PHILOSOPHY

Nevertheless, he who dismisses the question of Being as an idle question is philosophizing. For he unwittingly accepts a certain attitude towards Being or the totality of all that is. He a priori regards our attempt to arrive at an actual asking of the question of Being as futile and doomed to failure. The concept of *Being* does not function in our explanation of things, for neither our everyday world nor the world of the positive sciences has ever revealed such a thing as Being. We are surrounded, however, with particular *beings,* and the only thing that counts is to gain technological control of these beings in our universe. It is true that the question of Being has been the central question of more than twenty-five centuries of Western philosophy. But has it ever produced any useful knowledge, has it ever contributed to the progress of mankind, and does not all progress result from the rise of the positive sciences, of technology and industrialization?

Now, as we said, this negative attitude towards Being is itself a philosophy. And this philosophy is as common as it is unauthentic. It is a *philosophy* since it attempts to answer a fundamental question, namely, the question of the ultimate meaning of all that is. It is noteworthy, however, that this attitude which denies Being does not pronounce upon any particular being, upon any group of beings or even the sum total of all beings, but upon *being as being*. We can only deny Being by affirming it, just as one who ridicules philosophy can only do so by philosophizing. For his ridicule is not directed towards any particular being, but towards the totality of all that is insofar as it is, and thus he contradicts himself *in actu exercito*. For we cannot explicitly deny phenomena such as Being or philosophy without implicitly reaffirming them.

In addition, the negative attitude towards Being is an *unauthentic* philosophy. For it rests on the common misconception that only that is meaningful and real which reveals itself in everyday life or in the positive sciences, and that the ultimate standards of truth are dictated by the correct functioning of the logical reason. We have already exposed this attitude as the illogical dogma of rationalism. Once again we are confronted with such a dogmatic attitude. To conclude that Being is nonexistent because it is neither given in our everyday situation nor in any scientific situation implies the tacit assumption that this disjunction is complete, and that no third alternative, no other meaningful situation is possible. For the possibility of a third alternative would invalidate the inference of this disjunctive argument. Now, the impossibility of a third alternative, of a more fundamental situation or primordial openness towards Being is precisely *not given* in our everyday life or in the world of science. Consequently, the assumption that this disjunction is complete rests on a dogmatic prejudice. This prejudice is the common belief that only the positive sciences can satisfy the human mind by providing us with the fundamental knowledge of things as they really are. This dogmatic pseudo-philosophy, one of the many variations on the general theme of rationalism, is "scientism" or the dogma of the absolute supremacy of the scientific reason. That which cannot be the object of exact observation, of scientific analysis, of measurement and experimental verification is unknowable and even unreal. And, once again, the practical self-contradiction of this assumption reveals itself in the fact that scientism is highly *unscientific*. For the absolutism of this assertion is something which, by definition, is not subject to observation, measurement and experimental verification.

SCIENTISM, THE DOMINANT PERSUASION TODAY

We can hardly overestimate the influence of scientism on the life and thinking of our present age. For scientism is the dominant persuasion today. It has even pervaded the world of human labor where it tends to degrade technology, which is the application of positive science to human labor, into "technocracy." Technocracy makes man the slave of his own technological creations and induces man to expect the full satisfaction of *all* his human needs from technology. Of course, it would be foolish to hold modern science and technology responsible for the evils of our time such as the progressive dehumanization of man and the ever growing tendency to mechanize the authentic, specifically human and creative dimension of human existence. "It would be absurd," says Gabriel Marcel, "to hope to solve the present crisis by closing down the factories and laboratories for good and all. There is every reason to suppose, on the contrary, that such a step would be the starting point of an almost unimaginable regression for the human race."[7] Strictly speaking, there is never too much science and technology. But it is possible that science and technology are not sufficiently integrated in authentic human values, that they develop *at the expense of* the specifically human dimension of our existence. And this is precisely what characterizes our modern technocratic culture. Henri Bergson puts it well when he says that man's body has become too big for his soul. In other words, the outward technological progress has not been balanced by a comparable progress in self-discovery or by an exploration of the more fundamental regions of reality. This is why modern man has a predominantly controlling attitude towards reality based on his exclusively, utilitarian interests. It is true that man's mastery of nature results from the rise of the positive sciences and technology. But it is equally true that "man's mastery of nature is a mastery which has less and less control over *itself*."[8]

Scientism is the dominant persuasion today. Moreover, scientism is intolerant of any kind of reflection on its own nature since reflection would invalidate the absolutism of its standpoint. Modern man, therefore, is less and less aware of the fact that he is dominated by this pseudo-philosophy. Scientism, as a result, has become a collective *fixa-*

tion in the modern *Weltanschauung*. Now, a fixation is never a merely static state of being, but rather an *active* mechanism, a dynamic though unconscious *resistance* to the basic dynamisms of human existence. This explains why modern man is not merely "indifferent," but positively "impatient" when confronted with fundamental questions. Scientism is strictly anti-philosophical. Whoever dares to ask himself fundamental questions "lacks the 'scientific approach'," is "behind the times," is "old-fashioned," "irrational" or "dabbles in mysticism." Once again, "whoever transcends science offends science," is the most unscientific leitmotiv of our age. Our scientistic and technocratic culture, therefore, is characterized by its active "oblivion of Being" (Martin Heidegger) or its "atrophy of the sense of wonder" (Gabriel Marcel). Scientism tends to block the asking of the very questions we are trying to grasp in their authenticity. We are living in a situation which is unfavorable for philosophical questioning, and we are hardly aware of our situation. This is why we were compelled to reflect on scientism, and to expose its dogmatic presuppositions, its "lived" contradictions, and its irrational and highly unscientific nature. For we find ourselves in a given point in history, in a given culture and tradition and in a given *Weltanschauung*. Our thinking is influenced by the spirit of our age long before we become engaged in philosophy. Today this means that if we want to "listen to the voice of Being" (Martin Heidegger), we have to break away from the dogmatic presuppositions, the prefabricated perspectives and mental constructs of rationalism and scientism, and to "return to things themselves" (*Zu den Sachen selbst*—Edmund Husserl). To enable ourselves to "listen to the voice of Being" is precisely the purpose of this chapter. Now we are forewarned when we return to its main question: how can we enter into the actual asking of the question of Being? In what situation does this question arise?

"SITUATED" THINKING

In order to elucidate the actual asking of the question of Being we will make a brief and preliminary comparison between various situations of human existence and their respective potentialities with regard to the self-manifestation of Being. But, once again, our procedure raises some questions that seem to place it in a dubious light. To begin with, should we really look for "human situations"? Is not "objective reality" precisely that which is free from all "subjectivity" of human situations? And is it not "objective reality" we are looking for? Moreover, doesn't our procedure contain a vicious circle? For in order to demonstrate primordial Being we apparently are supposed to know it beforehand.

Now, a brief answer to these questions will not only show that they are still asked within the framework of scientism, but also that this framework is too narrow to be truly objective and realistic.

Man's thinking never begins from zero. Thinking is a *re-flection* in the etymological sense of the word, a "bending-back upon" that which is *immediately given* to our conscious existence. This "implicit" or "unreflected" experience precedes any kind of reflection or explicitation. The "immediately lived world" (*Lebenswelt*—Edmund Husserl) stands at the beginning of all our scientific and philosophical explorations. These reflective explorations have no aim or existence in themselves, but as "mediatizations" of the primary data of our consciousness they remain rooted in our immediately lived world. Our thinking, therefore, not only *starts in,* but also is *nourished by* our "lived" experience. The reflective knowledge of our intellect is not the primary form of knowing, since originally it is embedded in the integral experience of our conscious being-in-a-situation. "Human consciousness is not originally and primarily a "knowing" one in the narrow intellectualist sense of this word; it is first and foremost "being-with," a lived experience of presence."[9] Consequently, it is of the greatest importance to give an accurate account of the way a phenomenon is given in our pre-reflective situation before we try to grasp it in a reflective form of knowledge. We simply corrode the objectivity of our reflective thinking by not allowing reality to reveal itself the way it is in our pre-reflective situation, by not letting the facts "speak for themselves," or by prematurely eliminating certain aspects as "irrelevant." This way we do not reflect on reality, but on dogmatic prejudices, on artificial constructs, distorted perspectives and optical illusions.

Now, when man reflects upon his immediately lived experience, he discovers that whatever its specific content may be, it is always given to him "in a situation." To be sure, man can experience a great variety of situations, but it is impossible for him ever to pass entirely beyond all situations. The fundamental situation of man is precisely his "being-in-the-world." If it is important to give an accurate account of the phenomena as they are given in our pre-reflective situation, then it is *a fortiori* imperative to grasp our "being-in-a-situation" itself as it really manifests itself unadulterated by dogmatic preconceptions. To say that man is situated (L. *situs*—place, site) is to say that man always finds himself "already" involved in a certain body, in a certain position in space and time, in a certain condition with regard to circumstances and environment. His involvement, however, the "being-in" of his "being-in-the-world" is not the mere presence of a thing "among other things."

Man is not in the world as water is in a glass, or as a candy is in a box. Such a vision of man's "being-in-the-world" would reduce man to a thing, it would distort the pre-reflective data of human consciousness and fail to grasp the human situation as a unique but complex phenomenon. The candy does not do anything with the box, is not, literally speaking *in* the box, but rather surrounded by the box. The candy does not *find itself* in the box but remains unaware of its environment. Man, on the other hand, is not merely determined by the facticity of his situation, but also actively determining his determinations. Man literally *finds himself* in the situation, is an open relation to his environment and transcends it in creative participation. Man's situation is not merely the physical surroundings of his home, his school, his church, his traditions, his culture and his friends, but his situation *includes* the integral and lived experience of these surroundings and the various meanings he attaches to them. The human situation is the actual presence of that which surrounds to the integral experience of this presence which man *is*. Man's "being-in" is an active participation, a "living"-in-the-world in the sense of the Latin word: *habitare*. This is why our "being-in" manifests itself in various modes of *habitare,* such as to "dwell"; to "stay"; to "love"; to "understand"; to "care"; to "cultivate"; to "sojourn," etc.[10] Man's situation is a synthesis between what is imposed and what is willed (Heidegger), between *"fatalité et élan"* (Buytendijk), between immanency and transcendency.

"Ex-sistence" as Unity of Immanency and Transcendency

Man's "being-in-the-world" is a unitary structure, or a structural whole. The relation between man and world is unique and difficult to grasp. The relation of the "being-in" is not a *spatial* relation, not a relation man has *in addition* to his existence, not a mere *de facto* relation which we can make and unmake at will. The relation between man and world is an *essential* relation which exists *de jure,* it is a relation we *are,* a relation which *defines* man as "existence" in the etymological sense of the word: *to stand out, to emerge* (L. *ex* and *sistere*). "The relation between man and world," says Albert Dondeyne, "is a reciprocal one like that between 'container' and 'contained'. This is why it is impossible to understand man without considering the universe, just as it is impossible to describe the universe correctly without referring to man."[11] Man progressively cultivates and dominates the deterministic processes and forces of the physical world, and at the same time he depends on these material mechanisms for his very existence. "For there is no spiritual knowledge without sense perceptible objects, without brains, without physiological processes, without sense images or without words. There is no spiritual love without sensitive love. There is no personal conscience without a biological substructure. There is no artistic act without expression in matter."[12] The two terms of the relation, man and world, are mutually inclusive, and each is both "container" and "contained." Man is *immanent* in the material determinations of the world and at the same time dynamically *transcending* the material world by his creative openness towards the determinations. In other words, "the essence of man is his 'ex-sistence'."[13] A further exploration of man's "being-in-the-world" will be given later in this book where we will examine the various *modes* of being-in-the-world and its multidimensional structure. Our present reflection on the immediately lived world suffices to show that *all* our reflective knowledge has its primary and permanent *origin* (*Ursprung*—original leap) in an unreflected or implicit *situation,* that the fundamental situation is man's "being-in-the-world" and that there is no absolute priority of either the human subject or the material object since both are co-original as mutually inclusive terms of an essential relationship, as poles of a dialectical tension or as partners in the same dialogue.

SUBJECTIVISM?

From this it follows that we are fully justified by beginning our search for the primordial question of Being with an examination of human situations, provided that we understand the term "situation" in its primary meaning. But this still leaves unanswered the question about *objectivity.* Are we not objective to the extent that we are free from the "subjectivity" of human situations? And is it not precisely *objective reality* we are looking for? There is no doubt indeed that we are looking for objective reality. But in the light of our foregoing elucidation we have our serious doubts about the possibility of an objectivity which would not be involved in the subjectivity of human situations. For, as we have seen, our pre-reflective encounter with reality reveals that the human self and the world of objects are *co-original* and constitute a dialectical relationship. And this immediately lived world is a *primary datum* in which *all* knowledge is rooted. It is as much impossible to posit the existence of a "world-in-itself," of a world of "real objects" independent of the human mind, as it is to reflect on a world-less self, an acosmic ipseity or a pure and object-less consciousness. The world is not the sum total of external objects, nor is it an indifferent framework that we can accept or reject at will. The world is the unitary structure or original openness of "ex-sistence" in the light of which the self-manifestation of man and things becomes possible. In other words, the discovery of the world is anterior to the discovery of both the human self and the surrounding objects. Fundamentally we understand both the subject and the object in the natural light *(lumen naturale)* of the horizon of the world, and not the other way around. The world, therefore, is prior to the beings encountered in the world. Consequently, it is one-sided, and a contradiction of our fundamental situation to place the source of all knowledge and objectivity exclusively in the *human subject* as the rationalists and idealists do. But equally unacceptable is the assertion of scientism that explains the objectivity of the "real world" in terms of the *material objects* alone and relegates the meaning of the "phenomenal world" to the realm of myths and dreams. For any reflection on reality, whether starting in the human self or in the material objects, has posited the world already and takes place *within* the natural light of the subject-object *relationship*. Any doctrine which gives an absolute priority to either the human subject or the material object must be based on an absolute *opposition* between subject and object, and, therefore, distorts the primary data of our consciousness that constitute the original source of all reflective thinking. We shall have more to say about this later on.

Our question, "Are we not looking for objective reality?" implied the assumption of such a radical dichotomy between subject and object. For underlying this question was the presupposition that objective reality is *exclusively* the reality of *external objects* and that real objectivity is *entirely unrelated* to the human subject. Now, it seems that the physical scientist, and *only* the physical scientist fulfills the requirements for the knowledge of such an objective reality. Only his approach is the truly "scientific approach" since only his approach is truly impersonal, abstractive, objectifying and detached. Consequently, only that which can be discovered by the physical sciences is real and objective. There is no reality but scientific reality, there is no truth but scientific truth, there is no objectivity but scientific objectivity. The "real world" of the physical scientist completely replaces the "phenomenal world" of our immediately lived experience. In short, reality is what physical sciences reveal, and nothing but that. "Matters have gone so far in this respect that even the non-philosophizing public at large has slowly but surely become convinced that the world of the physicist and the chemist is *properly the only real and objective* world. Accordingly, the knowledge supplied by the physical sciences is true knowledge—the rest is poetry, romanticism or subjectivism."[14] Unfortunately, "the rest" are our most authentic and profoundly human realities such as love, beauty, moral responsibility, creativity, personal life, happiness and freedom. From the very beginning this approach restricts the "reality" and "objectivity" of that which reveals itself to the reality and objectivity of that which reveals itself within the framework of the physical sciences. Givenness as such is reduced to "scientific data." That which is not accessible to this "scientific approach" is slightingly relegated to the realm of dreams and fancies, and is considered to be of no importance whatsoever. It goes without saying that this attitude itself is not the "scientific approach," but rather *scientism* or the *unscientific* and sham philosophical dogma of the monopoly of the "scientific approach" in this restricted sense of the word.

VARIOUS MEANINGS OF THE TERMS "SUBJECTIVE" AND "OBJECTIVE"

Consequently, it is mainly under the influence of scientism that nowadays the term "objective" has a very restricted meaning, and is generally defined as "being independent of the human mind." And this illegitimate diminution of the meaning of "objectivity" has created a perfect babel of languages as to the meaning of the term "objective" and its correlative "subjective." We can distinguish at least three basically different meanings in the modern usage of these terms. *Firstly,* to be objective may mean "to pertain to the *object pole*" of our act of knowledge. And, of course, to be subjective in the correlated sense means "to pertain to the *subject pole*" of the same intentional act. This meaning of the terms "subjective" and "objective" is fully legitimate. For, as we have seen, the knowledge of human "ex-sistence" is essentially an "encounter" between subject and object, an unbreakable unity in opposition, a polar tension, or dialogical relationship. To be object, therefore, is to-appear-to-a-subject, and not to be a thing-in-itself which would exist independently of the human mind. To be subject means to-allow-an-object-to-appear, and not to be merely a passive receptacle which would be unrelated to the world of objects. Consequently, the terms "subjective" and "objective" taken in this sense are *not mutually exclusive,* but they necessarily include one another as correlative polar aspects of one and the same intentional act of knowledge.

Secondly, the terms "subjective" and "objective" may refer to the *truth aspect* of our knowledge. This also is a legitimate usage of these terms, provided that we understand them in their proper sense. Here, to be objective means "to know reality *as it is.*" Whereas the correlated term "subjective" indicates that we "know reality *as it is not.*" In other words, objective knowledge is *true* knowledge because it is founded on reality as it is, and subjective knowledge is *false* knowledge to the extent that it is founded on our own bias, on prejudices, disrupting emotions or preconceived ideas. Such a preconceived idea, for instance, is the misconception of scientism that reality "as it is" means reality "as it is *in-itself,* independently of the human mind." This misconception, as we will discuss in connection with the third meaning of "objectivity," not only restricts the meaning of "objectivity," but also destroys the possibility of having objective knowledge of the human subject, or, in fact, of having any knowledge at all. A proper understanding of the first two meanings of objectivity shows that we can have "objective" knowledge of the "subjective," in the sense of true knowledge of the subject pole. It also shows that objectivity in the sense of truth is *not primarily* found in the "agreement between the judgment and the object," or in the "adequation of the intellect and the thing." We say "not primarily" for we do not deny the validity of this kind of objectivity. We maintain, however, that *a special kind* of objectivity does not constitute objectivity *as such,* and cannot *define* the meaning of objectivity as truth. The agreement of the intellect with the thing is only a *special kind* of objectivity because it is not primary and *presupposes* a more fundamental situation in which such an agreement becomes possible. This fundamental situation is the very *openness* of the world of man's conscious "ex-sistence." This original openness of human "ex-sistence" and not the judgment is the primary *locus* of objectivity as truth. There can only be an agreement or disagreement between the intellect and the thing when *both* are *already* standing in the light of *the same original openness* of the world as unitary structure.[15] In other words, the original openness of man's being-in-the-world, which is the primary source of intelligibility, the *lumen naturale* or natural light of our "ex-sistence," is *never* constituted by *the object alone* (against empiricism, scientism and abstractionism) nor by the *human subject alone* (against Cartesian rationalism and monistic idealism). For this primary openness is *co-openness,* or the original light of "ex-sistence" mysteriously emerging out of concealment in the "encounter" between man and world. To put it differently again, the truth of agreement presupposes the more fundamental *truth of openness,* or the truth as unconcealment or *aletheia*[16] in which the objects have already been unveiled or taken out of obscurity by the uncovering activity of the human "ex-sistence," and in which man has already discovered himself as "ex-sistence" by allowing the objects to appear in the world-for-a-subject. *Objectivity as truth,* therefore, is primarily *the dynamic openness or unconcealment of human "ex-sistence" revealing reality as it is.* The objective *attitude* of the human subject, therefore, is a constitutive element of objective reality.

The objective attitude is the respectful openness of the whole of our "ex-sistence" which allows reality to reveal itself the way it is.[17]

Completely contradicting the first two meanings of the term "objec-tive" is the way in which objectivity is commonly understood today. Objectivity in this *third* sense means "being independent of the human mind." This meaning of objectivity is as illegitimate as it is destructive of the world of man. Here objectivity is defined in its radical *opposition* to the human subject, and absolute priority is given to the material "ob-ject" in the etymological sense of the word (L. *ob-jectum,* G. *Gegen-stand*—something standing over against). Only that is real and objec-tive which is "extramental," "other-than-the-subject," and a "thing-in-itself." The "real world" is the "world without man," and objectivity is understood in terms of the external object alone. Consequently, only the physical scientist is truly objective, since his impersonal attitude is exclusively concerned with the external world of physical objects. Only he knows the objects as they exist independently of the human mind, only his objectifying attitude can detect the "primary qualities" of the objects or the purely quantitative characteristics that can be known without any involvement on the part of the human subject. Objectivity, therefore, means more and more our submission to an impersonal net-work of functional and mathematical relationships. "The rest" is subjec-tive! Here, subjective is *always* understood in the sense of false, unreal or meaningless. Whatever does not fit in the framework of the physical sciences remains "without foundation in objective reality," and is "sub-jective" in the pejorative sense of the term.

THE CONTRADICTIONS OF "OBJECTIVISM"

We have already shown that this third meaning of "objective" is based on *scientism,* the unscientific and self-contradictory dogma of the ultimacy of the physical sciences. To understand objectivity in terms of the physical object alone is "objectivistic," which is unscientific, and, therefore subjective in the sense of *false.* Now, our question, "Are we not objective to the extent that we are free from all human situations?" was clearly based on "objectivism" or the false assumptions of scien-tism. The question itself, therefore, was wrong and illegitimate. Cer-tainly, we should look for objective reality, but this should not be understood in the objectivistic sense, in terms of the physical objects alone. The objectivism of scientism wrongly restricts the meaning of both reality and objectivity. Realities that include the subject pole, such as love, beauty, culture and personal responsibility are even more real and more truly objective than that which can be demonstrated mathematically and verified by experimental tests. In the following chapters we shall discuss how scientism also restricts the meaning of terms such as science, demonstration, verification, experience, universality and method.

The "objectivistic" understanding of objectivity is not only based on the self-contradiction of scientism but it also contains several other contradictions. First of all, it contradicts the fundamental source of all knowledge, the natural light of human "ex-sistence" which reveals the essential *co-originality* of the human subject and the world of objects. Objective knowledge can never be understood in terms of the external object alone. The same co-originality of the subject and the object, however, demonstrates that "subjectivism" is not the only alternative to "objectivism" as scientism wants us to believe. For it is also impossible to understand objectivity in terms of *the human subject alone,* no matter whether we interpret this in the idealistic sense of a world-less self or in the relativistic sense of arbitrary opinions or egotistic feelings and prejudices. All human knowledge is based on the "encounter" or the "polar unity" between subject and object. This is why the "objectivism" of scientism contradicts even the physical sciences themselves. Ever since the turn of the century great scientists such as Poincaré, Eddington, Einstein, Bohr and Heisenberg, to mention only a few, have emphasized the dependency of the physical sciences on the particular attitudes and exploratory activities of man. Heisenberg, for instance, says that the "ideal of a science which is completely independent of man is an illusion."[18] Moreover, the objectivistic ideal of *disinterested* knowledge contradicts the fundamental impossibility of such a knowledge. We are necessarily *interested* in the various objects of our knowledge, because we are always "involved" (L. *inter-esse*—to be present, to participate), and we are always involved, because it is our essence to "ex-sist" in the etymological sense of the word. The idea that we are more objective to the extent that we are less involved implies the conclusion which is not without humor drawn by Rollo May, "that he will most successfully discover truth who is not the slightest bit interested in it!"[19] This conclusion, of course, contradicts elementary laws in psychology and education. Furthermore, the objectivistic conception of objectivity as conformity to "extramental" reality destroys the very possibility of objectivity by contradicting the basic conditions for all knowledge. For, if the essential characteristic of objectivity becomes the object's "independency of the human mind" rather than its "self-present appearance" in the openness of human "ex-sistence," and if all light comes exclusively from the external object rather than from the natural light of its "appearing-in-the-world," then objectivity is reduced to an *exact re-presentation*. Now, an exact *re-presentation* is the pure mirroring of an external object, in which the object is no longer *self-present,* in which the object does not appear-to-a-subject, and, consequently, is not an object any more. The mirror is not a subject, is not involved and does not know what it reflects. If the most objective presence of the object is its total absence from the human mind, then not only objectivity but even all knowledge becomes impossible. We cannot know that which we are by definition unconscious of. Even if, for the sake of argument, we did accept the possibility of an exact image or mental copy, we could never be sure of possessing such an "objective" copy since the necessary comparison between the "mental" copy and the "extramental" original can never be made and is self-contradictory. And, finally, the objectivistic conception of the absolute priority of the external object over the human subject constitutes a *lived* contradiction between the "objective" world and the exigencies of the world of human "ex-sistence." Objectivism acts like the neutron bomb which leaves material structures intact but kills all forms of life. If man is only "objective" in his absolute submission to an impersonal network of functional relationships, then man becomes a disturbing factor in a universe that corrodes specifically human values such as love, beauty and mystery, that deprives man of the original light of his existence and leaves him the "stifling impression of sadness produced by this functionalized world."[20]

The Circularity of Fundamental Thinking

By showing that our question, "Are we not objective to the extent that we are free from human situations?" was based on objectivism, and, therefore, on *false* presuppositions, we have implicitly answered the other question, "Are we not moving in a vicious circle?" We certainly are moving in a circular fashion. But we don't have to apologize for it. Our question implies the tacit assumption that *any* circular movement in our thinking *ipso facto* constitutes a "vicious" circle, and, consequently, that there is only one legitimate mode of thinking, namely the "straight" thinking of the logical reason which is based on clear and distinct concepts. These clear and distinct concepts, however, are already "second-level constructions of the human mind,"[21] and to mistake these constructions for the foundations of *all* thinking is characteristic of *rationalism* or the dogma of the monopoly of the syllogistic reason. *Fundamental thinking, as we have seen, originates precisely in human situations,* in the immediately lived world of human "ex-sistence". Surprisingly enough, reflective thinking knows what it is looking for. We would not ask our fundamental questions without an immediately lived contact with our point in question. Fundamental questions are originally "lived" questions, and they "present themselves" in our experiential being-in-the-world. Our *re-flection* on these questions is a thematization of what was non-thematic, or an explicitation of what was implicitly present in our human "ex-sistence." This circular movement of the philosophical re-flection, of the "turning back upon" that which is immediately given, is not a "vicious" circle, since a *fundamental* demonstration is not a *syllogistic* demonstration. That which is to be demonstrated cannot be reduced to anything more original or more fundamental. A fundamental demonstration does not consist in a syllogistic proof (G. *beweisen*), but in "allowing the phenomena to show themselves" in the progressive self-enrichment of their immediate givenness (G. *aufweisen*). What is really "vicious" is the tenacious grip scientism holds on our modern minds.

HUMAN SITUATIONS AND THE QUESTION OF BEING

At long last we are prepared to proceed with our brief and preliminary comparison between various situations of human "ex-sistence" and their respective potentialities with regard to the primordial question of Being. Of course, we can only make this comparison in the light of primordial Being itself. We must recall, therefore, that a fundamental question is not made or approached *from without,* and that such a question is not truly asked except when it is asked in the *lived* experience of the primary data of our unreflective consciousness. Fortunately, we have already experienced such an initial contact with primordial Being. We, namely, encountered the primordial question of Being as the question which is implicitly asked in all fundamental questions, and, in fact, in any question at all. As the ultimate presupposition of all fundamental questions the primordial question of Being has a radical priority in fundamental thinking and is the beginning of philosophy. Meanwhile we have learned that this question cannot possibly be an *abstract* question. For a question that underlies fundamental or self-questioning and immediately lived questions must be a most *concrete* question itself. Moreover, in so far as the primordial question of Being is implicitly asked in any question at all, it is not restricted to any *particular* being or group of beings; this question is not a *particular* question, not a question among other questions. The primordial question of Being is truly *comprehensive* in the sense of *all-inclusive* or *all-encompassing.* Thus we have removed the only impediment that prevented us from seeing that the primordial question of Being and the act of *wonder* constitute one and the same reality. For the apparent antinomy between a concrete and unique experience of wonder and an abstract and general question of Being is nonexistent. The primordial question of Being is as concrete and unique as the act of wonder or the original discovery of the radical mysteriousness of *all that is*. The question of Being and wonder constitute one and the same beginning of philosophy. In other words, *the beginning of philosophy is the primordial question of Being, which is the original, concrete and all-encompassing experience of wonder at the radical mysteriousness of the totality of all that is in so far as it is.*

Everyday Situations

Now, in the light of this initial contact with the question of Being it becomes evident that this question cannot arise in the world of our *everyday situations*. For, although everyday situations are fully concrete, they cannot possibly be regarded as comprehensive in the sense of all-encompassing. In our everyday situations we are so concerned with the *particular* necessities of daily life that we do not perceive our "existence" in the *all-encompassing openness of Being,* but rather in the *perspectivistic openness* of the *particular* horizons of our workaday world. This world is not the authentic and comprehensive openness of Being or the openness of *the* world *(Welt),* but rather the unauthentic and particular openness of everyday situations or the openness of our *surrounding* world *(Umwelt).* This workaday world is the world of utilitarian values, of social functions and human labor—"it is the world of supply and demand, of our needs and their satisfaction."[22] To be sure, our everydayness still retains the fundamental structure of man's "ex-sistence" as being-in-the-world. But our everyday situation *conceals* the *authentic way* of being-in-the-world. This workaday world fragmentizes Being into beings, the comprehensive openness into particular concerns and the primordial act of wonder into questions about particulars. It goes without saying that in a situation where Being is not encountered the question of Being cannot arise. The question of Being is not an ordinary question, not a question among other questions and not a question that deals with any of our everyday concerns. The question of Being is not a useful question but a fundamental question. In our everyday situations the term Being remains an empty word, and the question of Being a meaningless question. This explains why the question of Being escapes the meaning of our everyday language, and why it is impossible to "popularize" philosophy.

Scientific Situations

The highly concrete and all-encompassing question of Being cannot arise in *scientific situations* either, since sciences to the extent that they are physical sciences are *abstract* and deal only with a *particular* segment of reality. The physical sciences deal only with *external* reality, and each individual science cuts off its own slice of external reality. Physics studies physical objects, chemistry chemical objects, astronomy astronomical objects etc. Science, therefore, only asks *particular* questions about particular beings or segments of reality, and never fundamental questions about the totality of all that is in so far as it is. The universality of the physical sciences, therefore, is never the *comprehensive* universality of the *all-encompassing* experience of fundamental questions. The *extensive* universality of the physical sciences is not authentic universality, but rather *generality*. The universality of physical laws is, strictly speaking, their *general validity*. A physical law applies to every case or every individual in a certain *class* of beings (L. *genus,* —kind, class). Even a physical law that would apply to the whole universe cannot be universal in the sense of comprehensive or all-encompassing, since it would apply to the class of *material* objects alone and not to the totality of all that is in so far as it is. Physical sciences, therefore, cannot raise the all-encompassing question of Being. Moreover, the knowledge of general laws presupposes a process of objectivization and abstraction. Now, since the question of Being is only concerned with reality in its all-encompassing totality, and with particular beings in the light of this totality, it cannot be asked in a merely abstract way. For, if we withdraw from reality, a *dichotomy,* an opposition between a knowing subject and a known object becomes unavoidable, and, consequently, we exclude our personal existence from the point in question. Although we can readily state that we are not a bookcase, not a mathematical formula, not a tree or a cosmic ray, we cannot seriously maintain that we *are not,* or that there is anything in us which is not in some way or another *involved* in the point in question: Being. The abstractive attitude of the physical sciences, therefore, will never originate the authentic question of Being. "Philosophy never arises out of science or through science and it can never be accorded equal rank with the sciences . . . Philosophy stands in a totally different realm and order."[23] Being does not reveal itself as an ob-ject (in the etymological sense of 'standing over against') to a knowing subject, since the subject itself is *also* involved in Being. Nor does Being reveal itself as *a being,* or as a particular *class* of beings or in any *particular* viewpoint or perspective. For Being implies the totality of all that is, and as the all-encompassing universality it transcends any kind of particularity, any fragmentary experience and even any opposition between subject and object.

Fixated Situations

However, the fact that the question of Being in its comprehensive universality cannot arise on the abstractive level of physical sciences, nor in the fragmentary and perspectivistic experience of our workaday world, does not imply that this question is either nonexistent or devoid of meaning. Such a conclusion does not follow from the mere absence of the question of Being from our workaday world or from the world of the physical sciences. Such a conclusion, therefore, must be based on a dogmatic attitude, on a pseudo-philosophical *fixation* of our fragmentary experience, on an artificial contraction of the whole of our "ex-sistence" and on a *refusal* to ever transcend the rigidity of this contraction. Scientism denies the question of *Being,* because in the physical sciences no such thing as Being is encountered. We have already exposed scientism as the self-contradictory, unscientific and sham philosophical *fixation* on the level of the physical sciences. Here we meet another and similar fixation, namely the "sound common sense" which denies the *question* of Being, because it regards being as self-evident. The "sound common sense" philosophy is a fixation on the level of our workaday world.[24] This "sound common sense" existence is characterized by its "bourgeois" feeling of security, its "detotalization" of totality, its total atrophy of the sense of wonder and its complete intolerance of fundamental questioning. The "sound common sense" attitude imprisons man in his everyday existence and mistakes *beings* for *Being.* Being is regarded as self-evident, for "everyone" knows what being is. The attempt to ask more fundamental questions is looked upon as meaningless and ridiculous. This mentality has inspired philosophers to give some humorous "common sense" definitions of philosophy, such as: "Common sense standing on its head" (Hegel); "the search by a blind man in a dark room for black cat which is not there" (James); "the systematic abuse of terms especially invented for the purpose" (Russell); or "the thinking of an abstract mind which keeps knowing less and less about more and more, until it finally knows nothing about everything."

Unfortunately, any attempt on the part of the philosopher to refute the "sound common sense" mentality is doomed to failure, and would fatally result in a fight between an elephant and a whale for lack of common ground. "Philosophy," says Heidegger, "can never refute common sense since common sense is deaf to the language of philosophy. Nor may it even wish to do so, since common sense is blind to the things which philosophy sets before her essence-seeking eyes."[25] Both scientism and common sense may "explain" things without any contradiction in terms or systematic contradiction. Within the narrow limits of their system, which is based on a contraction of the primary data of consciousness, their thinking is perfectly safe and irrefutable. What does not fit in their system is dismissed as "unimportant" and "irrelevant." Scientism is the thinking of the man "who has lost everything except his reason" (Chesterton), and common sense philosophy ignores everything that does not make "sense" (in the restricted sense of the term). The limits of their systems, however, do not coincide with the limits of reality, and their primary premises contradict the primary data of human consciousness. For fear of having to admit the unfathomable mysteries and inexhaustible depths of Being they escape into philosophical myopia. Neither scientism nor common sense philosophy can be convinced of their nearsightedness by means of the *reason alone*. Only through the experience of *lived* contradictions may they feel compelled to make the "primordial decision" to give up their *idée fixe,* and to allow Being and authentic "ex-sistence" to reveal themselves the way they are. Now, the *lived contradictions* are most acutely experienced in the *limit-situations,* in which the unquestioning securities of man's daily life, and *a fortiori* the dogmatic absolutes of his existential fixations disintegrate.

Limit-Situations

He who accepts the revelatory power of the *limit-situations (Grenzsituationen)*[26] transcends the boundaries of his everyday existence, prepares himself for the possibility of the self-manifestation of Being and places himself on the road that leads to authentic philosophizing. For in the limit-situations man loses his foothold in the realm of particular beings, becomes suddenly aware of the fundamental limitations of his existence and discovers the radical contingency, relativity and finitude of all beings encountered. We find ourselves thrown into these limit-situations in moments of great despair, of existential boredom and of profound suffering. Limit-situations are experienced in the face of death, in moments of anxiety, irony and human tragedy. Limit-situations arise through our awareness that we find ourselves inescapably in a situation, that we are historically determined, and that our freedom is always confronted with the restricting conditions of our environment. In short, limit-situations arise whenever we discover that fundamentally things escape our control, whenever our familiar world loses its solidity and its obviousness, whenever we are confronted with the insurmountable antinomies in the world of particular beings. In other words, the limit-situations show us the *fundamental limits* of any and all particular situations, they point within these situations to a possible transcendency, they indicate that there is something more fundamental without revealing what that "something more fundamental" really is. *In limit-situations Being announces itself without revealing itself.* Let us elucidate the revelatory power of the limit-situations by means of an example. A clear example would be the limit-situation of *existential boredom*. Existential boredom is not the ordinary boredom of our daily life which arises when a particular object or situation does not come up to our expectations, when a book, a play or a conversation bores us. Existential boredom is more fundamental. In existential boredom absolutely *nothing* can interest us any more. Everything seems to have lost its ultimate meaning, the reason of our very "ex-sistence" is called in question and our whole life is reduced to the empty experience of "nothing-ness." "This profound boredom," says Heidegger, "drifting hither and thither in the abysses of existence like a mute fog, draws all things, all men and oneself with them, together in a queer kind of indifference. This boredom reveals what-is in totality."[27] In the existential boredom we do not question the meaning of a particular thing, but within the world of things we experience the "no-thing-ness" of this world. In other words in the existential boredom we are informed about the possibility of transcending all particular situations towards the totality of all that is, we encounter the possibility of the comprehensive universality of Being, but only in its negativity, namely as the negation of all particularity, and we are provoked to ask the fundamental question, "Why is there anything at all and not rather nothing?" This question is a fundamental question, but not yet the primordial question of Being about which we are still completely in the dark. The passage from a limit-situation to the primordial situation still involves a leap. Limit-situations prepare and provoke man to make this leap, but man remains in a position where he can either accept or refuse to accept this provocation. All this is beautifully expressed by Albert Camus in his essay *The Myth of Sisyphus*. "It may happen that the whole environment collapses. Getting up, streetcar, four hours in the office or the factory, meal, streetcar, four hours of work, meal, sleep, and Monday Tuesday Wednesday Thursday Friday and Saturday always the same recurrence —this routine is easily followed most of the time. But one day the 'why' arises and everything begins in that boredom tinged with wonder. 'Begins'—this word is important. Boredom comes at the end of the activities of a mechanical existence, but at the same time it originates the vital impetus of our consciousness. It awakens consciousness and evokes the outcome. The outcome is either the unnoticed return into the chain or else it is the definite awakening."[28]

The Educational Significance of Limit-situations

We can hardly overestimate the importance of the limit-situations for the teaching of philosophy. Since all philosophy is a reflection upon our "immediately lived world" there can be no authentic teaching of philosophy unless the philosopher attempts to meet the student in his "situation," and starts from his actually "asked" questions. If the student simply does not transcend the everyday situations or the level of physical sciences, he will *not ask* himself fundamental questions. If, however, the student has become fixed in these situations, he will *refuse* to ask himself such questions respectively on the basis of the "self-evidence" or the "nonexistence" of their content. At any rate, as long as the student remains in these situations, and as long as the professor is unable to awaken fundamental questioning, his teaching will be doomed to failure for lack of common ground. We have seen, that questions *about* a question become only meaningful in the light of the actual asking of that question. As long as the student does not ask himself fundamental questions he will remain *outside* the meaning of the professor's philosophical language. He will be unable to engage in a dialogue with the philosophical questions and terms pouring from the professor's lips too often at full speed since the professor has to "finish his course." It goes without saying, that this pre-philosophical beginning is a precarious period in which the professor may make or break the philosophical future of his student. All depends on the philosophical authenticity and educational eminence of the professor. It is clear that an atmosphere of sterilizing verbalism or suffocating dogmatism, whether resulting from a fixation of the professor's own thought or from his impatient lack of reverence for the situation of his student, will kill the student's initiative, and will destroy both the possibility of his encounter with Being and his interest in philosophical study. Small wonder, therefore, that the student will regard philosophy as a juggling with empty words, as a matter of "merely academic interest" or a dull discipline he has to undergo because of the "requirements," when he is only offered premature answers to questions he does not have, skeleton-like structures that replace the riches of reality, or textbookish arrogance of omniscience and repulsive dogmatism instead of an open-minded reverence for the mysteries of Being and the actual situation of the student. His thinking is seriously in danger of coagulating into the fixations of "sound common sense" or of "scientism." He may lose his "sense of wonder," and may lose it forever.

Irony and Sarcasm

It is here that the pivotal importance of the *limit-situations* becomes manifest. For, as we have seen, it is precisely in the limit-situations that our everyday certainties lose their obviousness and that the dogmatic absolutes of our existential fixations disintegrate. Now, the professor may provoke in the student such a limit-situation by means of a tactful and respectful use of the *Socratic irony*. Socrates professed his own ignorance and interrogated his pupils in such a way that they became involved in unsolvable antinomies, and were compelled to give irreconcilable answers to the selfsame question and to transcend the level of merely logical reasoning. This dialectical maneuver induced the interlocuters to forsake their former fixations, to transcend their previous certainties and to admit their fundamental ignorance. "Irony," says Karl Jaspers, "is the glare of the thinking out of transcendency annihilating everything, and unsettling everything that could be fixed as valid."[29] Once irony has corroded the solidity of the student's everyday life, once it has revealed the non-ultimacy of his particular outlooks and his objectifying thinking, once it has dissolved his controlling attitude into an existential dizziness in which the meaning of everything remains in suspense, the student touches the comprehensive universality of Being without comprehending it. The student discovers that *no particular object* or outlook is self-sufficient or ultimate, that for a fundamental understanding of that which is he cannot rely on the world of particular objects but has to transcend this world of things, and that the "no-thingness" of this transcendency is no longer an object among the particular objects. Of course, at first the student will be frightened, shocked and irritated. He will think that he has lost everything. He is out of his depth and no longer knows where he is. His very existence is dislocated, and he moves within a sphere of relativity without finding any anchorage, without finding any trace of familiarity. All he knows is his fundamental ignorance.

It goes without saying that the rationalist will frown upon an educational device that *provokes* rather than solves a crisis. For the acceptance of the revelatory power of irony would undermine the fixities of his philosophical foundations. Moreover it would destroy his aim of education which is the perfect adjustment to an impersonal network of functional relationships. In addition, his acceptance of the fundamental relevancy of non-controllable reality would endanger his basic controlling attitude. And finally, it would be difficult for the rationalist not to degrade irony into sarcasm, which is a perverted form of irony. Rationalism as a fixation can only maintain itself by actively destroying anything that transcends it or is superior to it. And sarcasm serves such a purpose. The word sarcasm is derived from the Greek verb *sarkazein* which means "to tear flesh like dogs do" (Gr. *sarx*—flesh). The aim of both irony and sarcasm is to destroy. But whereas irony destroys the barriers that prevent us from engaging in an authentic *dialogue,* sarcasm destroys the very possibility of such a dialogue by humiliating the opponent in the *debate*. The sarcastic educator attempts to make his student feel inferior by heaping scornful, wounding, insulting and sardonic remarks on him. Irony contains humor, is constructive and inspired by the moral requirements of authentic philosophy, namely: love, humility and self-restraint.[30] Sarcasm contains ridicule, is merely destructive and inspired by contempt, dogmatic arrogance and an unrestrained desire to conceal one's weakness and to gain the victory over one's opponent at any cost. Irony makes free, invites to participation and prepares for "the definite awakening." Sarcasm enslaves, antagonizes and causes the "unnoticed return to the chain." Sarcasm causes this return since it forbids its victim to transcend, and compels him to ignore his fundamental ignorance and to withdraw into the complacency of his pseudo-philosophical fixations. True irony, on the other hand, provokes authentic ignorance which is not a sheer lack of knowledge, but rather a higher way of knowing, a "learned ignorance" proceeding from the awareness of one's transcendency and participating in the *dynamism* of this transcendency towards self-fulfillment.[31] This is why Socrates claimed that he was better off than the "intellectuals" of his time. Whereas these people fundamentally did not know anything, but thought they did, Socrates *knew* that he did not know anything. And this active ignorance placed him on the road to wisdom.[32]

The Primordial Situation

The limit-situations, then, are various ways of transcending the securities of everyday life, the particular outlooks of the sciences and their respective fixations. Moreover, the limit-situations make us aware of the philosophical importance of "germinal insights" into fundamental reality that are given to us in moments of despair or anxiety, in courses in art and literature, in personal contacts with the mysteries of birth and death or in the authentic experiences of love, morality and religion. In short, the limit-situations prepare us to hear the voice of Being and to take the leap into the primordial act of wonder. Unfortunately, some contemporary thinkers mistake the limit-situations for the primordial situation. They refuse to take the leap, become fixated at the level of the limit-situations and confuse the primordial situation of man with experiences such as anguish, boredom or despair. Although these philosophies of boredom and despair have a greater revelatory power than the pseudo-philosophies that restrict themselves to the everyday situations or the level of the physical sciences, they, none the less, do not fully escape the accusations of "psychologism." For their thinking is not sufficiently fundamental and has become fixated at a level where man thinks in the light of the *human subject* rather than in the light of *primordial Being*. In the various limit-situations the human subject experiences *within* a particular world the need to transcend anything particular. The source of this need, however, remains concealed, and it is in vain that man keeps looking for that particular "ob-ject" which could explain the origin of his limit-situation. For particular "ob-jects" and perspectivistic outlooks, special methods and even limit-situations are only *modes* of Being. And no *mode* of Being can disclose the comprehensive universality of Being in its authentic originality and uniqueness. In other words, although the limit-situations *prepare* us for an encounter with primordial Being, the actual passage from these situations into *the primordial situation* of our existence still involves a leap. "There are diverse ways and paths," writes Jacques Maritain, "leading towards the attainment of this intuition [the intuition of Being]. None is traced in advance, none is more legitimate than another—precisely because here there is no question of rational analysis or of an inductive or a deductive procedure, or of a syllogistic construction, but only of an intuition which is a primary fact."[33] This primary fact is our *primordial situation* in which Being reveals itself as the primordial act of wonder. A brief discussion of this primordial situation will be the theme of the next chapter.

CHAPTER III

THE PRIMORDIAL PHENOMENON OF WONDER

As we have seen, the question of Being is not concerned with particular beings as particular, but with Being or the totality of all that is and with particular beings in the light of this totality. It matters little, therefore, whether primordial wonder is awakened at the sight of a child's face or a sunset, or at the sudden realization of the precariousness of all that is; whether it proceeds from existential boredom or the despair over the meaning of life, or from moments of creative inspiration; whether it overwhelms us in the midst of our daily occupations or while attending the deathbed of a beloved friend or during the solitary hours of profound meditation or of irrevocable decisions. What matters is that we take the leap by opening up *the whole of our "ex-sistence"* in response to the call of primordial Being. For Being as the all-encompassing universality encompasses us; we do not encompass Being. Being can only be discovered where it reveals itself, namely, in the mysterious act of primordial wonder. And, as a result, any attempt to discover our primordial situation, to raise the question of Being, or to criticize or verify its authenticity *outside* the primordial act of wonder or apart from one's being-in-the-presence of Being, will paralyze our efforts and is doomed to failure. The certainty of being in the primordial situation is not given by anything other than the primordial situation itself.

PRIMORDIAL WONDER COMES UNSOLICITED

Since the question of Being encompasses Being as *all-inclusive universality,* it involves not only the object in question but also the questioner and even the question itself. This is why we are always deeply *involved* and personally *interested* in the question of Being. This is also the reason why the authentic question of Being can only arise *beyond the dichotomy between subject and object.* Strictly speaking, the authentic question of Being is *not of our own making;* this question *posits itself* and *makes us*. Being invites us to transcend the narrow limits of our particular individuality by revealing itself in and through the *primordial act of wonder*. This act of wonder is not so much the approach of man towards Being, but rather the approach of Being towards man. Wonder is an act of Being rather than the act of a psychological subject; wonder is "ontocentric" rather than "anthropocentric." We cannot create wonder at will, because only at certain "gifted" moments do we receive this unique phenomenon as a suddenly overwhelming and intensely inspirational experience.

No special talent or trait of character, no professional skill or logical excellence, not even our intellect alone can produce the primordial question of Being or awaken our authentic sense of wonder. Being as the all-inclusive *totality* does not reveal itself in any *special mode* of Being, profound as this mode may be. The philosophical intellect, for instance, tries to grasp Being in its real intelligibility, whereas the moral will attempts to realize its intelligible reality. The *initial* encounter with Being, however, transcends any distinction between intellect and will, object and subject, essence and existence. Any distinction is based on a differentiation of modes of Being and, as such, is excluded from an *immediate* experience of the totality as totality, from an unreflected being-in-the-presence–of-primordial-Being. The primordial question of Being, therefore, supposes everything but presupposes nothing; it is a *radical* beginning, a spontaneous question, a question which posits itself beyond any possible distinction.

This is why the primordial question of Being is not a question of any *special* human faculty, not even of man as knowing *subject* (as distinguished from a known object). It is rather a question of *the whole of our "ex-sistence,"* or, more exactly, of man as *the participant in the actuality of Being*. It is a question man *is* rather than a question man *has,* an astonishment of our whole personality rather than a merely intellectual inquiry, an existential act of wonder rather than a premeditated problem of research. If man is unwilling to abandon himself in favor of "overwhelming" reality, then Being refuses to reveal itself— not because Being is not ready for us, but rather because we are not ready for Being. Only the radical openness of our whole "ex-sistence" allows the all-encompassing totality of Being to reveal itself in wonder. And only the reverent and humble abandonment of our very self permits us to respond authentically to a reality which escapes our control and which transcends us "overwhelmingly." Being does not reveal itself except to the reverent, humble and genuinely enthusiastic openness of a person in his entirety.

How, then, can we define, describe and demonstrate this unique and original experience of wonder? This question, however, confronts us with an embarrassing dilemma. It seems impossible to do justice to both the nature of wonder and the legitimate desire of the human mind to rely on clearly defined ideas and proven certainties. We either mutilate the nature of a unique experience by defining and describing wonder, or else we leave the human mind unsatisfied.

Should not we distrust an experience which is undefinable and appears to escape our control? An experience which overwhelms us and is literally beyond description does not seem to be a solid foundation for objective thinking. How can subjective experiences such as wonder, enthusiasm and inspiration possibly be the point of departure for a sound and objective philosophy? Does not our reliance upon these philosophically irrelevant phenomena necessarily end in some kind of sham-philosophical subjectivism? We easily recognize these objections as coming from the rationalist camp. And, in effect, we have answered all of them already. Nevertheless, since the present objections are explicitly directed against the philosophical relevancy of our primordial situation, a brief answer to each objection will greatly help our understanding of the question of Being.

PRIMORDIAL WONDER IS UNDEFINABLE

That which is undefinable is not *ipso facto* philosophically irrelevant or unimportant. On the contrary, Being cannot be deduced from any preceding knowledge, for it reveals itself in a *primordial* experience. Nor can it be represented by proximate genus and specific difference, for it is the *all-encompassing universality* which reveals itself *beyond any distinction*. Being is not undefinable because of its emptiness which abstracts from everything, but because of the plenitude of its inexhaustible concreteness. Being is *comprehensive* universality, and as such it is illimitable and undefinable (L. *finis*—limit). One can never say that Being is *this* and not *that*. The definitum cannot be excluded from the definition since the parts of the definition are also parts of the comprehensive totality of Being.

Defining is the *logical* art of determining the precise "limits" of univocal concepts and material reality. Only over the realm of "classifia-ble" and "controllable" reality—in other words, over the world of science and technique—can logic wield its power of *divide et impera:* divide and rule. Being is not *a being* among other beings, and the question of Being is not *a question* among other questions. In the question of Being *everything* is at stake. No definition can exhaustively penetrate the all-inclusive comprehensiveness of primordial Being. No definition can possibly represent the mysterious depths of authentic Being and its original plenitude. The science of formal logic describes the rules for progressive thought, that is, of "calculative" thought in its various shades of abstraction. But logic does not probe into our more fundamental and concrete forms of thinking; nor does it ask for the ultimate "why" of its own rules in the light of Being. Logic never even encounters *Being,* it never transcends the realm of *beings.*

Authentic philosophizing, then, cannot consist in casting Being in a logical mould. This Procrustean method would subordinate Being to the rules of logic, or the whole to a subordinate part. The attempt to explain Being in the light of logic instead of logic in the light of Being results in some kind of intellectual sclerosis. It is the lack of existential openness, the petrifying prejudice underlying the rationalistic sham-philosophies of today. Wonder is not anti-logical but meta-logical, and it does not offend logic by transcending it. Philosophical thinking, there-fore, should be guided by the light of Being rather than by the tendency of "calculative" thinking to conceptualize, to define and classify reality. The original unity of philosophy or "originative" thinking is not so much the unity of classification or systematization, but rather the dynamic unity of the emerging comprehensive universality or primordial Being as it differentiates itself in its progressive self-explicitation through human "ex-sistence."

Primordial Wonder is Undescribable

The very fact that wonder originates *beyond any differentiation* makes this unique experience literally an *undescribable* phenomenon. We are unable to give an account of its "characteristics" or its "specific qualities," for the primordial self-revelation of Being transcends any such distinctions. Wonder cannot be elucidated in terms of anything other than itself. However, the impossibility of describing wonder—or in effect any original or fundamental phenomenon—does not impair its intelligibility. On the contrary, anything we want to describe has to be *immediately given* prior to the description. "Givenness" precedes description, or the immediacy of an original datum is fundamentally prior to its descriptive mediatization. Immediate or unreflected given-ness is the necessary presupposition of our descriptive activity, the un-describable stands at the beginning of any possible description. Descrip-tion is only a mediatization or a means to improve the "givenness" of an original "datum." Description never takes place apart from the unre-flected experience, it is never a thing in itself or an absolute beginning, but it is constantly nourished by the immediate experience. To mistake the intermediary for the original source of intelligibility, to absolutize the mediatization and regard it as a primary datum, and to completely forget the original experience of our *Lebenswelt* is typical of the spirit of abstraction of our technocratic age.

PRIMORDIAL WONDER IS INSPIRATIONAL

The undescribable experience of wonder, then, is also an *overwhelming* and profoundly *inspirational* experience. Our existential openness to the experience of the all-pervasive comprehensiveness of primordial Being far transcends our controlling attitude. This is why our original encounter with the totality of all that is escapes our control, and is given as a response to *the call of Being*. From this, however, it does not follow that our reliance upon wonder should result in some sort of *subjectivism*. On the contrary, this overwhelming and all-encompassing experience cannot possibly be subjective for the very reason that it arises *beyond the dichotomy* between subject and object. Man can never be a mere *subject* when dealing with questions of Being. Being, or the comprehensive universality does not reveal itself as something "standing over against" (ob-ject) man as a human subject, as something "faced" by man as a mere onlooker, as something that can be judged upon and controlled from the privileged standpoint of an "outsider" or a mere "spectator." Man does not encounter primordial Being as an indifferent human "subject" confronted with Being as a neutral "ob-ject," but rather as a "participant" in the self-revelation of this primordial phenomenon. He who claims to be indifferent to the question of Being merely proves that he has never really asked this primordial question. Man is deeply "inter-ested" in this question of Being because he is utterly "involved" in the question.

Strictly speaking, wonder is not a standpoint of man about Being, but rather the standpoint of Being in and through man. In wonder man is "overwhelmed" by Being which encompasses man and escapes his controlling attitude. Being reveals itself as a "given" reality, a reality which is received in our most "gifted moment," in the existential act of wonder. This primordial "givenness" of Being[34] is constitutive of our authentic "ex-sistence" and makes us fully what we are, namely, human beings. Of course, Being as the *all-encompassing* totality of all that is *gives itself only in the act by which it is fully received*, namely, in *wonder* or the *total openness and creative receptivity of man's whole personality*. Even our very openness, therefore, is received as a "gift" from Being. This is why the primordial act of wonder is at the same time our primordial act of *gratitude* since the whole of our "existence" is received *as a gift*. In wonder the primordial meaning of "gift" and of "gratitude" are undifferentiated. In other words, it is only in the active openness of our "ex-sistence" that Being "presents itself," and that the "present" of Being becomes constitutive of the "self-presence" of our authentic "ex-sistence" which is the most original "present" we can possibly receive, namely, *the present we are*. Being and not man takes the initiative. Being gives us a meaningful existence beyond the narrow limits of our subjective *Ego; man is essentially more than he is* as the participant in the self-revelation of Being. It goes without saying that this basic paradox of human "ex-sistence" is totally ignored by the spirit of abstraction which characterizes our technocratic age. Yet great thinkers of all times have recognized this fundamental paradox. For instance, as to wonder and activities originating in wonder Aristotle said they "might be justly regarded as beyond human power,"[35] and St. Thomas Aquinas stated that they are "not strictly speaking human, but rather superhuman."[36] Or as Pieper writes, " . . . man himself is in a measure superhuman and is, as Pascal says, infinitely above man."[37] This is also correctly given by Pieper as the reason why "every attempt to provide a smooth definition of man is bound to fail."[38]

Since man is more than he is as the participant in the actuality of Being, it is *impossible* for him to be the complete "possessor" of his authentic "ex-sistence," nor can he, strictly speaking, "control" the dynamism of its emergence. Consequently, our most authentic activities are *not* entirely *ours*. This is why artistic creativity, philosophical meditation, authentic love, moral heroism, etc. are characterized by features such as: "ecstasy" (Gr. *ek* and *stasis:* standing out, being beside oneself); "enthusiasm" (Gr. *en* and *theos:* 'being possessed' by a supreme Being); "inspiration" (L. *in* and *spirare:* to breathe into, to infuse by breathing); "gratuitousness" (L. *gratuitus:* spontaneous, given free, unexpected, overwhelming, not of our making) and "mystery" (Gr. *muoo:* to look through one's eyelashes, to see the unseen, to participate in the super-intelligible source of intelligibility).

Wonder, then, instead of being the source of subjectivity, calls man beyond his subjective Ego into the true universality of the all encompassing experience of primordial Being. In wonder man's thinking and action become authentic, or, to put it in another way, in wonder man's actions and insights are more of Being than of himself; they are guided by the self-manifestation of Being rather than by the subjectivity of his own *Ego*. Man is more than a thinking thing or a human subject that knows and controls physical ob-jects. To be the *locus* of the self-revelation of Being is constitutive of the being of man. Man is a being whose very essence it is to be the *open relation to Being* or to "exsist" in the etymological sense of the word.

PRIMORDIAL WONDER IS UNDEMONSTRABLE

Since, as we have seen, wonder *pre-supposes nothing* but itself, it is a *radical beginning* which posits itself beyond any kind of mediatization or discursiveness. Consequently, wonder is our *most original* and highest possible *immediacy* of insight and revelation. In wonder there is not even a differentiation given between man's openness to Being and the self-manifestation of Being to man. Wonder is strictly an act of intuitive self-evidence, provided that we understand the term self-evidence in the sense of seeing reality in its immediate "givenness" to our unreflected consciousness, and not in the rationalistic sense of an alleged pure self-transparency of the human consciousness or of clearly and distinctly perceived abstract principles. An *explicit* intuition of Being, however, would contradict the nature of man as "ex-sistence" or as emergence, as dynamic possibility of Being (*Seinkönnen*—Heidegger). Primordial Being remains the *implicit principle* and guiding light throughout its dialectical self-manifestation in man, a point which we shall discuss in the next chapter.

Wonder, then, the immediate self-manifestation of Being to our pre-reflective consciousness, or the implicit intuition of the all-encompassing universality, is by necessity a *primordial self-evidence*. And as such wonder is *undemonstrable*. For, being a primordial datum, wonder cannot be elucidated by anything other than itself, nor can it be derived from any previous knowledge. This primordial self-evidence of wonder cannot be proved—but it does not need to be. For wonder belongs to the "primary premises" of all thinking, and is, in effect, the *primordial premise* of fundamental thinking. Without the primordial experience of wonder, philosophical demonstrations would remain without foundation, and philosophical thinking would become a thinking *in vacuo*.

Some thinkers assume that nothing can be truly known unless it can be demonstrated. According to these thinkers the assumption of primary data or primary premises necessarily results in some kind of "dogmatism." Aristotle could already say in his time, "Some hold that, owing to the necessity of knowing the primary premises, there is no scientific knowledge. Others think there is scientific knowledge but that all truths are demonstrable."[39] But Aristotle immediately subjoins his own observations: "Neither doctrine is either true or a necessary deduction from the premises."[40] After all, to prove a truth is to make it more evident by means of a demonstration. Demonstration is an indirect intuition, a mediated immediacy, an immediately lived "giveness" which becomes more explicitly given by means of "discursiveness" (L. *discurrere:* to turn in different directions). But, as we have seen, all reflection, discursiveness and demonstration begins in the unreflected experience of the immediately lived world and is constantly nourished by it. Aristotle puts it succinctly when he states that "the starting-point of demonstration is not demonstration."[41]

If a demonstration is based on premises that in their turn are not immediately evident, then these premises too need to be proved. If, however, *demonstrability* were the *ultimate criterion of all truth,* we would become involved in an infinite regress, and truth could not be discovered at all. We cannot go on *ad infinitum:* we have to stop, as Aristotle says, in immediate truths. Let us quote the well known passage from *Posterior Analytics:* "Our own doctrine is that not all knowledge is demonstrative: on the contrary, knowledge of the immediate premises is independent of demonstration. The necessity of this is obvious: for since we must know the prior premises from which the demonstration is drawn, and since the regress must end in immediate truths, those truths must be undemonstrable."[42]

Our reliance, then, upon unproved and undemonstrable self-evidences or on primary data of the immediately lived world does not result in a dogmatic attitude. On the contrary, it is precisely the assertion that "demonstrability" is the ultimate criterion of all truths which is dogmatic. For, in order to be self-consistent, one who claims that every truth should be demonstrable, should be able to prove this assertion. The very attempt, however, to prove this thesis would involve this thinker in the crippling necessity of an "infinite regress" or of a "vicious circle." This thesis, therefore, cannot possibly be demonstrated and contains a lived contradiction.

What has been said about the necessity of primary self-evidences holds eminently true for the *primordial self-evidence of Being,* which is given in the existential act of wonder. Wonder as the primordial self-evidence of the comprehensive universality of Being cannot depend on anything else for its self-manifestation and is a radical beginning. For everything other than the all-inclusive experience of the totality of all that is, is simply nothing; and whatever is not nothing is included in wonder. This means that even the total openness of our "ex-sistence" in which primordial Being is perceived is an undifferentiated part of the act of wonder. In other words, *primordial Being reveals itself only to our unconditional acceptance of its self-manifestation, or it does not reveal itself at all.*

THE TRUSTWORTHINESS OF PRIMORDIAL WONDER

The primordial question of Being, then, cannot possibly be defined, described or demonstrated in terms of anything other than itself. Wonder is the undemonstrable point of departure of any philosophical demonstration. It is the undescribable source of any authentic description. And it stands as an undefinable and intuitive self-evidence at the beginning of all our fundamental thinking. Thus we have found the answers to the objections raised at the beginning of this section. By not being able to demonstrate, to define or even to describe the primordial experience of wonder, we certainly have to leave the human mind unsatisfied. Nothing is less satisfactory from the viewpoint of the merely logical frame of mind. But we have also found that merely "calculative" thinking does not satisfy the requirements for "originative" thinking. Unsatisfied, however, will also remain our "originative" thinking. But for a quite different reason. St. Augustine who said: "Our heart is restless until it rests in Thee, O Lord" was not speaking as a "maladjusted" man who was "unable to reduce his restlessness," but as a philosopher who expressed a profound truth of human nature. Since it is our essence to "ex-sist," we are fundamentally "emerging" or "becoming" beings. As Pieper writes: "We are essentially *viatores,* on the way, beings who are 'not yet.' "[43] In other words, as "ex-sistent" beings we are participants in the primordial event of Being which is the "presence of inexhaustible concreteness" (Marcel) or the "superintelligible source of intelligibility" (Maritain). *Fundamental answers,* therefore, although they increase the light of our originative thinking, also increase the intensity of our perpetual "not yet," and always return as deeper questions. This means that philosophical questions can never be answered with complete finality or to our full satisfaction. This fact, however, instead of blocking our quest for truth and ending philosophy at its very beginning, provides us with the vital impetus needed to start originative thinking and to continue its fundamental explorations into the promised land of Being. Consequently, instead of distrusting the undescribable, undefinable and undemonstrable act of wonder and its inspirational characteristics, we rather should distrust the arrogation to the merely logical frame of mind of philosophical ultimacy.

THE DIFFICULTY OF GRASPING WONDER IN ITS PRISTINE ORIGINALITY

Although the idea that wonder is the beginning of philosophy has become a commonplace in the history of philosophy, we will look in vain for a description of this undescribable experience. And this is to be expected, since any attempt to describe wonder either conceals its undecribable uniqueness or makes explicit what as primordial experience is implicit or immediately lived. The first allusion to wonder in the history of Western thinking is found in Plato's dialogue *Theaetetus*. Here wonder is hinted at as what we would call today "cosmic dizziness" or "oceanic feeling." The comprehensive universality is given and the comprehensive universality is in suspense. Consciousness steps out of the narrow bounds of the *Ego* and a transcendent intuition is awakened in which limitless horizons open up and foundations disintegrate, in which everything becomes at the same time infinitely remote and intimately close, and in which one's being is reduced to a drop in the infinite ocean while at the same time the infinite ocean seems to be contained in the drop. Things can no longer be localized in time and space, but seem to be freely floating while they are drawn into a whirlpool of a kind of mysterious omnipresence.[44] Plato was the first thinker who recognized the revelatory power of this primordial experience by calling wonder the beginning of philosophy. In his dialogue *Theaetetus* Plato describes how the old Socrates had tactfully applied his method of irony to the young mathematician Theaetetus. Theaetetus who is filled with awe, astonishment and cosmic dizziness exclaims: "Good heavens, Socrates, I am astonished when I think of the significance of these questions, and at times I become really dizzy when I try to probe into them." Then follows the famous answer of Socrates: "I see, my dear Theaetetus, that Theodorus hit the mark when he called you a philosopher. For wonder is the basic mood of a philosopher. Wonder, and nothing else is the beginning of philosophy."[45]

Let us give, by way of example, a more recent allusion to wonder. For instance, in his *The Degrees of Knowledge* Jacques Maritain quotes a close acquaintance of his as saying: ". . . it often happened that by a sudden intuition I experienced the reality of my own being, of the deepest, first principle that placed me outside nothingness. It was a powerful intuition and its violence often frightened me; that intuition gave me, for the first time, knowledge of a metaphysical absolute."[46] As a mere allusion to wonder this statement is perfectly acceptable. As a possible explicitation of wonder, however, it would not say enough, and as a description of this primordial experience it would say too much. For, as we will see in the next chapter, the explicitation of wonder differentiates this phenomenon into a multi-dimensional structure. The statement indicates only one dimension, namely the dimension of the "self" without making mention of any other basic dimension. This is clearly not enough. But as a description of wonder the statement would say too much. For wonder as the primordial self-revelation of the comprehensive totality as totality is unconcerned with any particular modes of Being. And since any differentiation implies a certain particularization or specialization of distinguishing characteristics, the primordial experience of wonder must be completely undifferentiated. The statement, however, indicates several distinguishing characteristics of wonder, such as the fact that wonder is sudden, intuitively perceived and unconditional, the fact that wonder is a primordial beginning, that it awakens anxiety, etc. As a description of primordial wonder, therefore, the statement would say too much. The shortest possible allusion to the undescribable act of wonder would be: *"I am!?"* And even this allusion would be too differentiated. For in this primordial experience no differentiation is given between the "self" and the "to be," or between the "exclamation mark" and the "question mark." No differentiation is given between the question and the questioner, between the phenomenon of Being and the Being of this phenomenon. Primordial wonder is an immediately "lived" astonishment of the whole of our "ex-sistence" rather than an explicitly asked question. Primordial wonder is the interiorizing self-transcendency of our all-inclusive openness as participants in the comprehensive universality of Being rather than an incidental encounter with anything particular as particular. The fact, however, that wonder is undefinable and undescribable makes it impossible to present this phenomenon by anything other than itself. It is, therefore, very difficult to grasp wonder in its original purity, and not to mistake Being for what it is not.

THE DANGER OF THE ATROPHY OF THE SENSE OF WONDER

In many thinkers the faculty of wonder has dried up by their premature systematization of philosophy, by substituting some particular mode of Being for primordial Being, and consequently, by leaving wonder as the beginning of philosophy behind. Now genuine philosophizing can never leave its original beginning behind, since primordial Being is all-inclusive. True philosophy cannot, strictly speaking, raise any questions "outside" the primordial experience of wonder, and in any philosophical question the totality of all that is presents itself and is at stake.

Philosophy is the differentiated self-explicitation of wonder or the dialectical self-manifestation of Being. This is why Plato called wonder the *basic mood* of the philosopher, and why Pieper writes: "Wonder is not just the starting point of philosophy in the sense of *initium,* of a prelude or preface. Wonder is the *principium,* the lasting source, the *fons et origo,* the immanent origin of philosophy. The philosopher does not cease 'wondering' at a certain point of his philosophizing—he does not cease to wonder unless, of course he ceases to philosophize in the true sense of the word."[47] Wonder focalizes strictly philosophical thinking, and as philosophy begins, so too it ends, namely in wonder. And this ending is always a renewed beginning, in wonder. Wonder is the oldest question in philosophy, and at the same time it is always the youngest question asked by any authentic philosopher. It is in this profound sense that we can say that a true philosopher is always a beginner. He who is first struck by the overwhelming experience of wonder is a "first" beginner; the "advanced" philosopher is a "greater" beginner. And a philosopher ceases to be a true philosopher to the extent that he ceases to wonder.

It is important not to mistake wonder for something other than wonder, since wonder is the permanent source of all originative thinking. On the other hand, it is difficult to grasp wonder in its primordial authenticity, since this unique phenomenon is an undefinable and undescribable experience. We will, therefore, conclude and summarize this chapter by summing up what wonder or the primordial question of Being *is not.* By contrasting wonder with its various historical substitutes we may be able to intensify our immediately lived awareness of its authentic manifestation. This, of course, can only be done in the light of at least an implicit experience of wonder. Now, it is precisely the awakening of this *implicit* experience of wonder which has been the aim of the present chapter. A progressive *explicitation* of the primordial act of wonder will be the task of the following chapters. This is why we should not regard the following statements as exhaustive and final. For, as we have seen, fundamental insights evoke a deepened sense of wonder, call for further explicitations, and return as more fundamental questions. The following statements, therefore, will be gradually elucidated and seen in deeper perspectives throughout our explicitations of wonder in the following chapters.

SUMMARIZING REMARKS

Wonder as the primordial question of Being is not an *explicit* question. Wonder reveals itself as the immediately lived experience of our primordial situation.

Wonder as the primordial question of Being is not an *abstract* question. An abstract question cannot encompass the all-inclusive universality of Being.

Wonder as the primordial question of Being is not a *particular* question. A particular question is not concerned with the comprehensive universality. Being is never this or that.

Wonder as the primordial question of Being is not an *irrational* question. An irrational question offends the reason. By transcending the reason and relating it to its superintelligible source wonder does not offend the reason but reveals its existential ground.

Wonder as the primordial question of Being is not a *disinterested* question. The questioner is utterly involved in the comprehensive universality of the question.

Wonder as the primordial question of Being is not a question *about* Being. This primordial question cannot be asked by anything other than itself.

Wonder as the primordial question of Being is not a question of the *intellect alone*. Primordial Being does not reveal itself in any mode of Being, but in the presence of the whole of our "ex-sistence" to the all-encompassing self-manifestation of Being.

Wonder as the primordial question of Being is not a *philosophical* question. Philosophy is an explicit "re-flection" on the primordial situation. Primordial Being is the implicit and pre-philosophical beginning of philosophy.

Wonder as the primordial question of Being is not an *ordinary* question. Ordinary questions are found among other questions in our everyday situation. The all-encompassing question of Being underlies all ordinary questions. And this unique primordial situation transcends all everyday situations.

Wonder as the primordial question of Being does not *withdraw from everyday situations*. The comprehensive universality of Being does not withdraw from anything. Transcending everyday situations means that they are viewed in a more fundamental light and lose their unquestioned obviousness.

Wonder as the primordial question of Being is not a question of the totality *as totality*. To know something *as such* requires explicit or thematic knowledge.

Wonder as the primordial question of Being is not a *subjective* question. Wonder is not a question of the human subject in opposition to an external object. The all-encompassing universality of Being transcends the dichotomy between subject and object.

Wonder as the question of Being is not a question *of specialists.* Specialists as such are unconcerned with the comprehensive totality of all that is.

Wonder as the primordial question of Being is not a question we *have.* Wonder as the astonishment of the whole of our "ex-sistence" constitutes the very root of this "ex-sistence," and is rather a question we *are.*

Wonder as the primordial question of Being is neither a question of the *philosophy of Being* nor a question of the *philosophy of knowledge.* Wonder is not a philosophical question at all. It is the pre-philosophical encounter with primordial Being in which knowledge and Being are given in their still undifferentiated and primary unity. No differentiation is given between the phenomenon of Being and the Being of the phenomenon.

Wonder as the primordial question of Being is neither a *judgment,* nor a *concept* or an *idea.* Primordial Being is the pre-predicative, unreflected and superintelligible source of all modes of intelligibility.

Wonder as the primordial question of Being is not a *dogmatic* question. It is precisely the denial of the possibility of this question which is based on the dogmatic absolutism of pseudo-philosophies.

Wonder as the primordial question of Being is not an *empty* question, which has to be filled by particular beings. Primordial Being is the inexhaustible source of concreteness which sheds a more fundamental light on particular beings.

Wonder as the primordial question of Being is not a *static self-evidence* in the sense of a completely transparent self-consciousness or of clear and distinct concepts. Primordial Being is self-evident in the sense that the all-encompassing universality needs nothing but itself to reveal itself *(selbstgegeben)* as the profoundly dynamic mystery of Being.

Wonder as the primordial question of Being is not a *sensation* or a being startled by something exciting or thrilling. The particularity of these experiences fails to impress the all-encompassing expectation of wonder. The sensational dulls the sense of wonder; whereas in wonder the sensational loses its fascination and man wonders at things usual which our everyday existence takes for granted.

Wonder as the primordial question of Being is not *disillusionment, anguish, boredom* or *despair.* These limit-situations, to be sure, prepare man for the act of wonder by freeing him from illusions and sham absolutes. But the transition from these situations to wonder still involves a leap.

Wonder as the primordial question of Being is not *doubt*. Primordial Being reveals itself only to the unconditional acceptance of its self-manifestation or it does not reveal itself at all. Moreover, doubt presupposes differentiation and choice which is precisely not given in wonder.

Wonder as the primordial question of Being is not merely the beginning of philosophy in the sense of a *prelude* or a pre-established framework of reference. Wonder is the lasting principle and immanent source of philosophical thinking, or, for that matter, of all aspects of our authentic or mature "ex-sistence," such as moral responsibility, authentic love, religious life etc.

All this implies that the primordial question of Being does not read as follows:

"What is Being?" This is an explicit, and, therefore, philosophical question.

"Is there such a thing as Being?" This question remains outside the primordial question of Being.

"Am I?" This question shows that Being is not given because it is not received.

"Why is there anything at all rather than nothing?" This question arises from limit-situations such as boredom and despair. The transition to the primordial question of Being still involves a leap. Moreover, what seems to be self-evident and immediately given is *nothingness* and not *Being.*[48]

Descartes' startingpoint: "I think, therefore, I am," makes abstraction from the world, and is a static, self-enclosed evidence which does not reveal the all-encompassing universality of primordial Being. Descartes' *dualism* underlies our modern empiricism and rationalism, which both contradict our primordial situation by detotalizing the comprehensive openness of human "ex-sistence."[49]

CHAPTER IV

WONDER AND
PHILOSOPHICAL AUTHENTICITY

The claim that philosophy begins in wonder has become a commonplace in the history of philosophy. Unfortunately, however, it has been a common practice *not to begin* philosophy in wonder. Wonder has merely functioned as a catalyzer which remains untouched by the philosophical reaction it produces, or as a trigger which sets the mechanism of a philosophical mind in action but plays no role in the construction of a philosophical system and its appropriate method. In other words, wonder ceases to have any revelatory power as soon as a rigorous method has been found and the first outlines of a philosophical system are taking shape. Method and system are substituted for wonder, and wonder is no longer the permanent source of philosophical thinking.

Nevertheless, we discovered in the preceding chapter that wonder is the immanent and lasting source of fundamental thinking, and that the philosopher ceases to philosophize to the extent that he ceases to wonder. Plato, who called wonder the beginning of philosophy, also emphasized that this primordial experience is the "basic mood" (Gr. *pathos*) of the philosopher. In this connection it is worth noting that Plato employed the Greek word *arkhe* to indicate the relationship between wonder and philosophy.[50] Wonder is not merely the "beginning" of philosophy in the sense of "initial stage," but wonder is also the "governing" principle of fundamental thinking. Wonder not only "begins" philosophy but also remains its "guiding" light throughout. In other words, *wonder focalizes philosophical authenticity*. A philosophy which does not actually begin in wonder is from the very start out of focus. A philosophy which does not actually begin in wonder distorts the fundamental "way of thinking" or philosophical *method* (Gr. *meta* and *hodos:* "way after"), falsifies philosophical "strictness" and becomes one-sided by overemphasizing one aspect of fundamental thinking at the expense of other, co-original aspects. It will, therefore, be our task in this chapter to reflect on *the actual beginning of philosophy in wonder.* This actual beginning will reveal the strictly philosophical "way of thinking" or the appropriate *strictness of philosophy as method* (Chapter V). The philosophical reflection on wonder differentiates this undifferentiated primordial experience into the "dialectical self-manifestation of Being" or *logos.* It is only as *logos* that philosophy unfolds in a strictly philosophical way, and that the co-original aspects of philosophy as method preserve their philosophical authenticity as *the interplay of ontology, phenomenology and dialectics* (Chapter VI).

THE ACTUAL BEGINNING OF PHILOSOPHY

The most *decisive* moment in philosophy is its actual beginning. Primordial wonder, as we have seen, is the undifferentiated, immediately lived and pre-reflective question of primordial Being. And since every question is the beginning of its answer, wonder as the primordial question of Being contains the implicit affirmation of Being as its initial answer. This first answer, however, remains fully implicit, and is not yet differentiated from the primordial question itself. In other words, this first answer is not yet known *as* answer, this first affirmation is not yet known *as* affirmation and Being is not yet known *as* Being. *As such* primordial wonder, strictly speaking, is nothing. This makes us *wonder at the primordial experience of wonder.* We ask ourselves the fundamental question what wonder ultimately *is.*

Now, when we wonder at primordial wonder we actually *re-flect* on this primordial experience. *Re-flection,* however, as a "turning back upon" presupposes a certain *distance,* a certain *differentiation.* In other words, our wonder at primordial wonder does *not fully* coincide with this primordial experience itself. Our undifferentiated "wonder-consciousness" changes into a *consciousness of* wonder. A certain thematization takes place in which *primordial* wonder becomes the *theme* of *reflective* wonder. Primordial wonder differentiates into an "intentional act" with a subject pole and an object pole. *This intentional act of reflective wonder is our "primitive cognitive intention"* (Dondeyne) *and actually begins our philosophical thinking.* However, the oppositional unity between an object pole and a subject pole is not the only differentiation resulting from our first reflection on wonder. This primitive cognitive intention differentiates primordial wonder into a *multi-dimensional structure* of original phenomena or an *articulated whole* of primary philosophical data. It goes without saying that because of the polar *unity* of the intentional act both the object pole and the subject pole of the primitive cognitive intention are affected by this articulation. Being (the object pole) manifests itself (subject pole) in a differentiated or dialectical way. And this is to be expected since on the one hand reflective wonder is no longer the undifferentiated awareness of primordial Being, and on the other hand an explicit consciousness of Being would contradict the nature of man as "ex-sistence," as "emergence" or *homo viator,* and would require a kind of deification of human "ex-sistence."[51]

THE PRIMARY DATA OF PHILOSOPHY

Now, re-flecting upon primordial wonder I find-myself-being-together-with-others-in-the-world.[52] The way Being manifests itself in the primitive cognitive intention is different from the way it reveals itself in primordial wonder. Our re-flection on primordial wonder "ex-plicates," or "un-folds" this undifferentiated experience into the unitary structure of "ex-sistence" in the etymological sense of the word. Consequently, an accurate description of this "ex-sistence" in the light of primordial Being is our only access to the philosophical question of Being. In other words, the fundamental dis-covery of our "ex-sistence" as the multi-dimensional openness focalized by our essential openness towards Being is the actual beginning and central reference-point of all our philosophical thinking. To put it differently again, the actual beginning of philosophy is a re-flection on the pre-philosophical experience of Being which reveals the fundamental phenomena of "ex-sistence" as the primary data of philosophical thinking.

The *primary data* of philosophical thinking are *original* phenomena. This means that they are *beginnings* in their own right, they *reveal themselves,* are *self-given (selbstgegeben)* and cannot be reduced to anything more fundamental. They cannot be deduced from primordial Being since primordial Being does not contain anything differentiated, and they cannot be induced from particular beings since the mere knowledge of particular beings lacks the *com-prehension* (grasping-together) which defines "ex-sistence" as differentiated Being. In other words, the philosopher does not construct or make the primary data of philosophy, but the primary data of philosophy make the philosopher. The philosopher, instead of constructing the primary data of philosophy, rather "encounters" them in his primitive cognitive intention. He has to recognize and to respect them and to allow them to reveal themselves the way they are. Now, they reveal themselves neither as one single and isolated phenomenon, nor as many separated and unconnected phenomena, but as the *unitary structure* of "ex-sistence" which is the actual beginning of philosophy. The actual beginning of philosophy, therefore, is neither the one, nor the many, but a *polar tension* between the one and the many, an *existential dialogue* between differentiated wonder and primordial wonder. The "actual" beginning of philosophy is a dialogue with the "pre-philosophical" beginning of philosophy, and philosophy points "from the very beginning" *beyond* philosophy. This paradox, this tension between immanency and transcendency is the actual beginning of philosophy and the mainspring of all our philosophical explorations. To ignore this paradoxical tension is to "detotalize" the *integral whole* of "ex-sistence" as the actual beginning of philosophy. Those who mistake one single and isolated phenomenon for the "first principle" of philosophy are as much detotalizing the actual beginning of philosophy as are those who start from many unrelated "first principles." And since philosophy is a re-flection on its beginning, a detotalized beginning will begin a philosophical "deviation," or a philosophy which turns aside from the authentic philosophical way of thinking.

THE QUESTION OF PRESUPPOSITIONLESS PHILOSOPHY

It is sometimes said that philosophy as our most fundamental and autonomous way of thinking should be *free from all presuppositions*. This freedom from presuppositions *(Voraussetzungslosigkeit),* however, can easily be misunderstood. If we mean that philosophy should begin in a strictly philosophical way, free from any *dogmatic* presuppositions, from pre-fabricated concepts, free from anything that is not "actually given" in the primitive cognitive intention, then we merely express an essential characteristic of philosophical "strictness." If, however, we mean that philosophy starts from absolute zero we contradict the nature of the primitive cognitive intention. For, philosophy is actually beginning as a "re-flection" on primordial wonder. Primordial wonder, therefore, is presupposed by this reflection. Moreover, it is precisely in this first re-flection that the primary data of philosophical thinking manifest themselves as the first spontaneous and immediately lived differentiations of primordial Being. Also the primary data of "ex-sistence," therefore, as integral parts of the differentiated self-manifestation of Being belong to the presuppositions of philosophical re-flection. In other words, although the beginning of philosophy as a spontaneous encounter between fundamental phenomena and primordial Being is a primary datum which cannot be reduced to anything more fundamental and remains the lasting source of all philosophical reflection, *this philosophical re-flection itself presupposes the philosophical beginning as al-*

ready "given." To put it differently again, the very moment we begin to philosophize we are "already" engaged, we are "already" *on the way.* The beginning of philosophy is a *re-flective spontaneity,* an *immanent dialectics,* a *circular movement.*

The beginning of philosophy as the first *re-flection* on the comprehensive universality of Being is *differentiated from* or *other than* primordial wonder. But at the same time, as a reflection on *the comprehensive universality* of Being the beginning of philosophy *cannot possibly be different from* or *other than* wonder. For, strictly speaking, there can be *nothing outside* the comprehensive universality of all that is. In other words, philosophical re-flection, far from leading us *away from* primordial wonder brings us back *into it.* Philosophical wonder *does not replace* primordial wonder but *mediates* it. Philosophy is the progressive self-mediation, the dialectical self-manifestation, or the differentiated interiorizing self-transcendency of the primordial light of Being. Every philosophical question is a self-mediation of the all-inclusive immediacy of Being, every philosophical question questions the integral totality of all that is, every philosophical question involves the whole of philosophy. "The truth is the whole," says Hegel.[53] The immediacy of primordial wonder remains the focal point and guiding light of all the self-mediations of the immediacy of primordial Being. A question is precisely philosophical to the extent that it involves wonder in its immanent dialectics. Primordial wonder, therefore, *focalizes philosophical authenticity.*

PHILOSOPHICAL AUTHENTICITY

Philosophy is *authentic* when it is "strictly" philosophical. And philosophy is *strictly* philosophical in so far as it develops in undeviating conformity to its own principles, standards and conditions (L. *stringere*—to draw tight). Generally speaking, thinking is strict when it 1) holds its *own* 2) in the undeviating *way* (method) 3) in which its dynamism proceeds from its *proper beginning.* The "strictness" of a science determines its authenticity by the appropriate way in which it mediates the immediate data of its beginning, or by the undeviating firmness of its fidelity to its own first principles. It goes without saying that any science deserving the name should be *strict,* but also that the *kind of strictness differs* from science to science. Those who mistake one specific kind of strictness for the prototype of strictness as such misunderstand the very nature of strictness, blur the distinctions between the various sciences and impair sciential authenticity. The English word "authentic" is derived from the Greek *authentes,* one who does things himself, one who acts with authority or is the actual origin of something. Something is "authentic" when it is of original stock, genuine, really proceeding from its reputed source or author, authoritative. Now, philosophy is authentic when it really proceeds from its beginning as the "strict" self-mediation of primordial wonder, or when it "un-folds" primordial wonder in *undeviating fidelity* to its *actual beginnings* which is *the re-flection on the dialectical self-manifestation of Being* or *logos*. In other words, philosophy is authentic when its *reflective way of thinking* (method) is differentiated into three co-original aspects, namely: *ontology* (Gr. *on*—Being, and *logos*), *phenomenology* (Gr. *phenomenon*—that which manifest itself, and *logos*) and *dialectics* (Gr. *dia*—apart, differentiated, and *logos*). Those who ignore the interdependency of these equiprimordial aspects of the philosophical way of thinking and employ one aspect at the expense of the others are unfaithful to the actual beginning of philosophy and corrode philosophical authenticity.

Another aspect of the philosophical "strictness" is the undeviating fidelity of the philosophical way of thinking to its actual beginning *as reflection*. The actual beginning, as we have seen, is the *re-flection* on the dialectical self-manifestation of Being. And this re-flection, instead of leading us away from the actual beginning, brings us back into it. In other words, philosophy actually begins in a *circular* fashion, begins as a *re-flection* on the beginning, and in this re-flection the actual beginning becomes the *pro-ject* of philosophical reflection (L. *projicere*—to throw forward). Philosophy *is* the differentiated returning upon itself of the fundamental meaning of the integral totality of all that is. Philosophy *is* the self-questioning of its primitive cognitive intention or the self-questioning of its actual beginning. Philosophy is "arche-ology" (Husserl) in the etymological sense of the word, is "the *logos* of beginnings." Once again, the actual beginning in philosophical wonder is not only a preface, but it remains the lasting source, the pro-ject, the aim, the immanent finality, the guiding light and the philosophical question *par excellence* throughout our philosophical explorations. The scope of philosophy is its progressive self-foundation, its ever renewed and enriched self-beginning, its deeper and deeper self-questioning of its primary data. The actual beginning of philosophy determines its aim and scope, and the beginning *is* the end, but in a beginning way, namely as *immanent finality*. Philosophy never leads us out of primordial wonder, but instead it makes us probe more deeply into the originality of this mysterious experience. In the fundamental or self-questioning questions of philosophy *everything remains at stake,* and in the first place *philoso-*

phy itself. Now, as we learned in the preceding chapter, the fact that philosophy moves in a circular fashion does not imply that fundamental thinking goes around in a "vicious circle." Indeed, in *logic* circular thinking is vicious since *nothing is gained.* But the circular movement of the *logos enriches and illuminates everything.* The *straight* thinking of the logical reason is essentially *non-reflective.* It does not reflect on its nature, its beginning and its ontological foundations. The *circular* way of thinking of the *logos* on the other hand is essentially *self-reflective.* That which is reflected upon and the reflection itself constitute *the selfsame reality.* A philosophical question is self-questioning since it is a question "which encroaches upon its own data," which is its own "research pro-ject" in the etymological sense of the words. Such a question always returns as a deeper and enriched question, but can never be answered with exhaustive finality. Gabriel Marcel calls such a question "which encroaches upon its own data," and cannot be answered with perfect finality: "the ontological *mystery.*"[54] We will return to this later on.

PHILOSOPHICAL CREATIVITY

At the present we are mainly concerned with the fact that self-questioning questions, or essentially re-flective ways of thinking are "from the very beginning" self-enriching and *creative.* In so far as the initial philosophical *re-flection* presupposes the primary data of philosophy as "already given," it *re-*flects on that which is "already there," on that which is "pre-given," and not of our own making. The *facticity* which is encountered by the initial re-flection "before" it can emerge as *re-*flection is the ontic "past" of this re-flection. On the other hand, these primary "data" do not *reveal themselves philosophically,* they are not *philosophical phenomena* unless they reveal themselves in the act in which they are received, namely in the primitive cognitive intention with its openness towards Being. In other words, our being-together-with-others-in-the-world cannot become the object pole of our initial reflection unless the phenomena of this unitary structure are comprehended (grasped together) by the differentiated directedness towards Being which defines our "ex-sistence" as subject pole. Of course, the term "ex-sistence" here is taken in its etymological sense and expresses the essence of man as being *subject to* the all-encompassing universality of Being, rather than the human subject in its opposition to a thing-like ob-ject *(Gegenstand).* Now, it is precisely the "encounter" (dialectics) between the primary phenomena of our primitive cognitive intention (phenomenology) and the re-flective attempt to com-prehend (grasp—

together) these fundamental phenomena in the light of Being (ontology) which con-stitutes (sets—together) the "actual" beginning of philosophy and of all fundamental meanings. In the beginning of philosophy the differentiated totality of all that is reveals itself as "given," as "not of our own making" or as "thrown" (*geworfen*— Heidegger). Yet, the selfsame differentiated totality of all that is becomes the *pro-ject* (*Entwurf*—Heidegger) of the actual beginning of philosophy as initial *re*-flection. The actual beginning of philosophy *projects* itself into its authentic past, *throws* light "ahead of itself" into its origin, or goes out into its "past" as something "to come," as its authentic "future" (G. *Zukunft*—future). Philosophy "actually" begins, becomes "present" or "presents itself" by "presenting" its "past" as possibility for the "future," by "presenting" its source as "re-search project," by "re-newing" the old, by "re-peating" (G. *Wiederholung*) its original data as immanent finality or by the self-enriching "ad-venture" (L. *ad, venire*—to come to) of going back into its own foundations. Philosophy comes into its own as a dialogue between coming out of its past and going back into its past as future possibility, as a dialogue between "having part in" and "taking part in" the differentiated self-manifestation of the totality of all that is.[55] Philosophy "actually" begins as an *act* (L. *agere*) of self-transcendency, as an act of self-enrichment or *self-creation*. Now, the discovery of the actual beginning of philosophy as an act of self-creation may easily give rise to two serious misconceptions. The self-creation of philosophy may be interpreted as an *absolute creation* or a *pure aseity*. Or the "self" of the self-creation may be mistaken for a disembodied and *world-less self* reflecting upon itself in an act of pure self-consciousness. Both views, however, contradict the actual beginning of philosophy. It will not be difficult in the light of the foregoing discussions to show how these views are unfaithful to the actual beginning of philosophy, and how they deviate from the "strictness" of philosophical authenticity.

Two Misconceptions

The beginning of philosophy, as we have seen, is not the absolute source of its own being. Philosophy does not start from absolute zero, but *presupposes* the primary data as "already given," as not of our own making or as *facticity*. In order to be faithful to its beginning philosophy has to develop in accurate conformity to its facticity, or to the "givenness" of its primary "data." Human creativity always presupposes the data of the immediately lived world as pre given and is never *absolute creativity*. Or, as Heidegger puts it, "All authentic pro-jection

(*Entwurf*)—and, consequently, all "creative" activity of man—is *thrown (geworfen)*."[56] In other words, all human creativity presupposes "givenness," presupposes "participation in" the *facticity* of the experiential world. We, therefore, contradict the primary data of the actual beginning of philosophy by mistaking this act of *relative* self-creation for an act of *absolute* self-creation, or for an *absolute aseity* à la Fichte and Hegel. Philosophy has to be faithful to this facticity by allowing its primary data to *reveal themselves* the way they are, or by *accurately describing* the self-manifestation of these phenomena. On the other hand, a *mere description* of fundamental phenomena *is not yet philosophy*. For philosophy actually begins as a *re-flection* on its fundamental phenomena. We can only describe the primary data with *philosophical accuracy* after they have become an *integral* part of this initial re-flection by which they are transformed into the pro-ject of our fundamental intention to com-prehend Being. Or, to put it differently again, fundamental phenomena are not philosophical in so far as they are *merely given*, but in so far as they are creatively transformed, re-newed, enriched and illuminated by the projective intention of the initial reflection. Philosophical phenomena are not exhausted by the mere phenomenality of their appearances, but they are rooted in the inexhaustible experience of wonder as the trans-phenomenal source of their being and their immanent finality. Philosophy, then, develops in "undeviating conformity" to its principles and is "strictly" philosophical neither by accepting its original data with rigid and unchanging fidelity, nor by producing them in an act of absolute creativity, but by adhering to its primary data with "creative fidelity" (Gabriel Marcel).[57] Moreover, the "creative fidelity" of the philosophical way of thinking is not the rectilinear deduction of the logical reason, but the *circular* movement of a relative *self*-creation. The "self," however, of this self-creation may not be interpreted as the reflection of a self-contained self upon itself, as the turning back of a disembodied and acosmic entity on itself, or as the clear and distinct presence-to-itself of an unhampered self-consciousness. "Reflection," says Dondeyne, "is not just a turning back of the self on itself; it is rather *the intentional act par excellence*. To reflect is to sally forth to conquer the concrete; it is to make an effort to uncover the why and the wherefore, *the general structure of reality*."[58] Creative fidelity as re-flection is not the unhampered self-reflection of an isolated and world-less self-consciousness à la Descartes, but the creative and *multi-dimensional openness* of "ex-sistence" re-flecting on the differentiated self-manifestation of Being. This "ex-static pro-jection" into primordial wonder defines our authentic "ex-sistence" as *creative emergence.* Fundamental thinking, then, is "strictly" philosophical in so far as it remains faithful to the actual beginning of philosophy. And it remains faithful to this beginning by "holding on" in a *creative* and *differentiated* way of the *factual data* of the primitive cognitive intention. In other words, *philosophy is authentic when it creatively mediates the all-encompassing light of primordial wonder in its re-flection on our multi-dimensional being-in-the-world.* Fundamental thinking is existential thinking!

THE DECISIVENESS OF THE ACTUAL BEGINNING

Our statement made at the beginning of this chapter that the most *decisive* moment in philosophy is *its actual beginning* becomes highly significant in the light of the preceding elucidations. The word "decisive" here is taken in both its etymological sense and with all its possible connotations. The word "de-cision" is etymologically derived from the Latin *decidere* which means: to cut off, to separate, to decide (*de,* off, from—*caedere,* to cut). Now, the actual beginning of philosophy as the "ex-static pro-jection" into primordial Being is our fundamental *de-cision* (setting apart, decision) to respond to the differentiated call of primordial wonder, and this de-cision *constitutes* (sets together) our authentic "ex-sistence." Consequently, this fundamental decision is not so much a decision *we make,* but rather a decision which *makes us.* Being, as we have seen, gives itself only in the act in which it is fully received, namely in the total openness of the whole of our "ex-sistence." In other words, it is *one and the same intentional act* which gives birth to the *differentiated self-manifestation of Being (logos),* and to our *fundamental de-cision* to accept this comprehensive openness of Being as the ground of our authentic "ex-sistence." *The philosophical re-flection on Being is at the same time the philosophical re-flection on the essence of man as "ex-sistence."* It goes without saying that our fundamental de-cision is not a particular decision to act or to judge. On the contrary, our fundamental de-cision "opens up" the *comprehensive universality* of Being, and, as such, constitutes the authentic human *will* which is the "will-to-be," the will to allow Being to reveal itself the way it is. Here we find for the first time the role of our universal will in the beginning of philosophy. This authentic will as our fundamental de-cision is not a particular decision to act, but rather the permanent source of all our particular actions, judgments and decisions which opens up the very possibility of all our theoretical and practical knowledge.

Moreover, the term *decisive* also carries the connotation of *critical* in the sense of dangerous or risky (Gr. *krinoo*—to separate, to decide, to judge). The actual beginning of philosophy is a decisive moment, for it is the critical "turning point" of the initial re-flection on the differentiated self-manifestation of Being, and always involves the danger of mistaking a particular phenomenon for the all-embracing totality of Being or of substituting a part for the whole. "The danger continually threatening us here," says Dondeyne, "is that of taking as our basic intention, primordial and all-embracing, some particular function of consciousness."[59] Our fundamental thinking will be out of focus, and no longer "strictly" philosophical, the very moment we mistake our openness to Being for the perception of a thing, of a physical fact, of a logical concept or the self-identity of a world-less self-consciousness. The *birth* of philosophy as the "separation" from the womb of primordial Being is a critical "turning point," a crisis fraught with danger. It is the de-cisive "moment" on which the "future" life of philosophy depends as the re-flection on its "past."

Furthermore, the actual beginning of philosophy is its *most decisive moment* in the sense that it *decides upon* its authenticity *at any stage of its development*. This re-flection on the differentiated self-manifestation of Being *decides upon* the philosophical "strictness" of our fundamental thinking. In other words, the actual beginning of philosophy as "the thinking of the *logos*" is the *criterion* (*krinoo*—"that by which something is decided upon") of all "true" philosophizing, and *ascertains* (*krinoo*) the philosophical truth. And, of course, since the actual beginning of philosophy is the criterion of philosophical authenticity, philosophy itself as the re-flection on its beginning, *remains essentially a critical way of thinking*.

And, finally, the term *decisive* also carries the connotation of *resolute* (L. *resolvere*—to separate into constituent parts, to solve or settle a question). The actual beginning of philosophy is its *most decisive moment* in the sense that it presents philosophy with its *terra firma*, its "solid ground" on which to build its authentic *certainty* which is the *"firm"* assent to philosophical self-evidence. The actual beginning of philosophy is the criterion which *ascertains* philosophical truth. As the creative *fidelity* to the primary "data" or *self-evidences*, the actual beginning presents philosophy with its fundamental evidences to "hold on to," to "stand on" or to "trust." In other words, the actual beginning gives philosophy its "stability" (L. *stare*—to stand), its "re-liability" (L. *religare*—to bind back), its "trust-worthiness" (ON. *traust*—"firmness") or its "certainty" (L. *certus*—decisive, settled, reliable). Now, the actual beginning of philosophy as re-flection is the *fidelity* or "firm assent." (subject pole) to the *differentiated self-manifestation* or "primary self-evidences" of Being (object pole) which "con-stitutes" (sets together) the criterion of philosophical *truth* (OE. *treowth*—reliability, trustworthiness). *It is the element of reliability rather than that of conformity which defines the veracity of truth.* The conformity between a judgment and an object is true because it is a *reliable* conformity. *Fundamental truth is the creative de-cision to be bound by the differentiated self-manifestation of Being, or the creative fidelity to the dynamic unconcealment of the logos (aletheia).* Philosophy comes into its "own," receives the "firmness," "stability," and "permanence" of its "self-presence" by "binding" back upon its "past" as the *ground* of its "future" possibilities. In other words, the "solid ground" of philosophy is a self-grounding ground, and its "stability" is its pro-jecting "understanding" of Being (standing under), rather than the standing *on* a ground of unchanging and massive solidity. The solid ground of strictly philosophical certainty, therefore, is neither the compact solidity and unquestioning obviousness of our everyday certainties, nor the unchanging solidity of the clear and distinct conception of abstract principles. If this were so, there would either be no need for philosophical questioning, or else the "un-folding" of philosophy would be degraded to the mere "unfurling" of a fan, or the mere "application" of perfectly known principles to some particular instances. Unquestioning certainties such as these may have their value in particular situations, but they are definitely *not fundamental*. What is unquestioning is not *ipso facto* unquestionable. On the contrary, we have discovered that *what is fundamentally unquestionable is that everything is fundamentally questionable*. The fundamental certainty by which fundamental thinking is focalized is precisely that Being manifests itself as *wonder,* that the *logos* is our fundamental "re-search pro-ject," and that nothing can be settled with perfect finality. Wonder is both the *self-manifestation* and the *question* of the totality of all that is. Wonder as the lasting source of philosophical authenticity remains the "binding criterion" and *terra firma* of the trustworthiness of philosophical truth. This is why philosophy remains in the literal sense of the terms both our most "wonderful" and most "suspense-ful" "ad-venture" in our search for a fundamental "com-prehension" of the integral totality of all that is. He who builds his fundamental thinking on the massive solidity of rigid and unquestioning certainties is really building on sand, and he ceases to be a philosopher to the extent that he loses his sense of the wonderful.[60]

"STRICTNESS" AND "EXACTNESS"

Scientism, of course, disqualifies wonder and philosophy from having any fundamental importance. According to scientism these phenomena are unscientific and unable to produce objective truth, since they lack "the scientific approach" and are highly "inexact." "But this," says Heidegger ironically, "is a misfortune only so long as one supposes that scientific thinking [in the sense of mathematical science] is the only authentic rigorous thought, and that it alone can and must be made into the standard of philosophical thinking."[61] And, then, he makes the surprising statement: "But the reverse is true."[62] This means that the "exactness" of mathematical and physical thinking is *less rigorous* than the "strictness" of fundamental thinking. To our modern minds, indoctrinated as they are by scientism and technocracy, this statement may sound nonsensical or even blasphemous. Nevertheless, this statement is simply true. For science, as we have seen, is rigorous or "strict" to the extent that it is authentic, to the degree in which it holds its own by the undeviating way in which it "holds on" to its proper beginning and standards, or by the appropriate way in which it mediates its own immediately given data. Now, as Heidegger puts it elsewhere, " 'Exact' thinking is never the strictest thinking, if the essence of strictness lies in the strenuousness with which knowledge keeps in touch with the essential features of what-is. 'Exact' thinking binds itself to the calculation of what-is and ministers to this alone."[63] The strictness of "exact" thinking is *unreflective,* leaves its beginning behind, and keeps less and less in touch with its immediate data which it merely "calculates" and "translates" into symbolic language. The strictness of fundamental thinking, on the other hand, is *reflective,* "turns back upon" its own immediate data which it penetrates and enriches. "Exact" thinking is *abstractive* and reaches its object so to speak *from without,* whereas the strictness of fundamental thinking is *concrete* and reaches its object *from within.* All this, of course, should not be construed as a depreciation of the value of the "exact sciences." On the contrary, it is precisely in a fundamental re-flection on the nature of "exactness" that we discover its "strictly scientific" character. For it is the specific "strictness" of a science, the way in which it mediates its immediate data, or the undeviating way in which it is faithful to its own principles, standards and viewpoints which determines its scientific authenticity. Now, the *exactness* of the mathematical sciences is a *special form of strictness.* Exactness is the scientific strictness of those sciences that deal with the world of material bodies from a quantifying viewpoint. Mathematics, of course, is the prototype of exact thinking. The less mathematically determined a science is, the less "exact" it will be. For example, exactness decreases from mathematics to physics, from physics to biology, from biology to history and from history to philosophy. But from this it does not follow that the "strictness" of these respective sciences decreases accordingly. A science is not less scientific to the extent that it is less mathematical. As we have seen, rather the reverse is true. It is, therefore, "strictly" unscientific to determine the scientific character *of a science* on the basis of its mathematical exactness, rather than using the criterion of "strictness" as the norm by which to decide on the specific authenticity of a given science.

THE VIEWPOINT OF SCIENTISM

And this is precisely what the pseudo-philosophy of *scientism* (not science) fails to see. Scientism *mistakes strictness for an inexact form of exactness.* In other words, according to scientism whatever is *non-exact* is *ipso facto inexact,* or whatever *transcends* exactness, *offends* exactness. This attitude, of course implies the tacit assumption that non-exact sciences are *faulty* sciences, that exactness or "quantitative precision" determines the scientific character *of any science,* and that whatever does not admit of *quantifying treatment* should be *eliminated* from *truly scientific inquiry.* In short, scientism identifies scientific authenticity with mathematical demonstrability. Here we easily recognize scientism as a variation on the general theme of rationalism which is the dogmatic assumption of the ultimacy of correct deductive and inductive thinking. Our refutation of rationalism in the first chapter also applies to the sham-identification of "science" with "mathematical exactness." By making absolute assertions about the nature of the non-exact sciences scientism contradicts its very own premises which identify scientific objectivity with mathematical intelligibility. There is a lived contradiction in the assertion that whatever is non-exact, or cannot be the object of exact observation, mathematical measurement and experimental verification is scientifically "meaningless," and cannot be known in any objective or valid way. For the absolutism of this assertion is by definition non-exact, and is not subject to the methods of exact observation and mathematical measurement. Moreover, the claim that science is inexact and faulty to the extent that it is non-exact, mistakes the contradictory for the contrary, and dogmatically monopolizes the methods of the exact sciences.

Now, it is precisely this dogmatic belief in the monopoly of the methods of the exact sciences which has led our modern world into a serious confusion with respect to the strict "demonstrability" of various sciences. It is characteristic of the exact sciences as abstractive sciences to leave the immediately lived world behind, and to follow basically the same methodic demands of exact observation, mathematical measurement and experimental verification regardless of the particular problem under consideration. But *scientism* oversteps the limits of the exact sciences by *hypostatizing their methods of exact demonstration,* and by making them to *the ultimate norm of all scientific meaning,* rather than regarding these methods as merely *a specific way · of demonstration,* namely as the appropriate method of demonstrating *mathematical* and *physical data.* This way scientism mistakes a particular scientific approach for "*the* scientific approach," and "exactness" for the prototype of scientific "strictness." This scientistic sham-identification of "science" with "mathematical demonstrability" results from its failure to understand that the authenticity of a science is determined by its "strictness," and not by its "exactness," and that "exactness" is only the criterion of scientific authenticity for some sciences, because their "strictness" or undeviating conformity to their viewpoints and original data requires "mathematical precision." Long ago Aristotle warned his contemporaries that mathematical precision is not to be demanded in all sciences.[64] In short, scientism fails to see that "strictness" is not to be defined in terms of method or demonstration alone, and that "strictness" is codetermined by the *immediate data* which it mediates in an appropriate way. The "strictness" of a scientific method or demonstration is never a "thing-in-itself," is never a separate entity, and can never be determined in isolation from the specific viewpoint, initial data and original scope of a given science. In other words, we cannot possibly, as scientism does, identify scientific "strictness" as such with the monolithic use of the method of demonstration of *one particular type of science.* "Strictness" is, fundamentally speaking, a dialogue between a given immediacy and its appropriate mediation, and this mediation or method of demonstration *alone* can never function as the criterion of scientific authenticity. As *mediated immediacy* true "strictness" *differs from science to science,* and imparts to every science its own characteristic uniqueness and relative autonomy.

COMMON GROUND AND THE APPROPRIATE WAY OF DEMONSTRATION

The fact that scientific "strictness" is *appropriately mediated immediacy* has two important implications. In the first place, by the mere use of the appropriate method of demonstration we cannot prove anything to anyone unless the other is also rooted in the same immediacy of experience and insight, unless we have a *common ground*. A philosophical demonstration is meaningless to a five-year-old child. A textbook of "differential calculus" remains a "closed book" for a student without any knowledge of elementary mathematics. The argumentation of an idealist philosopher may have no validity for his empiricist colleague. A discussion cannot possibly be successful as long as the participants in the discussion have no "common ground," as long as they do not participate in the same immediacy of principles, premises, evidences or beliefs. For discursiveness is mediated *immediacy,* and discussion is intersubjective discursiveness. Without at least some initial point of contact in the discussion, there cannot be any hope for a final agreement either. Even the perfect use of the correct methods and appropriate demonstrations will be of no avail, since mediation that cannot be understood as mediation of a *common immediacy* cannot be understood as meaningful discursiveness at all. The participants in such a discussion will arrive at only one conclusion, namely that they have never started a real discussion, that they have only been talking at cross-purposes, and that it is better to break up something that has actually never begun for lack of common ground.

There is a second implication in the fact that "strictness" is *appropriately mediated immediacy.* If it is true that we must participate in a *common immediacy* of insight in order to arrive at a successful form of discussion, it seems, inversely, to be equally true that we must make use of an *appropriate form of mediation or discursiveness* in order to advance in common immediacy of insight. This is not simply putting the same proposition in a reverse order. For a former assertion stressed the need of a *common initial insight,* whereas the latter statement points to the necessity of employing an *appropriate form of demonstration.* As we have seen, scientism hypostatizes demonstration, isolates it from its natural foundation in immediacy, makes it the ultimate norm, rather than the appropriate way of development of scientific meaning, and leads up to a monolithic use of the "exact" methods of demonstration. Scientism completely overlooks the fact that the method of demonstration is mediated *immediacy,* and does not understand that each science has its own kind of "strictness," its own irreducible and autonomous way of demonstration and its own characteristic authority. For scientism there is no other authority than that of the methods of demonstration of the "exact" sciences, and no other method can lay claim to the prerogatives of "the scientific approach." It is under the influence of scientism that several "non-exact" sciences are induced to quantify their basically non-quantifiable data. For instance, many modern psychologists, sociologists and even philosophers feel guilty at not being exact scientists. They attempt to overcome their inferiority complexes by imitating the exact sciences in their own respective fields and to dance to the music of "the scientific approach." The monolithic use of the "exact" methods has led many "non-exact" scientists into the belief that the scientific authenticity of their studies is determined by the number of equations, diagrams, graphs and statistics that fill their scientific books. They are no longer aware of the fact that, as Sorokin puts it, "their 'precise' measurements are only a pseudo-mathematical screen hiding the arbitrary assumptions of the metromanic numerologists."[65] Instead of ascertaining the authenticity of their own sciences by means of such sham-quantifications, these scientists impair the specific strictness and proper authority of their own methods of demonstration. We are, of course, not trying to deny the existence of an "exact" *aspect* in some of these sciences, nor do we overlook the fact that these quantifiable aspects can become the "strict" object of "exact" studies. All we want to stress is the fact that the specific strictness of a science cannot be the exactness of the mathematical sciences to the extent that the "human factor" or the "ontological factor" is its predominant concern, and that by being *non-exact* this science *does not become inexact or less strictly scientific.*

Another common source of the pseudo-philosophical hypostatization of a particular method of scientific demonstration is the force of *habit.* It is a typical professional disease of specialists and experts to become so accustomed to their special field of research that they take it for granted that their particular approach is "the scientific approach." They dogmatically monopolize their own method of inquiry, mistake it for the criterion of scientific authenticity and assume an attitude of condescending superiority with regard to any other method of demonstration. Long ago Aristotle wrote, "Thus some people do not listen to a speaker unless he speaks mathematically, others unless he gives instances, while others expect him to cite a poet as witness."[66] Of course, this monopolizing by a particular method of demonstration has created a great deal of confusion with respect to the proper objects and the specific methods of demonstration of various sciences. Psychology, for instance, is more than "psychophysics"; physics is more than "an inadequate knowledge of the mathematical structure of the universe"; sociology is more than "social chemistry"; history is more than "applied psychology"; and philosophy is more than "science that deals with wider generalizations than the special sciences." Historical facts do not admit of mathematical demonstration, whereas in mathematics historical arguments have little value. But from this it does not follow that either history or mathematics should be called unscientific. All that follows is that both mathematics and history have their very own and irreducible kind of scientific strictness, and that by not respecting their respective autonomies we destroy their scientific authenticity. A fundamental reflection on the differentiated self-manifestation of primordial wonder does not satisfy the requirements of "exact" thinking. But this does not prevent this reflection from being "strictly philosophical." The "non-exactness" of philosophical thinking does not impair its autonomous "strictness," nor does it infringe upon its truly scientific authenticity. And the criterion of this authenticity is not to be determined by any science other than the strictly philosophical way in which the fundamental re-flection un-folds the primary data of the primitive cognitive intention. This philosophical strictness is not the rectilinear and mechanical conformity to some abstract principles, but rather the creative fidelity to the differentiated self-manifestation of primordial wonder.

CHAPTER V

WONDER AND
PHILOSOPHICAL METHOD

In the previous chapter we have examined the *authenticity* of our fundamental or philosophical "way of thinking." And we discovered that philosophy is authentic when it creatively mediates the all-encompassing light of primordial wonder in its re-flection on our multi-dimensional being-in-the-world. In this chapter, we want to explore further the philosophical way of thinking as *way,* or philosophy as *method.* We shall attempt to answer some basic questions about the philosophical method. Does the philosophical method replace wonder, or is it rather nourished and guided by this primordial experience? What is the nature and structure of the philosophical method? Is there an essential difference between the philosophical method and the methods of the positive sciences?

It goes without saying that we ask our questions about the philosophical method fundamentally, i.e. philosophically. Now, in the preceding chapter we have made the actual beginning of philosophy; we are "on the way." This enables us to re-flect philosophically on our philosophical "way of thinking," or on philosophy as *method.* For, although pedagogically a reflection on method may precede a science in its presentation, genetically it follows the actual beginning of a science. And it is precisely the actual beginning and the depth and scope of its original intention which determine the specific kind of method to be followed by any given "way of thinking."

METHOD AND METHODOLOGY

Etymologically the word "method" is derived from the Greek *methodos* (*meta* and *hodos*—way after) and means: "a way to something," "a going after," "an investigation." The current English word "method" signifies: "a regular manner of doing anything," "an orderly procedure of arriving at a certain end," "a systematic way of investigation" or "a

set of directives that guide a process to a result." In the modern usage
of the term it is essential that we have a *preconception* of the plan to be
followed.[67]

Nowadays, we have even established a *science of methods* which is
called "methodology," and which applies the laws and principles of
logic to the principles and processes that guide scientific inquiry in
general and the special modes of demonstration of different sciences in
particular. And as such, of course, methodology is usually considered as
a branch of logic. As a branch of logic, however, methodology can only
cope with the methods of the calculative, abstractive and objectifying
ways of thinking of the *exact* sciences. Methodology, at least in so far
as it is regarded as a part of formal and mathematical logic, remains
fully unconcerned with that which transcends the logical reason and the
supra-logical methods of demonstration. And this is perfectly legitimate
as long as methodology does not pronounce upon the methods of the
non-exact and more fundamental ways of thinking by considering them
unscientific. In this case methodology would overstep the limits of its
own compentency, and once again we would be confronted with scientism, the dominant pseudo-philosophy of today.

THE NON-METHODICAL BEGINNING

It should be remembered—and we have briefly touched on this point
in the previous chapter—that no method can be hypostatized or regarded as a separate entity which could decide upon the strictness of
any given science apart from its actual beginning in the immediately
lived world. On the contrary, scientific strictness is rather determined by
the appropriate way in which a method mediates the original immediacy of its actual beginning. In other words, the actual beginning of any
method, even of the methods of logic and of methodology, is *nonmethodical,* and is like any beginning an unforeseeable, original and
creative moment in the spontaneity of our immediately lived experience. It is precisely the non-methodical beginning and the depth and
scope of its original intention that determine the characteristic strictness
of any methodical way of thinking. Consequently, that which determines the specific method of any given science cannot be arrived at by
employing this very same method, or, strictly speaking, by any method
at all. Instead of distrusting the scientific value of non-methodical originality, we should rather distrust the pseudo-philosophy of those who
disregard the methodological importance of our immediately lived
world.

If it is true that all our methods originate in a non-methodical and original intention experienced in our immediately lived world, then it is *a fortiori* true for our most fundamental and most original way of thinking: *the philosophical method*. The strictly philosophical way of thinking, as we have seen, is focalized by *primordial wonder* or the undefinable, undescribable and undemonstrable self-manifestation of all that is. Wonder as the primordial self-revelation of Being is a radical beginning, a pure spontaneity not determined by anything other than itself. There is nothing "outside" this all-encompassing phenomenon, nothing prior or more fundamental that could lead up to its self-manifestation. Wonder reveals Being without any premeditation on the part of man, without any systematic way of arriving at it, without any method, skill or technique. Wonder is strictly non-methodical, over-whelming and original. Wonder cannot be taught or passed down from generation to generation. Whoever begins to philosophize in wonder makes a new historical beginning in philosophy.

SCIENTIFIC AND PHILOSOPHICAL METHODS

Generally speaking, all methodical ways of thinking resemble one another in so far as they are orderly and strictly systematic ways of mediating the data of their actual beginnings. They differ, however, to the extent that the original intentions of the actual beginnings differ in depth and scope. The actual beginning of a method is the criterion which both determines its nature and distinguishes it from any other method.

Now, the actual beginning of philosophy, as we have seen, is the re-flection on the dialectical self-manifestation of primordial wonder, or on our multi-dimensional being-in-the-world focalized by our essential openness towards Being. Consequently, the depth and scope of the original intention of the actual beginning of the philosophical way of thinking is the *fundamental and differentiated com-prehension of primordial wonder*. This, therefore, is the criterion which both determines the nature and structure of the philosophical method of thinking, and distinguishes it from any other scientific method.

It goes without saying that there is a certain resemblance between the philosophical method and the methods of the positive sciences in so far as both have to be "strict." Both have to "hold on" to their actual beginning by mediating it in an appropriate way. But they differ radically as to the *nature* of their respective strictness. The philosophical method is strict when it creatively re-flects on *the differentiated self-manifestation of Being*. In other words, the strictly philosophical method is characterized by its creative fidelity, its comprehensive universality, its fundamental concreteness, the circular movement of its self-questioning, and the co-originality of its ontological, phenomenological and dialectical aspects. Each of the positive sciences, on the other hand, studies only the *material* universe from its own *particular* viewpoint. Reality has to be "reduced" in such a way that it appears to the human mind as an *ob-ject* in the etymological sense of the word, as something that is standing-over-against the mind in such a manner that it becomes accessible to exact observation, measurement, mathematical calculation and empirical verification. Contrary to the common belief, reality does not spontaneously present itself in the form of "observable and quantifiable ob-jects." Only by *actively* dis-engaging himself from his immediately lived and prescientific "involvement" in the world can the scientist arrive at his "ob-jectifying way" of being-in-the-world. The scientific situation is a particular situation, a particular mode of being-in-the-world, which requires a particular approach on the part of the scientist. This "scientific approach" consists fundamentally in *delimiting* a certain segment of the material universe, and interrogating this particular segment from a *particular viewpoint*. This viewpoint is particular since positive science studies only *one particular aspect* of reality. The scientist as scientist does not examine reality from the practical viewpoint of his immediately experienced "involvement" nor does he ask fundamental questions about his scientific "ob-jects." The positive scientist studies material reality from the viewpoint of "mere ob-jectivity," from the viewpoint of "pure quantity." This viewpoint requires on the part of the scientist a *quantifying and abstractive attitude* by means of which he dis-engages himself from the qualitative concreteness of his everyday world and constitutes the abstract network of mathematical and functional relationships of his scientific world. The scientific way of being-in-the-world, therefore, or the "attitude" of the positive scientist determines the ob-jectifying, abstractive, limiting and quantifying characteristics of the "methods" of the positive sciences. In other words, the specific "strictness" of the methods of the positive sciences is the *exactness* of their inductive and deductive processes.

We cannot here attempt to discuss all the complex problems involved in scientific methodology. It will be helpful for our purposes, however, to draw a further parallel between the methods of the positive sciences on the one hand and the philosophical method on the other.

The Myth of "Pure Facts"

In the first place, the "scientific facts" as presented to us by the exact methods of the mathematico-physical sciences are neither the "only real facts," nor are they the "most fundamental facts" as scientism would have us to believe. They are not even "pure facts." The positive sciences, to be sure, provide us with a true explanation of the reality which they study. The purely "ob-jective" face of reality is a true "aspect" of the material world. This aspect, however, does not represent the exhaustive and only possible meaning of this world. On the contrary, the purely "ob-jective" side is inherent in the material world only as an *as-pect* (L. *ad* and *spicere*—to look at), only reveals itself to the extent that this world is being "looked at" from the quantifying viewpoint of the positive sciences. The merely "ob-jective" dimension of reality, therefore, is not an independent thing-in-itself, but is essentially related to the *abstractive viewpoint of the scientist.* It is the object pole constituted (not created) by the viewpoint of the scientist as subject pole. In other words, the "ob-jective" dimension of reality and the scientific attitude of the scientist are correlative, they are a particular form of *encounter* which constitutes the *scientific world,* and no scientific fact reveals itself outside this world. No scientific fact is a "pure fact," or a fact that would reveal itself to no attitude whatsoever on the part of the scientist.

The scientific world is neither our only real world, nor is it our immediately given or our most fundamental world. The scientific world *does not replace* our other modes of being-in-the-world, but rather *complements* and *presupposes* them. The scientific world is the *particular* world in which the scientist through his ob-jectifying attitude disengages himself from his immediately lived world, and in which he interrogates his scientific "ob-jects" from an abstractive and quantifying viewpoint. His abstract questions are not the concrete questions of his everyday world and his fundamental ex-sistence. Abstraction, however, presupposes that which we abstract from. The ob-jectifying abstraction of the scientist presupposes the prescientific and immediately lived experience of the everyday world. The chemist has to know water as drinking water and wash water before he is able to know water as a compound of hydrogen and oxygen. The chemical formula which expresses water in terms of H_2O is chemically true, but also, *only chemically* meaningful. Only by "ob-jectifying" his prescientific experience of "water" is the chemist able to arrive at his formula H_2O, and only by keeping in touch with this everyday experience does he know that his formula applies to a colorless, odorless, tasteless and transparent liquid. Only in his chemical world does the scientist know that two atoms of hydrogen combined with one atom of oxygen form one molecule of water. Only in his everyday world does the scientist know that water is colorless and odorless, tasteless and transparent, that it can occur as rain water, spring water or river water, that it can be used as drinking water or wash water, and that it can have a cooling and refreshing effect. These characteristics cannot be expressed in terms of a chemical formula since they are constitutionally unobjectifiable. Nevertheless, it would be utterly nonsensical to state that water is exclusively what science discovers it to be, that "in reality" water is "nothing but" H_2O, and that this formula expresses "the truth, the whole truth and nothing but the truth" about water. "In reality" water has also all these un-objectifiable characteristics. The "chemical fact" that water is H_2O *does not replace* the "everyday fact" that we can use it for washing or drinking purposes, nor does it relegate to the domain of sheer roman-ticism the cooling effects of water, or make it meaningless to say that water is transparent or that it can occur as rain water or river water.

In addition, the chemical fact that water is H_2O does not answer or even ask the most fundamental question about water. Indeed, both the chemist and the philosopher may ask the question "What is water?" Yet, despite the appearance to the contrary, the chemist and the philos-opher are asking radically different questions. And the questions are different since they are being asked from different viewpoints, in the light of different horizons, in different worlds anticipating different kinds of answers. When the chemist asks himself the question "What is water," he is interrogating water from his ob-jectifying and abstractive viewpoint, and anticipates an answer as to the chemical make-up of water. When the philosopher, however, asks himself seemingly the same question, he is *de facto* asking a radically different question. His ques-tion is guided by his intention to know Being. What constitutes the being of water to the extent that it *is*? What kind of "being" is water, what is its "is-ness," what is it in the light of the totality of all that is? This question is evidently asked in the light of primordial wonder which is not a particular and abstractive viewpoint, but rather the concrete encounter with the comprehensive universality of Being. It is not the particular horizon of a particular world, but the primordial experience of the horizon of all horizons, the unobjectifiable re-flection on the all-encompassing self-revelation of *the* world. And the philosopher antici-pates an answer about the "being" of water, i.e. a fundamental answer in the light of the totality of all that is.

From the foregoing elucidations it has become abundantly clear that the potentiality to present us with the "only real," "truly objective" and "pure" facts cannot possibly be the criterion by which we distinguish between scientific and philosophical methodology. The reason is simply that such a potentiality does not exist. As we have seen in Chapter Two, and once again in the present chapter, every way of knowing reality is a mode of being-in-the-world, is an encounter between a subject pole and an object pole within an existential situation, and is, fundamentally speaking, always *a way of* "ex-sistence." Now, this "ex-sistence" as we also have seen is "pluralistic," i.e. various ways of "ex-sistence," various levels of intentionality, various modes of being-in-the-world, various existential situations are possible. Consequently, there is not one single way of knowing which is the only means of access to our knowledge of reality, there is not one exclusive kind of objectivity that relegates all other kinds to the realm of subjectivism, and there are no "pure" facts that reveal themselves independently of the human mind, unrelated to the respective world of the perceiving subject, apart from any mode of "ex-sistence." There is no fact which does not reveal itself within the horizon of a certain world, within the perspective of a certain intentionality. In other words—and this is a thorn in the flesh of scientism—the *same* fact becomes a *different* fact in a different world. A fact reveals itself only to the extent that it appears as an object for a subject, and the intentionality of the world of the subject co-determines the *kind* of objectivity of the perceived fact. Water reveals itself "objectively" as refreshing from the everyday viewpoint, it manifests itself "objectively" as H_2O in the world of chemistry, and in the light of philosophy it appears to be "objectively" a material sort of being. All these meanings are truly "objective," but from a different "standpoint." These different kinds of objectivity cannot replace one another, nor do they exclude each other. They are simply complementary means of access to knowledge of reality, they are irreducible ways of thinking corresponding to the pluralistic nature of human "ex-sistence."

The Pluralism of Human Thinking

Human thinking is always a mode of being-in-the-world. And just as there are fundamentally different ways of being-in-the-world, so there are basically *different ways of thinking,* different ways of mediating reality, or different scientific methods. These basically different methods are not solely determined by the "objects," nor are they completely separable from that which they mediate or merely dependent on the "standpoint" taken by the subject pole. Misconceptions such as these are based on the false presuppositions of Cartesian dualism or on the radical separation between man and world. This dualism, however, contradicts the primary data of human "ex-sistence" as "being-in-the-world," and makes the gap between the human mind and the "outer world" unbridgeable. There is no such thing as the one and only universally applicable method that presents us with the "pure objects" or with objects that have been constituted as such outside the human world, independent of human "ex-sistence," independent of any involvement of the human mind. On the contrary, there is, as we have seen, no object which does not reveal itself as object pole to a subject pole, which is not constituted by an encounter between a datum and an intention, which is not given in the perspective of a certain human world. Our different methods of thinking are rooted in our different possible ways of being-in-the-world. Consequently, our various methods of thinking are fundamentally as irreducible as our various ways of being-in-the-world. It is impossible to find the interconnection between the various methods of thinking by means of the use of any particular kind of methodological research. For each particular method of thinking is a mode of "ex-sistence," and as such has an irreducible originality of its own. Fundamentally the interconnection between the various methods of thinking can only be found in the pluralistic nature of human "ex-sistence." It is not the respective approximation of the various methods to the alleged absolute objectivity and absolute exactness of mathematical methods which explains the *analogy* of our different methods of thinking, but rather the fact that they represent different modes of being-in-the-world of the same "ex-sistence."

Moreover, it is interesting in this context to realize that even the modern sciences themselves reject this spurious idea of absolute objectivity from which the world of man and the attitudes of the knowing subject are completely excluded. Modern sciences have in this century discovered that the observer always *co-determines* the results of his observations, that man always intervenes in his experiments, that an absolute world-view in which the human factor plays no role is a fundamental impossibility and that nature is never fully objectifiable *in principle*. The dogmatic belief of classical physics in absolute objectivity, in absolute predictability, in absolute deterministic causality, in absolute space and absolute motion, in absolute simultaneity and absolute exactness etc. has been thoroughly undermined by discoveries such as Bohr's Principle of Complementarity, Einstein's Theory of Relativity, Heisenberg's Principle of Indeterminacy in physics and Gödel's Incompleteness Theorem in mathematics.

An "Impoverishment" of Human Nature?

All this has some interesting implications. The fact that all methods of human thinking represent various modes of human "ex-sistence",

various ways of "being-in-the-world" and various kinds of "involvement" of the human mind explains why *no scientific method can be
regarded as an "impoverishment" of human nature*. All methods of
human thinking are simply irreducible but complementary ways of access to an ever growing com-prehension of the pluralistic nature of
human "ex-sistence." No scientific method can be absolutized without
distorting the fundamental structure of *human* "ex-sistence," no scientific method can be ignored without atrophying truly *human* possibilities. Whereas scientism and positivism tend to look upon non-exact
methods as an "impoverishment" of reality, some modern forms of non-
exact (but strict!) thinking attempt to dismiss the exact sciences as an
"impoverishment" of human ex-sistence.[68] Both attitudes, however, are
extremes and result from the same mistake. Scientism tends to absolutize the exact methods, which, as we have seen, is unscientific, and
some forms of phenomenology tend to absolutize the non-exact methods
which is unphenomenological. For the exact methods of physics and
mathematics are not *only* physical and mathematical possibilities; fundamentally they reveal themselves (Gr. *phainesthai*—to appear) as *human* phenomena, as possible modes of being-in-the-world, as *possibilities of human ex-sistence*.[69] The exact methods, to be sure, ob-jectify the
material world, dichotomize the subject-object relationship and make
abstraction from man's concrete personal, aesthetic and everyday situations. This, however, is not an "impoverishment" of human ex-sistence,
but a realization of one of its basic potentialities. On the contrary, it
would be an "impoverishment" of human ex-sistence to deny man the
actualization of his abstractive mode of ex-sistence, for it would distort
the harmony of his pluralistic nature and impair the growth of his
culture. This is why Gabriel Marcel is right in saying that "it would be
absurd to hope to solve the present crisis by closing down the factories
and laboratories for good and all. There is every reason to suppose that
such a step would be the startingpoint of an almost unimaginable regression for the human race."[70] Not science is to be blamed for the
impoverishment of human ex-sistence which has caused the crisis of our
present age, but *scientism* or the absolutism of the exact methods of
thinking. Our attempt to solve the present crisis by dismissing the existential value of the exact sciences altogether would cure the absolutism
of the exact methods with the absolutism of the non-exact methods of
thinking and replace one distortion of human ex-sistence with another.
This, however, is casting out the devil with Beelzebub. Neither the
exact nor the non-exact sciences result in an "impoverishment" of reality, for both are complementary ways in which the various possible

levels of thinking move towards a differentiated understanding of the poly.morphous totality of human ex-sistence. What does lead to catastrophe is the monistic acceptance of one method to the exclusion of every other method.

THE IMPOSSIBILITY OF DISINTERESTED THINKING

There is another interesting implication of the fact that all methods of thinking are modes of being-in-the-world, and that no method whatsoever can be regarded as a nonhuman procedure, as an "autonomous entity" that is free from even the slightest trace of reference to human ex-sistence. This second implication is that *"disinterested knowledge" is a fundamental impossibility,* and that, therefore, "disinterestedness" can never be used as the criterion of scientific objectivity. The belief in even the desirability of disinterested knowledge rests on the illusion that the ideal of methodical thinking is to arrive at the "absolute objectivity" of "pure facts," or of facts that can be grasped in their total independency of the human mind. Now, our discovery that all methods of thinking are ways of being-in-the-world, that the existential attitude of the observer co-determines the appearance of the object, and that "pure facts" are a myth corrodes the belief that disinterestedness is an essential characteristic of scientific objectivity. The human mind is always "involved" in the object of thinking, but the *kind* of involvement is different in different modes of ex-sistence. Consequently, the human ways of thinking are always *interested* ways of thinking (L. *inter* and *esse*—to participate, to be involved), but the *kind of interest* depends on the mode of existential involvement. It is false to call the exact sciences "pure sciences" because of their alleged disinterestedness, for absolute disinterestedness is contrary to their very nature. The purity of a science or the distinctive characteristic of scientific objectivity is not to be found in its disinterestedness, but rather in the *appropriation* of its respective kind of interest to the characteristic involvement of the corresponding mode of ex-sistence.

Both the philosopher and the exact scientist are essentially interested in their respective fields of concentration. Their interest, however, is of a radically different nature. The philosopher is involved *with the whole of his ex-sistence* in the all-encompassing world of his "re-search project." As existential thinker he is experientially affected by his encounter with the dialectical self-manifestation of all that is. He is "tuned in" to the overwhelming experience of primordial wonder. This existential involvement of the philosopher results in a primordial sort of interest which we call: *primordial enthusiasm.*[71] We will revert to this primordial enthusiasm later on. The exact scientist, on the other hand, is involved (inter-ested) in a particular segment of all that is from a particular viewpoint. He is involved through his abstractive intentionality by which he allows the "ob-jective" face of the material world to reveal itself. Hence it is incorrect to call this "scientific approach" a "neutral" or "disinterested" approach. Underlying this common misconception is the prejudice of classical mechanistic physics which teaches that reality reveals itself independently of the human mind. To be sure, the passionate interest of the scientist in science and in the scientific activity is not the primordial enthusiasm of the philosopher, but it is not its absolute opposite either. For, if it be granted that the world of science is a derivative mode of the primordial world of wonder, it follows that scientific enthusiasm is a derivative mode of primordial enthusiasm and ultimately grounded on this inspirational experience. The scientist, as we have seen, is not completely divorced from the objects of his study. On the contrary, he constitutes the objects of his science *as* scientific objects by being actively involved through the ob-jectifying attitude of his scientific approach. The world of science is always at the same time the world of the scientist.

If it is true that the "laboratory spirit" of the scientist is not the "personal" involvement of the philosopher, it is equally true that the "impersonal" involvement of the scientist does not result in a non-human or even inhuman sort of interest. The scientist as scientist does not dis-engage himself from the world, but merely from his experiential involvement in the world. He does not step out of his ex-sistence, but merely actualizes a particular possibility of this ex-sistence. He is still together-with-others-in-the-world. This world, however, is not the primordial world of wonder, but the particular world of scientific ob-jects in which he makes the quantitative face of reality accessible to himself as a scientist and to a community of scientific observers. As the actualization of a possible mode of being-in-the-world the impersonal attitude of the scientist is a truly *human* way of ex-sistence. And its impersonal involvement in scientific ob-jects originates a truly *human* sort of interest.

It is precisely because our scientific being-in-the-world is a derivative mode of our authentic being-in-the-world that the scientist as scientist has his own particular kind of interest and enthusiasm. And it is only to the extent in which this enthusiasm is permitted to enter into a dialectical relationship with the various modes of being-in-the-world of our pluralistic ex-sistence that our scientific interest can fully function in the integral self-realization of this ex-sistence. The biographies of all great scientists of both the past and the present show that their scientific activities have not been impaired but rather improved by their genuine interest in art, philosophy and humanities. The pluralistic nature of human ex-sistence allows for a great variety of simultaneous motivations that tend to re-enforce one another as long as we prevent one single motivation or interest from becoming fixed and enclosed within itself and monopolizing the integral structure of our variegated ex-sistence. For such a fixation or monopoly would turn our multi-dimensional creativity into possessive fanaticism. For instance, a denial of the revelatory power of primordial wonder would not only result in a rejection of our philosophical thinking, but in a progressive atrophy of our creativeness in science as well. Directly or indirectly our whole ex-sistence is affected by the absolutism of one particular field of interest. This is the meaning of the often quoted saying of Albert Einstein: "The most beautiful and most profound emotion we can experience is the awareness of the mysterious. It is the source of all true science. He who is unfamiliar with this experience, and can no longer wonder or stand rapt in awe, is all but dead."

FORMALIZATION

It goes without saying that the *way* (method) in which the scientist and the philosopher relate themselves to their respective fields of interest is essentially different. In the exact sciences the methods can be formalized, in philosophy never. In the exact sciences the scientist disengages himself from his experiential involvement in reality. His way of thinking (method) is an abstractive process which dissolves the experiential world of the scientist into a world of physical ob-jects facing the scientist as an impersonal *observer*. The mathematico-empirical sciences are *strictly* scientific (*stringere*—to hold tight) by holding on to their data in an appropriate way. This way is the method of quantifying *observations (servare*—to hold; *ob*—over against). In other words, the method of the exact sciences dictates the scientist to hold on to his data in such a way that they reveal themselves as physical *ob-jects (jacere*—to throw; *ob*—over against), or as data standing "over against" the scientist as ob-server. This quantifying ob-servation allows the physical ob-jects to progressively reveal their quantitative face, and makes the physical sciences strictly "exact." This quantifying ob-servation also creates a dichotomy between the physical ob-jects and the scientific ob-server. Both the world of physical ob-jects and the subject of the scientist as ob-server become detached from the experiential world of the scientist as a personality. In the abstractive attitude of quantifying observation the subject and the ob-ject are no longer "standing together" in the concrete experiential unity of the immediately lived world. On the contrary, there is characteristic *di-stance* (*stare*—to stand; *dis*—apart) between the scientific ob-jects and the scientific ob-server. The subject of the scientist is reduced to a mere *apriori condition* for the self-manifestation of quantifiable ob-jects, and as such the subject can never become a physical object. This characteristic di-stance between the scientist and his ob-jects of research entails the possibility of a *formalization* of the methods of the physical sciences. The deductive and inductive processes of our logical ways of thinking can be formalized, i.e., given a definite form apart from any concrete world of ob-jects and apart from the experiential world of the scientist. Thus methodology tends to become an autonomous thing with its own laws that can be studied for its own sake. This is why a scientific method can be "applied" and why, as we have seen, it is characteristic of our modern conception of method that we must have a *preconception* of the plan to be followed or to be applied.

Things are essentially different in philosophy. The philosophical method of thinking cannot be formalized. Ob-jectivation and dichotomy are the necessary conditions for the possible formalization of a scientific method. Philosophy, however, neither ob-jectifies nor dichotomizes its data, but rather restores the experiential world of the thinker in its original unity. Existential thinking transcends the dichotomy between subject and object, and relates to the totality of all that is. Existential thinking does not submit itself to the abstractive and ob-jectifying processes of reductive analysis. The primordial question of Being does not admit of abstraction. Every philosophical question involves the question of Being. Every philosophical question is a self-questioning question in which the whole of philosophy is at stake. Every philosophical question involves the ex-sistence of the thinker in its entirety. Hence the philosophical *way* of thinking *(meta—hodos)* is completely inseparable from the philosophical content: the dialectical self-manifestation of primordial wonder in our human ex-sistence. The philosophical method never replaces primordial wonder, but is constantly nourished and guided by this indwelling phenomenon. It is utterly impossible to formalize the philosophical method and to deal with it as a ready-made structure that can be "applied" to the facts of reality. An "applied philosophy" is a contradiction in terms. Strictly speaking philosophy does not *have* a method, but *is* a method. The philosophical *way* of thinking *is* the dialectical self-manifestation of primordial Being. The philosophical method *is* the very movement of the *logos*. Philosophy does not have a formalized methodology since the *logos* of its method is the method (road) of the *logos*.

"THE ROAD THAT WALKS"

We might use in this case the simile of a "road." The methods of the exact sciences, as we have seen, can be formalized and studied as definite structures in their own right. Moreover, since the exact sciences are determined by their quantifying ob-servation, their methods become more and more quantitatively determined too. The method of an exact science becomes more and more literally a "road" to be followed, where, starting from a certain point "successive steps" have to be taken towards an "end" which is often not "in sight" yet.

The philosophical method, on the other hand, cannot be formalized or divorced from its content: the dialectical self-manifestation of primordial Being. The philosophical road of thinking *(meta-hodos)* is its creative fidelity to the all-encompassing experience of primordial wonder. Philosophy, therefore, does not follow "a beaten path," but it creatively pro-jects its own road. Philosophy as a road, says Henri Bergson, is being "created *pari passu* with the act of traveling over it, being nothing but the direction of this act itself."[72] The philosophical way of thinking does not find its road laid out on a map, but it constantly has to "pave its own way." The philosophical traveler never takes a scheduled trip, since his proper way of traveling is that of an adventurous "explorer." Philosophy does not "walk on" a road, but it is "a road that walks."[73] Philosophy "begins" as "being on the way" towards its own beginning. Philosophy is "being on the way" towards the explicit asking of the primordial question of wonder as the mysterious ground of all its fundamental questions.

In the following chapter we will further differentiate our understanding of the philosophical method by making a dialectical comparison between logic and *logos*. This comparison cannot be based on a formal philosophical methodology for the simple reason that it is impossible to formalize the philosophical method. Such a comparison is possible only because we have already made our actual beginning in philosophical thinking. We are "on the way." Our primary purpose in the next chapter is not so much to discover the essence of logic, but rather to differentiate and to deepen our insight into the structure of the *logos* as the unique method of philosophical thinking. The structure of philosophical thinking is the structure of primordial wonder as it dialectically demonstrates itself in man.

CHAPTER VI

LOGIC AND LOGOS

It is interesting to find a certain resemblance between the deductive and inductive dialectics of the logical sciences on the one hand, and the ontological, phenomenological and dialectical aspects of the *logos* on the other. This is to be expected, since both logic and *logos* are thinking ways of being-in-the-world. They are essentially different, however, insofar as the respective worlds in which they are found reveal a radical difference. In this chapter, we shall attempt to make a comparison between the deduction, the induction and the dialectics of the logical sciences with the ontological, the phenomenological and the dialectical aspects of existential thinking respectively. This comparison will enable us to probe deeper into the different ways in which the logical sciences and the existential thinking of the *logos* arrive at their judgments, their definitions and their systematizations.

LOGICAL DEDUCTION AND THE ONTOLOGICAL ASPECT OF EXISTENTIAL THINKING

In the first place, the *deduction* of the logical sciences has a certain resemblance to the *ontological* aspect of the fundamental way of thinking of the *logos*. In the deductive method of thinking a conclusion is inferred which follows with strictly logical necessity from given premises. As to our existential way of thinking or philosophical method, no way of acquiring fundamental insights is valid which does not follow with strictly philosophical necessity from the primary data of philosophy. But here is where the comparison ends. For there is an essential difference between the way in which conclusions *follow* from logical premises and the way in which fundamental insights *follow* from the primary data of philosophy.

Straight Thinking and Circular Thinking

In deduction the logical way of thinking argues *forward* from princi-ples and premises to conclusions of which we were often ignorant. Moreover, deduction does not verify its own premises and principles, it does not justify its own starting-point. In other words, deductive think-ing is essentially unreflective thinking, and it leaves its starting-point behind. To put it differently again, deductive thinking is "straight" thinking. Straight thinking is rectilinear and not circular, it is a "road" to be followed, where, starting from a certain point "successive steps" have to be taken, and where the "end" is often not in sight yet.

Now, as we have seen in Chapter Four, the strictly philosophical way in which new fundamental insights originate from the primary data of philosophy differs *toto caelo* from the deductive way of logical thinking. Philosophical thinking is strict when it creatively mediates the all-encompassing light of *primordial wonder* in its re-flection on our multi-dimensional being-in-the-world. The ontological aspect of existential thinking instead of leading us away from this primordial phenomenon brings us back into it. The *rectilinearity* or the "straight" thinking of the deductive sciences differs both from the *circularity* and the *multi-dimensionality* of existential thinking. Philosophy never leaves its start-ing-point behind, since primordial wonder remains the immanent origin and guiding light of all our philosophical explorations. Philosophical thinking develops *within* rather than *from* its point of departure. And as the *logos* of its beginning existential thinking is the progressive self-foundation of its own primary data.

In addition, the various steps to be taken in philosophy are never "successive" steps in the sense of separate steps following one another in space and time. Existential thinking is never piecemeal thinking. Every philosophical question is a self-mediation of the all-inclusive im-mediacy of primordial wonder. Every philosophical question questions the integral totality of all that is. Every philosophical question brings the whole of philosophy into play. Consequently, all steps to be taken in philosophy are mutually interdependent, each particular step involves all the others, and each move collects the whole of our philosophical explorations.

Finally, there is the fact that as contrasted with deductive methods philosophical thinking has continually "the end in sight." We are never totally ignorant of the "end" of philosophical thinking precisely because the "end" is the "beginning" as "re-search pro-ject." We discovered in Chapter Four that the actual beginning of philosophy determines its aim and scope, and that the beginning *is* the end, but in a beginning way. It should be clear that the word "end" in this context does not have the meaning of a mere cessation, or of the "ending" of a road that "stops," but is used in the sense of an immanent aim, a dynamic intention or authentic finality.

Authentic Finality

The *authentic finality* of existential thinking is never the mere realization of an idea, an object, a model or a thing that is ready-made and perfectly perceived in advance. If this were the case, the "aim" of existential thinking would have the nature of a "blueprint," and fundamental thinking would be reduced to "instrumental" thinking. Philosophy would solely consist in the constructing of a road towards a "fixed" end or in the procuring of the means for the attainment of a ready-made result. This, however, would contradict the basic findings of our fundamental thinking. For philosophy is the progressive self-questioning of its primary data, and as such it adheres to these data with creative fidelity. Fundamental thinking does away with the separation between the result and the process of arriving at it. In fundamental thinking there is a fusion of means and aim, of method and content, of beginning and end. The authentic finality of existential thinking throws light "ahead of itself" into its "origin," and goes out into its "past" as something "to come" (*Zukunft*—future). The authentic finality of philosophy is the creative interiorizing self-transcendency of the natural light of Being. Authentic finality is not a finished concept before our eyes, but it overtakes us from behind so to speak. Authentic finality is inspirational, and is "given" in our innermost ontological experience as the ever growing self-realization of the *mystery* of Being. Authentic finality reveals itself in philosophy as the very creativity of the ontological aspect of our primitive cognitive intention. We, therefore, are not the makers of true finality; we are its discoverers. We do not construct or control authentic finality, but authentic finality "inspires" us, and "attracts" us to make the leap into the unknown depth of known Being. Authentic finality *moves* us not by motives of force but by motives of appeal. Authentic finality "invites" us to make the leap into the unknown depth of Being, and this leap *makes us* by constituting our authentic "future," or by constituting our authentic ex-sistence as adventure. The attraction of authentic finality, therefore, is never the physical "pull" of *finalism* which would merely be the reverse of the blind "push" of *mechanistic causality*. "Finalism thus understood," says Henri Bergson, "is only inverted mechanism."[74]

Logical Verification and Ontological Self-verification

In deductive thinking the proof is our only assurance that the conclusion is true. And this proof presents itself as an accomplished fact. The process of verification is essentially different in existential thinking. In existential thinking the truth is found in the *beginning*, whereas in deductive thinking it is found in the *end*, which is the "result" of the deductive process. The truth of deductive reasoning "results from" the correct use of logical syllogisms *(beweisen)*, and is "verified" by checking the correctness of our procedure against the rules of deductive thinking as they are described by formalized methodology. Philosophy, on the other hand, finds its truth right in the *beginning*, namely in the critical moment of its primitive cognitive intention. Hence the truth of ontological demonstration *(aufweisen)* does not "result from" this demonstration, but it *is* this demonstration as the dialectical self-manifestation of its beginning: primordial wonder. In other words, ontological demonstration by making the truth more and more true, is its own *veri-fication* in the etymological sense of making the truth truer or more trustworthy *(verum*—truth; *facere*—to make). This self-verification of existential thinking does not present itself as an accomplished fact, but it is the never ending ad-venture of our authentic ex-sistence.

LOGICAL INDUCTION AND THE PHENOMENOLOGICAL ASPECT OF EXISTENTIAL THINKING

A similar parallel could be drawn between the *induction* of the logico-empirical sciences on the one hand, and the phenomenological aspect of philosophy on the other. Induction presents certain analogies with phenomonology, but their respective differences are far more basic.

Empirical and Experiential "Data"

Inductive argumentation seeks to establish universal propositions by reasoning from particular facts or individual cases to (more) general conclusions. Induction consults data "from without" in order to convert this fragmentary knowledge into a more universal validity. In this respect there is a resemblance between inductive thinking and the phenomenological aspect of philosophical thinking. For also the phenomena of phenomenology are "data" that are interrogated as to their "universal" meaning. Also the phenomena of phenomenology are "data" that in a sense are consulted "from without" in regard to the primordial question of ontology. The "primitive cognitive intention," as we have seen,[75] differentiates primordial wonder into a multi-dimensional structure of *original* phenomena that as such are not given in the undifferentiated experience of this primordial phenomenon. The primitive cognitive intention reveals itself as a unitary structure, in which I find myself-being-together-with-others-in-the-world. Phenomena such as the "self," the "others," and the "world" are among the *primary data* of philosophy, and as such they "reveal themselves" as *original* phenomena. This means that they are *beginnings* in their own right, that they are *self-given (selbstgegeben)* and *cannot be deduced* from primordial Being. In other words, the phenomena of philosophical thinking reveal a certain "otherness" or "opposition" in regard to the primordial phenomenon of wonder. Since also in philosophy the phenomena are in a sense given "from without," existential thinking must respect the tendency of Being to differentiate and to include that which is "other." But, once again, here is where the comparison ends. For the meaning of terms such as "data," "from without," "universality," etc. is fundamentally different in inductive thinking and in its phenomenological counterpart.

In the first place, the *givenness* of the "data" (L. *datum*—what is given) of inductive thinking is radically different from the "givenness" of the phenomena of phenomonology. The inductive thinking of *empiricism à la* Francis Bacon admits exclusively the type of givenness which is presented by our sense perception as the data from which all our thinking derives. This limits "givenness" as such to the *empirical data* of the immediacy of the vital order. The typical data of the *natural sciences* are the controlled data of exact ob-servation as the basis on which the scientific processes rest. Scientific facts are the verifiable, *experimental data* of the ob-jective order. The phenomenological data of *philosophical* thinking are neither the merely fragmentary experiences of the everyday world, nor the ob-jectified facts of the abstractive world of science. Philosophical data are the phenomena that *manifest themselves* in the primordial light of Being. Philosophical phenomena reveal themselves as *experiential data* in the totality of the existential order. Their "givenness" is always co-original with the givenness of *the* world, or the primordial condition for the discoverability of any beings or systems of beings encountered *(Ur-gestalt)*. The givenness of the philosophical phenomena, therefore, is also co-original with the experiential totality of man's ex-sistence as participant in the actuality of *the* world.

Both the "data" of our everyday existence and the scientific "facts" of our logico-empirical thinking have their own respective kind of truth. But it would be an illegitimate restriction of the nature of our thinking and a dogmatic arrogation to philosophical ultimacy when we mistake the givenness of such a particular kind of truth for the primary "data" of fundamental thinking. For instance, a theory which restricts its conception of "givenness" to the data of sense experience by regarding them as the only source of valuable knowledge, contradicts itself because of its inability to base itself on *any* experience. "The prejudice involved here," says Dietrich von Hildebrand, "arises from the idea that sensations have, in their being given, a superiority over other data, a superiority which precisely is not given, but which is rather the postulate of an arbitrary theory."[76] Among such arbitrary theories are empiricism and scientism. Both empiricism and scientism are pseudo-philosophies in so far as they dogmatically believe in the philosophical ultimacy of, respectively, empirical and experimental data, and regard these data as the only legitimate source of knowledge. Edmund Husserl, the father of phenomenology,[77] in an attack upon empiricism and scientism makes the following succinct statement: "We do not, indeed, let ourselves be deprived by *any* authority of the right to recognize all kinds of intuition as legitimate sources of knowledge—not even by the authority of the 'modern natural sciences'."[78] Both empiricism and scientism are pseudo-fundamental. For although they claim to be fundamental thinking, they pass over the "original givenness" of fundamental perception by starting from data that are already second-level constructions of the human mind. And if we understand the term "positive" (L. *ponere*—to place) in the fundamental sense of our unqualified being placed in reality, our downright presence to what is without any standpoint or prejudice, or our pre-reflective awareness of the given situation, then both scientism and empiricism are characterized by their *lack of positivity.* "If we mean by *positivism,*" says Husserl, "the absolute unprejudiced founding of all sciences on what is 'positive', i.e. what is to be perceived in its original givenness, then it is *we* who are the real positivists."[79] The positivity of our original perception will be further discussed in the following chapter.

Generality and Universality

Secondly, inductive reasoning aims at a kind of "universality" which is essentially different from the universality of philosophical phenomenology. The data of inductive thinking are individual facts, isolated events or particular objects. And the aim of inductive reasoning is to arrive at more "universal" conclusions. Apart from the fact that the conclusion of a "perfect" induction never really arrives at universal statements, never goes beyond the facts observed, but is merely an accumulative assertion "concerning all the entities of a collection on the basis of examination of each and every one of them,"[80] the ampliative inference of ordinary induction does not, as it is often stated, arrive at universal statements either. Ordinarily induction attempts to arrive with a certain degree of probability at a *general* assertion concerning all the members of a *class* (L. *genus*—class) from the observation of only some of them. Logical thinking is never truly "universal" in the fundamental sense of "all-inclusive." Logic only deals with beings or with the objectifiable segment of reality, and never arrives at the all-encompassing universality of the *logos*. The phenomenological aspect of the *logos* is an interiorizing "in-scription" of its "data" in the *com-prehensive universality* of primordial Being, and not the inductive *generalizing* "description" of unrelated and particular facts. The phenomenological aspects of the *logos* interrogates its data as to their universal meaning by probing deeper and deeper into the qualitative plenitude of their participation in the primordial universality of Being and thus differs radically from the abstractive generalization of logical induction.

Physical and Phenomenological "Di-stance"

Thirdly, inductive thinking receives its data "from without." The phenomena of phenomenology are also in a sense given "from without" in regard to primordial Being. This "from without," however, means something basically different in logical induction and in phenomenology. In ob-jectifying thinking, as we have seen, both the ob-ject and the ob-serving subject become detached from the experiential world of the thinker. The ob-servable facts for logical induction are literally external to the scientist. Inductive thinking receives its data "from without" in the sense of a *quantitative di-stance*. This, however, is essentially different in the phenomenological aspect of *logos*-thinking. The phenomena of phenomeno-logy are not identical with the primordial phenomenon of Being. In this sense they reveal themselves "from without" in regard to this primordial experience. Yet, this "from without" does not indicate a quantitative di-stance, but rather the interiorizing self-transcendency of the phenomena into the primordial depth of Being. We will revert to this primordial depth later on in this chapter.

As we know, the phenomena of phenomenology are never isolated data, they are never unconnected with one another, or unrelated to primordial Being and the experiential world of the philosopher. On the contrary, the phenomena of phenomenology are only truly philosophical to the extent in which they mediate the immediacy of primordial wonder. In fact they *are* the dialectical self-manifestation of this primordial phenomenon. No philosophical phenomenon, therefore, can strictly speaking manifest itself "outside" the com-prehensive universality of

Being. Philosophy precisely begins as a unity in opposition, as a polar tension or existential dialogue between the phenomenon of Being and the Being of the phenomena. The all-inclusive phenomenon of primordial wonder remains the immanent source and inspiring light of all our philosophical explorations. Phenomena are not philosophically "given" unless they manifest "themselves" as "participants" in the primordial act of wonder. This *dialectical* relationship between the phenomenological and the ontological aspects of the philosophical way of thinking is a constituent of the philosophical method. At this point it will be possible and helpful to draw a third parallel between the logical ways of thinking and the fundamental thinking of the *logos*.

LOGICAL DIALECTICS AND THE DIALETICAL ASPECT OF EXISTENTIAL THINKING

Once again, there is a certain resemblance between the *dialectics* of the logical sciences on the one hand, and the *dialectical aspect* of philosophical thinking on the other. For, generally speaking, dialectics indicates a certain *articulation* of our thought process, and both logic and philosophy are articulated ways of thinking. The foregoing elucidations, however, have made it abundantly clear that there is an essential difference between the kind of articulation of these respective ways of thinking.

The dialectics of logic is the articulation of a series of logical steps to be taken in inductive and deductive inferences. The dialectics of philosophy, on the other hand, is the articulation of the *differentiated* self-manifestation of Being. Whereas the dialectics of logic is an abstractive, reductive and mechanical process, philosophical dialectics is an experiential encounter, a creative interplay of polar opposites, or a truly existential *dialogue* (Gr. *dia*—between; *legesthai*—to speak).

The Equiprimordiality of Ontology, Phenomenology and Dialectics

Philosophy begins as a dialogue. For, as we have seen, the actual beginning of philosophy is the existential interplay *(dia)* between primordial wonder and differentiated wonder *(logos)*.[81] This "dia-lectical" tension between the phenomenological and the ontological aspects of *logos*-thinking is the mainspring of our philosophical dynamism. In the very beginning of philosophy the ontological meaning of the primary phenomena is "dialectically" given. In other words, *the ontological, the phenomenological and the dialectical aspects of the philosophical method are equiprimordial.* A one-sided understanding or application of one aspect to the exclusion of the others would lead our whole philosophical thinking astray. Ontology, phenomenology and dialectics are not three *separate methods* in philosophy, but as "differentiated" dimensions of the self-manifestation of Being they are "distinct" *aspects* of the *logos* that stand or fall together.

Differences between Logical and Ontological Dialectics

Philosophical dialectics *is* the articulation (differentiation) of the self-manifestation of primordial wonder. As contrasted with logical dialectics, the dialectics of the *logos* is experiential rather than abstractive, creative rather than mechanical, and circular rather than rectilinear. Philosophical dialectics is reflective and self-questioning, and can never be formalized or separated from its phenomenal content. Philosophical dialectics is never only *about Being;* it *is* Being in its articulated self-movement. Philosophical dialectics is never a formal procedure that can be "applied" to our philosophical questions, but it is an integral part of our philosophical questioning itself. In each dialectical move the whole of Being comes into play, and in each philosophical question the whole of dialectics is at stake. Philosophical dialectics cannot possibly coagulate into the fixity of a closed system without ceasing to be truly philosophical. Each dialectical move of the *logos* is an articulation of the primordial openness of wonder and brings the whole of philosophical dialectics into play.

Philosophical dialectics is the creative multi-polarity of our ex-sistence as the multi-dimensional articulation of the self-manifestation of primordial Being. The discursiveness, the unity-in-difference, the polar tension of this multifarious self-manifestation is not a rectilinear movement from premises to conclusions in a series of logical steps, but rather an authentic discourse, an ex-sistential dia-logue. The *logos* brings the primordial word of wonder up for discussion. And this discussion is in the most fundamental sense of the word an ex-sistential "dis-course" (*dis*—between, in different directions; *currere*—to run). The dialectics of the *logos* begins as a multi-dimensional dialogue between our primary phenomena and the primordial phenomenon of Being. And in this dialogue all the participants are both speaking and listening in a relationship of mutual interdependency. Listening is constitutive for the ex-sistential dialogue we *are*. For authentic listening is the ex-sistential openness of man as participant in the primordial word of wonder to the immanent opposition of original phenomena as the constitutive anti-words (answers) to his wondering ex-sistence. Only he who wonders can *truly* listen. The "primordial listening" of wonder constitutes the ex-sistential "openness" of our human personality. In the pre-ontological experience of wonder the primordial listening of man is the still un-differentiated answer to the primordial word of Being. The differentiation of this primordial listening initiates our "original perceptions" of reality.[82] And the fact that primordial listening remains the guiding principle of our philosophical dialectics prevents this dialectics from ever becoming fixated into a closed system. A closed philosophical system has ceased to listen and to wonder, and, therefore, has ceased to be truly philosophical.

The movement, then, of the *logos* as the existential dialogue is basically different from the "straight" thinking of logic. Philosophical dialectics is the "circular" motion of word and anti-word in a never ending ascendancy. This circular motion of philosophical dialectics is truly an ontological "pro-motion" of all the phenomena of phenomeno-logy. Philosophical phenomena are never merely "self-given," they never reveal themselves in their isolation as philosophical. Philosophical phenomena manifest themselves only in a mutual interdependency of giving and receiving, of speaking and listening. The phenomena of phenomenology are always "co-given" and "co-giving." They con-stitute philosophical *meaning* only in their dialectical togetherness in the context of *the* world, in their differentiated encounter with primordial wonder, or in the experiential dialogue of authentic human ex-sistence.

The Origin of Fundamental Meaning

Philosophical intelligibility or *fundamental meaning* originates in our "primitive cognitive intention" as the *experiential encounter* between primary philosophical phenomena and the primordial phenomenon of wonder.[83] In other words, philosophical meaning gives itself from the very beginning *in a dialectical way.* Philosophical meaning does not exist "outside" the existential thinker as a property of the "thing-in-itself." Nor does it pre-exist as a static essence that merely needs to be recognized and to which the dialectical method can be "applied." In fact, we have already seen in the previous chapter,[84] that not a single meaningful datum manifests itself independently of our human ex-sistence. There are no "pure facts," there are no facts that reveal themselves "outside" the horizon of a human world, unrelated to the perspective of a certain intentionality. Meaning is constituted by an encounter between a datum and an intentional act, and arises as a dialectical mode of our being-in-the-world. Philosophical meaning is constituted by the fundamental "encounter" (dialectics) between the primordial act of wonder (ontology) and the primary data of our human ex-sistence (phenomenology). Philosophical dialectics, therefore, is a constituent of philosophical meaning insofar as this meaning reveals itself as the articulated com-prehension of primordial wonder *(logos)*. Phenomena have no philosophical meaning unless they manifest themselves in the articulated context of *the* world *(logos)* as the horizon of all fundamental meanings. Fundamental meaning is rooted in the meaning of Being, and without the Being of this meaning there would *be* no fundamental meaning at all. Philosophical phenomena are never received in a merely passive way. Nor are they the result of an act of pure creativity. The phenomena of philosophical phenomeno-logy are con-stituted by the dialectical unrest of our human ex-sistence as the creative fidelity to the differentiated phenomenon of wonder.

In other words, by collecting the philosophical phenomena in the primordial light of wonder the *logos* (G. *legein*—to gather, to speak) "con-stitutes" the world of fundamental meanings (*con*—together; *statuere*—to set up, to found, to pass judgment). The *logos* gives rise to *the world* by setting primordial wonder apart into a multiplicity of "self-given" phenomena, and by founding their permanent togetherness on the primordial unity of Being. This seems to be the meaning of the well-known saying of Heracleitus of Ephesus (Fragment 53): *"polemos pantoon pater esti,"* "Conflict is the father of all things." Commenting on this text, Martin Heidegger says: "This conflict, as Heracleitus thought it, first caused the realm of being to separate into opposites; it first gave rise to position and order and rank. In such separation cleavages, intervals, distances and joints opened. In the conflict [*Auseinandersetzung,* setting-apart] a world comes into being. (Conflict does not split, much less destroy unity. It constitutes unity, it is a binding-together, *logos. Polemos* and *logos* are the same.)"[85] Now, the *logos* as that which "de-cides" (sets-apart) the ontological stature of phenomena in their primordial collectedness of Being is philosophy *as a system.* The *logos* as that which passes judgment on the meaning of phenomena in the com-prehensive universality of the context of fundamental meaning is *philisophical judgment.* And the *logos* as that which "de-limits" philosophical phenomena in their primordial light of Being is *philosophical de-finition.* We shall continue our comparison between logic and *logos* by examining the different ways in which they form their respective judgments, definitions and systems. And again, our primary aim in drawing this parallel is not so much to arrive at an understanding of formal logic, but rather to further our fundamental explicitation of existential thinking.

BASIC CONTRASTS BETWEEN LOGICAL AND ONTOLOGICAL JUDGMENTS

Although there is a certain resemblance between the judgments of logic and those of the *logos,* their respective differences are much more striking. A logical judgment bears upon particular beings or *classes* of beings. It never relates to the totality of all that is. A logical judgment is never fundamental. The *logos* as judgment, on the other hand, is always fundamental, differentiates the primordial totality of all that is and always involves the whole of Being. The *logos* as judgment reveals, not in a legalistic, but in a profoundly ontological way, the etymological origin of the word "judge-ment." The *logos* as judgment is the primordial judge of the Supreme Court of Being who hears and passes fundamental judgment on the ontological meaning, the proper place and essential limits of all philosophical phenomena.[86] The *logos* de-limits these phenomena in the context of their structural totality *(Urgestalt).* Thus the *logos* is the *primordial judgment* which con-stitutes *the world* as the actual possibility of the self-manifestation of the essence of phenomena in their primordial context of fundamental meaning.

Logos *as "Pre-judgment" or "Hypo-thesis"*

The *logos* as the primordial judgment is our ontological *pre-judice.* The term pre-judice here is evidently not taken in its pejorative and subjectivistic sense of bias, but in the ontological sense of *pre-judgment* in which the prefix "pre" indicates an existential primordiality. The *logos* as primordial judgment is ontologically prior to any fundamental phenomena encountered in the primordial context of the world. The *logos* as primordial judgment is the ground and "pre-supposition" of the very manifestation of philosophical phenomena, and is implicitly given in all our fundamental judgments. It is only in this unique and fundamental sense that we can regard the *logos* as the *hypo-thesis* of all our existential thinking. In the methodology of the natural sciences a hypothesis is the conditional explanation of a fact or group of facts as a starting-point for further investigation. The *logos* as the hypothesis of philosophical thinking (*hypo*—under; *tithenai*-—to posit) "posits itself" unconditionally as the all-encompassing ground of all our philosophical investigations. Thus the *logos* "underlies" all our philosophical phenomena and judgments as their self-grounding ground. The hypothesis of existential thinking is this very thinking in its *fundamental* "position" or "primordial positivity."

Logical Negation and Ontological "Nihilation"

There is another difference between logical and ontological judgments that draws our attention. In traditional logic a judgment is generally defined as a mental act which unites by affirmation or separates by negation, or in modern logic, as an affirmation or a negation of a relation among certain terms. This definition underlies one of the divisions of logical judgments, namely the division in affirmative and negative judgments. Also the *logos,* as we have seen, separates and unites. This, however, does not divide the *logos* into negative and affirmative judgments. On the contrary, in the *logos* there is a peculiar intimacy of relationship between the two movements that separate things and that hold them together in their primordial unity-in-difference. Heracleitus of Ephesus expressed this as follows (Fragment 60): "hodos anoo katoo mia kai hooute," "the way up and down is one and the same."

The *logos* sets primordial wonder apart into original phenomena by delimiting them in their primordial collectedness of Being. This is why the *logos* does not bifurcate the primordial experience of wonder into affirmative and negative judgments about Being. The *logos* as the differentiated self-manifestation of primordial wonder permits all beings to reveal themselves in their proper relationship to this all-encompassing phenomenon, and thus *reveals* the primordial openness of Being. Yet, by the very same token, the *logos conceals* Being insofar as its unconcealment takes place in a dialectical opposition with that which is "other" than the unstructured phenomenon of primordial wonder. The very dialectics of the *logos* which allows Being to reveal itself also conceals it. In other words, Being can only be revealed as concealed. The *logos* lets the exclamatory experience of primordial wonder appear *as the onto-logical mystery of Being.* The *logos* differentiates the undifferentiated experience of primordial wonder into the *mysterium tremens et fascinans,* the "dreadful and fascinating mystery" of Being. The *logos* differentiates the primordial phenomenon of wonder into a secret union of two distinct elements: the element of *fascination* and the element of *awe.* There is the experience of profound joy, enchantment, rapture or fascination insofar as we witness the *self-revelation* of primordial Being. And there is the experience of suspense, shudder, awe or anxiety insofar as we witness its primordial *concealment* or authentic Nothingness. We write Nothingness in a capital letter to indicate that authentic Nothingness is neither absolute nothingness (nothing at all) nor the mere dis-appearance of all particular and individual things (no-thing-ness). Authentic Nothingness over and above being "no-thing-ness" is more fundamentally "no-Being-ness" or *primordial Being as concealed*. "Nothingness," as Heidegger puts it, "is the veil of Being."[87]

Those who have degraded philosophical thinking to the thinking of particular beings or mere things ridicule the very idea of a Nothingness that has a fundamental meaning at the heart of philosophy. For them "no-thing-ness" can only mean one thing, namely: nothing at all. And to think of nothing at all is self-contradictory and, therefore, illogical. Who can deny this? But the claim that nothingness can only be understood in the sense of no-thing-ness is also illogical. For this claim would imply the dogmatic arrogation to logic of philosophical primordiality. We found that the *logos* as primordial judgment *de facto* reveals authentic Nothingness as a constituent of the mystery of Being. This Nothingness is not only "no-thing-ness" and nothing else. It is "no-Being-ness" which reveals itself at the heart of the mystery of Being, and thus *transcends* as "no-thing-ness" the mere appearance of things as things. And since authentic Nothingness reveals itself in the *logos* as primordial judgment we do not arrive at it by means of a negative judgment subsequent to the self-revelation of Being. On the contrary, Nothingness manifests itself as the intrinsic condition of the very occurrence of this self-revelation. Being and Nothingness are co-original, and only when Nothingness "nihilates" can Being reveal itself. It is evident that this "nihilation" is neither an "annihilation" nor a "negation" of Being. The "nihilating" action of authentic Nothingness does not "annihilate" Being, but is a constituent of its very self-manifestation. The "nihilating" action of authentic Nothingness is not a "negation" of Being, but as a constituent of the *logos* as primordial judgment it co-originates the "primordial positivity" of all our existential thinking.[88] To quote Heidegger again, "Nothingness is the origin of negation, and not the other way around."[89]

In other words, Nothingness does not divide the *logos* as primordial judgment into affirmative and negative judgments about Being, but the *logos* differentiates primordial wonder into a secret union of Being and Nothingness. This union of Being and Nothingness permeates as the *onto-logical mystery* every step of our *logos*-thinking, and, therefore, every philosophical judgment. Every philosophical judgment, every philosophical question, every dialectical move involves both Being and Nothingness, and transcends itself into the *primordial depth* of the onto-logical mystery. Every philosophical judgment is aroused by its own depth, stirred by its own strangeness and wonders at the very mystery of

its own Being. "Only because of wonder—i.e. the revelation of Nothingness—does the "why?" originate."[90] And since every philosophical
judgment remains rooted in wonder, every philosophical judgment remains a self-questioning question, and no philosophical judgment can
ever be regarded as final, as achieved or as an "established premise"
from which further conclusions can be drawn. In every philosophical
judgment the whole of the *logos* is always being called into question.
Every philosophical judgment involves the com-prehensive *universality*
of the *logos* as primordial judgment, and transcends all logical judgments both in depth and in comprehension.

Problem and Mystery

Consequently, no philosophical insight, no philosophical judgment or
question has ever closed boundaries or precise limits. A philosophizing
that wants to remain faithful to itself has to think the "unknown-
known," the all-pervading experience of wonder and the unfathomable
depth of the ontological mystery. Henri Bergson was right in distinguishing two kinds of clarity. On the one hand there is the clarity of the
"clear and distinct" ideas or the "define-able" concepts of logical thinking. But as Bergson puts it, these ideas "keep their light for themselves." On the other hand, there is the clarity of philosophical thinking
which is "itself obscure," but "illuminates the whole region of thought
and dissipates obscurities."[91] Both kinds of clarity result from a perspective of "di-stance," from a "standing-apart," from a "going beyond," or
from a "transcendence." The clarity of the logico-empirical sciences is
created by the abstractive and objectifying intentionality of the scientist.
The scientist, as we have seen, detaches both his "ob-ject" and himself
from his experiential involvement in the world. This creates a *spatial*
"di-stance" in which the "ob-jects" are questioned but the status of the
questioner remains unquestioned. "Questioned ob-jects" standing over
against the scientific "ob-server" are called "pro-blems" (*pro*—over
against; *balloo*—to throw).[92] Now, the characteristic fidelity of the scientist to his data is that of "exact ob-servation." The scientific "ob-server"
(ob—servare) holds his ob-ject at a di-stance in such a way that it
progressively reveals its quantitative face, and becomes more and more
accessible to the use of mathematical methods. This quantifying reduction leads to the univocity and the unambiguity of physical concepts
and the exactness of their mathematical descriptions, which accounts
for the peculiar clarity of scientific thinking.

In philosophizing the situation is different. The world of the philosopher is not the world of scientific *problems,* but the world of the onto-

logical *mystery* of Being. In this fundamental questioning the philoso-pher is involved with the whole of his ex-sistence. Philosophical think-ing is ex-sistential thinking. The "di-stance" which also characterizes the philosophical kind of clarity is not the spatial di-stance of scientific *pro-blems,* but rather the interiorizing self-transcendency of the *primor-dial depth* of the *mystery* of Being. All di-stances of the spatial dimen-sions melt into one another in this primordial di-stance of depth. The "going beyond" of this primordial di-stance is rather a "being its own beyond." In the dimension of primordial depth the "here" and the "there," the "now" and the "then," the "close" and the "far" tend to merge.[93] It goes without saying that the primordial and all-inclusive depth of the mystery of Being does not have the fixed limits and definite contours of logical thinking. The clarity of philosophical thinking is not the clarity of the inert contours of physical concepts and logical de-finitions. Philosophical clarity is a clarity of depth, a clarity of twilight, a clarity in which light and darkness blend into the *mystery* of Being. Primordial depth gives to existential thinking its all-pervasive and en-during *chiaroscuro.* An authentic philosophical insight has the onto-logical dimension of depth which makes it a "wonder-ful" experience. A "wonder-ful" insight originates a fundamental "why?" and maintains itself only by advancing. We have a fundamental urge to go back to a deep insight in order to explore deeper and deeper the inexhaustibility of its "wonder-ful" meaning.[94]

LOGICAL AND ONTOLOGICAL DEFINITIONS

Different Perspectives

This difference of clarity is also reflected in the different ways in which logical and philosophical thinking *define* the essences of their respective data. According to traditional logic a real definition expresses the essence of a thing by indicating its proximate genus and specific difference. Etymologically, to "de-fine" means to fix the *limits (finis)* of something, to set down the boundaries of something, to differentiate or to distinguish. In logic things are strictly "define-able" and can be confined within well-determined contours. For, as we have seen, the device of logic is: *divide et impera,* "divide and rule." The ob-jectifying intentionality of logical thinking atomizes the unity of the experiential world, and makes the de-limited data accessible to univocal and exact thinking by setting them down in their precise and closed boundaries.

As contrasted with logical thinking, the *logos* is constantly nourished by the primordial experience of wonder which is a completely undefinable phenomenon.[95] On the other hand, the *logos is* the differentiating self-manifestation of primordial wonder. And in this sense the *logos* de-fines the undefinable in a very unique way. The *logos,* as the differentiating self-manifestation of primordial Being sets all beings apart in their *limits (finis)* by gathering them in their original togetherness in the primordial *finality (finis)* towards Being. By setting all beings in their *limits* in the primordial context of fundamental meaning the *logos* reveals these beings in their *ontological essence.* The dialectics of the *logos is* the "de-finition" of ontological data which sets them in the proper limits of their own finality. It is only in the light of the primordial phenomenon of Being that the essence (be-ing) of fundamental phenomena comes into appearance. It is only in the dialectics of the *logos* that philosophical phenomena manifest their onto-logical unity-in-difference, and that they "essentiate" by truly *be-ing* what they *are.*

Essences and Presences

Whereas in logic the essence of a thing is de-fined in terms of its proximate genus and specific difference, or in terms of the sum total of predicates attributed to a certain subject, in philosophy the situation is radically different. The essence as de-fined by the *logos* is never static, definite, univocal, abstract and confined within closed boundaries. On the contrary, the "essence" of a philosophical datum as "de-fined" by the *logos* is *the dynamic appearance of its true "be-ing."*[96] And the true "be-ing" of a philosophical essence reveals itself only in an experiential dialogue with primordial wonder as the inexhaustible context of all fundamental meanings. Ontologically "de-fined" phenomena (essences) are never "static essences" or dead-ends on the way to Being. Philosophical de-finitions are not boundaries but beacons. Their unity-in opposition with primordial wonder is the mainspring of our philosophical dynamism and the guiding light on our way to philosophical insight.[97] Philosophical phenomena (essences) are the dynamic and dialectically interconnected self-manifestations of the all-encompassing phenomenon of wonder. They "con-stitute" as *logos* the dialectical self-revelation of this primordial experience, and always de-fine themselves within the mystery of Being. Philosophical essences are "pre-sences" (*prae*—before; *esse*—to be). For they "present themselves" in the "presence" of primordial *Be-ing.* And thus they *"present* themselves" in the "presence" of one another as original "data" (gifts—"presents"). Philosophical essences "present *themselves"* by presenting "their own be-ing" as autonomous participations in the heteronomy of primordial

Be-ing. Philosophical essences (phenomena) *are* differentiating self-manifestations of the *logos*.

Implications for Phenomenology

All this has some important implications for a truly philosophical understanding of phenomenology. *In the first place,* philosophical phenomena (essences) do not reveal themselves as "standing over against" man as a *human subject,* but they rather reveal themselves in man as the *participant in the actuality of Being.* To say, therefore, that philosophical phenomena always come into the world "through" man is correct if we mean by this "with" man, and not exclusively "by" man.[98]

Secondly, philosophical phenomena are not *mere appearances.* Behind the mere phenomenality of the philosophical phenomena are the ontological and dialectical aspects of existential thinking. But behind the phenomena as dialectical self-manifestations of primordial Be-ing there is nothing else. Those who restrict the whole of philosophical thinking to the phenomenological aspect alone, overlook the *trans-phenomenal be-ing* of the phenomena, and distort philosophy as method. They are unable to raise the ontological question about the being of phenomenology. A phenomenology which does not respect its dialectical beginning in primordial wonder tends to turn into an uprooted neo-essentialism,[99] just as an ontology which does not respect original phenomena turns into the sterile and formalistic apriorism of rationalistic dialectics.[100] And the respective disappearance or petrifaction of philosophical dialectics resulting from this separation between ontology and phenomenology not only paralyzes the *dynamism* of philosophical comprehension, it also destroys the *com-prehensive* character of philosophical dynamism. This trans-phenomenal be-ing of philosophical phenomena is not a world of unknowable "noumena" hiding behind the phenomena, but rather their being rooted in the ontological and dialectical aspects of the *logos*. Philosophical phenomenology is not only a dialectics of the appearances of beings, but also of the beings of the appearances. In other words, the question about the transphenomenal being of phenomena should be raised, but the question about their trans-phenomeno-logical being is meaningless.[101]

Thirdly, there will always be the fundamental distinction or immanent polarity between the phenomenon of Being and the Being of phenomena. No phenomenon *is fully* what it reveals, no being *reveals fully* what it is. This polar tension underlies the classical distinction between "essence" (what-ness) and "existence" (that-ness), and it is only in the

light of this polar tension that the distinction is philosophically meaningful. We will return to this in a later chapter.

Fourthly, no philosophical essence can be de-fined in its isolation,
since each philosophical phenomenon gathers in its own way the totality
of all that is. Each philosophical essence is a "part-whole" and, in a
sense, "re-defines" the whole of philosophy. The *logos* as the dialectical
self-manifestation of Being is the ever growing *self-definition* of existential thinking. This dynamic self-definition creates the "con-sistency"
(*con*—together; *sistere*—to stand) of existential thinking, and de-fines
philosophy as a "sys-tem" (*sun*—together; *histanai*—to set). And this
brings us to a final point of comparison between logic and *logos.* Both
are systematic ways of thinking, but in an essentially different way.

IS SYSTEMATIZATION CONTRARY TO EXISTENTIAL THINKING

Contemporary Attack upon Systematization

Ever since the period of the great rationalist and idealist system-
builders in Continental Europe the very idea of a *philosophical system*
has been under severe attack. It began with Søren Kierkegaard of Co-
penhagen. "The systematic tendency," he writes, "promises everything
and keeps nothing."[102] And, elsewhere, he states that "System and
finality correspond to one another, but existence is precisely the opposite of finality."[103] This is why, according to Kierkegaard, it is possible
to have a logical system, but not an existential system.[104] As an existing
individual Kierkegaard refuses to be "a paragraph in a system," or to
be put "into a systematic straitjacket."[105] The systematist can say "I do
not know whether I am a human being—but I have understood the
System." Says Kierkegaard: "I for my part would rather say: 'I know
that I am a human being, and I know that I have not understood the
System'."[106]

More recent times have echoed the voice of Kierkegaard. "It is of no
use," says Henri Bergson, "to hold up before our eyes the dazzling
prospect of a universal mathematic; we cannot sacrifice experience to
the requirements of a system."[107] For Gabriel Marcel the building of a
philosophical system is always done at the expense of the truth. He
makes this clear where he writes: "my general tendency to bring out
difficulties instead of concealing them helped to develop my distrust of
systems of philosophy of whatever kind: for there is no system that does
not involve the temptation to declare *a priori* that this or that difficulty
is to be judged unimportant and consequently set aside."[108] And

Maurice Merleau-Ponty states it flatly: "Philosophy," he says, "is contrary to systematization."[109]

Reasons for Distrusting Systematization

The reluctance of these thinkers to systematize philosophy clearly results from their fear of fixating the flexibility and the dynamism of philosophical thinking. A system, so they say, claims finality, and this is incompatible with the creative emergence of fundamental thinking. A system claims completeness, but this is incompatible with the primordial openness and inexhaustibility of the ontological mystery. A truth which resists inclusion in the system would simply be declared to be "irrelevant." A system claims universal applicability. In philosophy this would amount to a Procrustean method which tries to fit original phenomena into the single mould of the univocity of straight thinking. But straight thinking is abstract thinking, and abstract thinking encapsules the universe in a few abstract principles and logical deductions. The rigidity of this procedure, however, is incompatible with the dynamic openness of the *logos* in which every step means a new beginning, every move redefines the whole, and every re-flection remains open to new incursions of experience.

Logical and Ontological Systems

Now, generally speaking, a *system* (*sun*—together; *histanai*—to set) is any set or arrangement of things so connected as to form a consistent unity or an articulated whole. A system is a structural unity-in-multiplicity. And a scientific system is a set of facts, principles, laws and methods classified and arranged in a consistent way so as to show a logical plan of thinking. It is evident that those who reject the idea of philosophy as a system are not attacking the value of a logical or scientific system. Nor do they reject the open and dynamic unity of philosophical "com-prehension." What they are really attacking is the idea of philosophy as a *closed* system or the *substitution* for existential thinking of the merely logical kind of systematization.

Once again, there is a certain resemblance between the ways in which both logic and the *logos* systematize their respective data. Both the logical sciences and the existential thinking of the *logos* are *consistent ways* of arranging and organizing articulated thought processes into structural wholes. Both logic and the *logos* set things together into the permanency of a unitary structure. Both logic and the *logos* organize themselves as thinking ways of being-in-the-world. But since their respective modes of being-in-the-world are essentially different, the depth and the scope of their organized thinking are essentially different too. The ob-jectifying intentionality of logical thinking makes it possible for the logical sciences to divorce their method from their content, and to formalize their systems into more or less uniform patterns that have universal applicability. Logical thinking is systematic in that it follows step by step the outline of a pre-arranged plan. In philosophy such an abstractive procedure is simply impossible. In philosophy, as we have seen, it is the originality of the *logos* that sets primordial wonder apart into a *multiplicity* of "self-given" phenomena, and that founds their permanent *unity* on the primitive cognitive intention towards Being. In other words, it is the *logos* that *con-stitutes* the primordial unity-in-multiplicity or the unique sys-tem that philosophy *is*. The philosophical *sys-tem* is the dialectical interplay between phenomenological diversity and ontological unity of intention. Philosophy as a system *is* the dialectical self-manifestation of primordial wonder. Primordial wonder is *at the same time* the source of the *unity* of philosophical thinking and the source of its phenomenological *openness* at any point of its development. Both the merely haphazard way of philosophical thinking and the fixity of a closed philosophical systematization result from a common failure. It is the failure on the part of the philosopher to focus his existential thinking on the primordial experience of wonder. Neither random thinking nor closed systems are faithful to the primary data of philosophy. For the primordial openness of wonder is the permanent ontological horizon within which the multiplicity of philosophical phenomena find their dialectical unity.

Philosophical System as Ontological "Con-sistency"

Primordial wonder is the only perspective in which philosophy as a sys-tem finds its strictly philosophical *con-sistency* (*cum*—together; *sistere*—to stand). A philosophical system is not true because it is consistent, but it is consistent because it is philosophically true. And a philosophical system is true to the extent in which the phenomena are dialectically standing together in the transcending light of the mystery of Being. A philosophical system is true to the extent in which its data are gathered in the dynamic openness of primordial wonder. Neither the truth as correspondence nor the truth as coherency are as such sufficiently fundamental to constitute the truth of a philosophical system. A philosophical system is true when its coherency corresponds to the *dialectical unconcealment of primordial wonder* as the truth *(aletheia)* of the *logos*.[110]

The *logos* is a system *sui generis*. The *logos* as philosophical system is unique, original and constantly both unified and kept open by primordial wonder. Consequently, the con-sistency of the *logos* can never crystallize into the finished product of a closed system. Every step in philosophy has the nature of a quest, every dialectical move re-defines the whole, every answer returns as a deeper question. Philosophical answers are never definite intellectual achievements that could exist apart from the experiential context of our fundamental questioning. Philosophical answers are always given within the inexhaustible context of the mystery of Being. Philosophical answers cannot be crystallized into the fixity of a definite system. They are only given in the *actual* explorations of the *logos*. A philosopher who puts his thoughts into writing does not first have to wait until he has finished his system. If he does, he either will never write his book at all, or else his book will turn out to be strictly unphilosophical. The true philosopher is always caught between the beginning and the end. He can only write in the process of his actual explorations. The true philosopher can only be faithful to his primary data by leaving the doors of the future open, by actually searching while he is writing, and by presenting his answers in the form of questions for further re-search. Every philosophical answer opens new depths and original perspectives, every philosophical answer re-kindles our fundamental questioning, and, in a sense, re-begins the whole of our philosophical explorations. Philosophy is an existential discourse in which none of the participants ever has the last word.

CONCLUDING REMARKS

In conclusion, it cannot be emphasized too strongly that the parallel we have drawn between logic and the *logos* was by no means an attempt to discredit our logical way of thinking. In our world today, dominated as it is by the uncritically accepted and illogical prejudice of the absolute priority of logical thinking, such a parallel is almost systematically misunderstood. Any attempt to transcend logic, and to ask fundamental questions about its scope, its meaning and its place in the universe of thought is branded as illogical and unscientific. In earlier chapters, however, we had the opportunity to demonstrate the illogicality of this position. But the task of fully liberating logic from the pseudo-philosophies that are imposed on it today, had to wait until the end of the present chapter. For such a task requires beforehand a fundamental understanding of the *logos* and of its "primordial position" in the pluralistic world of our human ex-sistence.

Priority of the Logos

No logical thinking can produce the *logos*. For the *logos* is its primordial premise. There is no ascent to existential thinking as if it were the conclusion of logical premises. On the contrary, it is only in the fundamental light of the *logos* that we can understand the meaning of the parallel between logic and *logos,* and the nature of logic as a *derivative* mode of thinking. Not only has logic never shed any light on the mysterious dialectics of the *logos,* but it is in principle unable to do so. The logician as such is non-philosophical. The logician as logician is unable either to ask or to silence the questions of existential thinking. The respective ways of thinking of the *logos* and of logic are literally "worlds apart." They are, as we have seen,[111] fundamentally different and irreducible ways of being-in-the-world. And they find their interconnection only through the pluralistic structure of our human existence. Logic is the method of thinking of our objectifying way of being-in-the-world. The *logos* is the method of thinking of our fundamental way of being-in-the-world. The transition from the world of logic to the world of the *logos* is not a matter of having expert knowledge of logic, but of changing one's level of intentionality or of stepping into another world.

Consequently, the condescending superiority assumed by those who on the basis of their expert knowledge of logic deride any attempt to transcend logic is illogical. For all their expert knowledge of logic, or for that matter of mathematics, logicians are neither more nor less capable of *logos*-thinking than any other human beings. Logic as such is neither for nor against the *logos.* Those who see in the world of existential thinking, which they condemn for its illogicality, a mere object of derision are really ridiculing the illogicality of their own attitude. For this attitude is not based upon their logical thinking as logical, but on their illogical arrogation to logical thinking of philosophical primordiality. By turning logic into a pseudo-philosophy they first falsify the very nature of logical thinking, and then they brand as illogical or meaningless any assertion which disagrees with their own illogical attitude towards logic.[112] From the viewpoint of logic the *logos* is "meaningless" (without meaning), but from the viewpoint of scientism and logical positivism the *logos* is "nonsensical" (perverted meaning). Small wonder that logical positivism and scientism, the predominant persuasions of today, attack existential thinking for being anti-logical, anti-scientific

and anti-rational. They accuse existential thinking of being disrespectful
of logical thinking. But it is obvious (except to the logical positivists)
that the counter-attacks of the existential thinkers are not at all directed
against logic or science as such, but against those who illegitimately
transgress the domain of logical or scientific thinking.

No Attack upon Logic as such

Gabriel Marcel, for instance, regards "the spirit of abstraction" as
the source of the destructive elements in our contemporary world. But
when he calls his own philosophy of existence "an untiring battle
against the spirit of abstraction,"[113] he is not attacking abstract thinking
as such, but abstract thinkers who exceed the scope of their competence. According to John Wild, only "a provincially-minded fanatic"
may interpret existential thinking as an attack upon logic as such.[114]
Yet, Wild is rightly disturbed by the "imposing claims" that are made
for the possible applications of logic and science, and states that "so far
they seem relevant only to the construction of calculating machines."[115]
And elsewhere he continues: "No doubt, this is interesting and important. But there is another task that is even more important, no matter
what we name it. This is to study the intentional structure of living
discourse, and to devise a humane discipline for its guidance."[116] The
need for transcending the "spirit of abstraction" or the absolutism of
logical thinking by devising a "humane logic" is also clearly expressed
by Karl Jaspers. In his provocative book *The Future of Mankind* Jaspers proposes a "new way of thinking" as a way out of the modern
dilemma between "final destruction of human existence by the atom
bomb, and final destruction of the human essence by totalitarianism."[117]
This "new way of thinking" no longer permits the exclusive use of
logical thinking which "places the objects of thinking—things and people—at a distance where the thought no longer involves the thinker."[118]
On the contrary, this "new way of thinking" is simply "the way of a
thinking man who is himself."[119] It is a truly "humane logic," for it alone
"confirms, broadly and deeply, the human content which everyone harbors within himself, seeks in reflection, and finds in the realization of
his existence."[120]

True Respect for Logic

The existential thinker does not attack logic, but puts it in its proper
place in the pluralistic universe of man. And putting logic in its proper
place is not being disrespectful of logic. On the contrary, to understand
logic in the light of the *logos,* and to ask fundamental questions about

its meaning, its structure and its scope is a truly respectful attitude towards logic. For it allows logic to be. It allows logic to be logic, to be a useful instrument *(Organon)* in the human universe of thought. This is what Karl Jaspers means when he states "The spirit of philosophy is what gives meaning to science. It wants science to be. It knows the life of knowledge as the dignity of man."[121] The *logos* reveals the very essence of logic by setting it in its proper limits in the primordial context of fundamental meaning. It is precisely our modern positivistic and scientistic persuasions that are disrespectful of logic. For they do not allow logic to be logical or to reveal its true essence. Instead, they force logic into becoming illogical by dogmatically assuming philosophical ultimacy and thus exceeding the scope of its competence. The result is that ultimately logic is no longer a useful instrument in the universe of man, but that man becomes a disturbing factor in the universe of logic.

To be sure, the *logos* does not create the structure of logical thinking, but it makes it possible for us to understand this structure in a more fundamental perspective. It is in the light of the *logos* as our fundamental way of thinking-being-in-the-world that logic becomes intelligible as a *derivative mode* of thinking-being-in-the-world. Moreover, it is in the same light that the similarities and the essential dissimilarities between logical thinking and existential thinking become meaningful. Our comparison between logic and the *logos,* however, was not so much intended to shed light on the ontological nature of logical thinking, but rather to bring out by way of contrast the unique and fundamental structure of existential thinking. An existential phenomenology of logical and scientific thinking is beyond the scope of this study, and is, in fact, still almost completely lacking in the otherwise extensive phenomenological literature.

Suggestions for a Philosophy of Logic

Nevertheless, in the present chapter we have encountered some basic suggestions for an existential phenomenology of logic and of science. In the first place, the question of the fundamental "why?" of the structure of logical thinking *should be asked*. Logic should again be grounded on its long forgotten ontological roots: the dialectical self-manifestation of Being *(logos)*.[122] Secondly, the structural similarities between logic and the *logos* are due to the fact that logic as a derivative mode of thinking is ultimately rooted in the fundamental thinking of the *logos*. Thirdly, the essential difference between these two modes of thinking originates from the essential differences between their respective scope and depth of intentionality. Fourthly, the difference of intentionality consists in this, that logical thinking is calculative, whereas the thinking of the *logos* differentiates primordial Being. The quantifying objectification of logic is molded on the solidity of "ob-jects," whereas the fundamental re-flection of the *logos* is molded on the primordial dynamism of wonder. Fifthly, the structural characteristics of both ways of thinking becomes intelligible in the light of the faithfulness of their respective intentionalities to their proper data. Thus logical thinking is rectilinear, atomizing, unreflective, abstractive. Logical thinking leaves its starting point behind, never verifies its own premises and results in conclusions that are accomplished facts. *Logos*-thinking, on the other hand, is circular, com-prehensive, multi-dimensional and experiential. *Logos*-thinking never leaves its starting point behind, never results in final conclusions and is the self-verification of primordial wonder in a never ending ascendency. And, finally, logic is the controlling and controllable thinking of man as the scientific subject whose experiential world is not involved in his scientific thought. Logic is the reason man *has*.[123] The *logos,* on the other hand, is the overwhelming, all-encompassing and inspirational thinking of man as the participant in Being and involves his ex-sistence in its entirety. The *logos,* therefore, is rather the reason man *is*. Or, to put it even more accurately, the *logos* is the reason *which has man!*[124] For it is in the *logos* that man "essentiates." It is in the *logos* that man essentially "ex-sists" as man by fundamentally *going beyond himself* into the primordial depth of Being. The immanency and transcendency of the *logos* constitute the fundamental paradox of our human ex-sistence and of our existential thinking. And it is to this paradox and the questions it raises for our existential thinking that we must now turn in the two succeeding chapters.

CHAPTER VII

THE IMMANENCY OF EXISTENTIAL THINKING

In the previous chapter we found that the *logos* sets the philosophical data together in their primordial unity of wonder, and constitutes philosophy as a sys-tem. The fact, however, that the immanency of philosophical phenomena finds its systematic unity in the inspirational transcendency of primordial wonder raises a serious question as to the nature of existential thinking. Does existential thinking after all consist in some sort of *philosophical quietism?* Can we just say: "Leave it to the *logos* and everything will be 'in perfect order'?" Does the *logos* reveal to us in a single stroke the essences of all beings, even of those beings we have never encountered? Does the *logos* eliminate in a single stroke all our prejudices, all our pre-fabricated concepts, mental constructs and uncritically accepted self-evidences? Don't we have to know or to do anything on our part? Can we philosophize without having a rich and mature experience of life, without knowing any sciences, without possessing a wealth of phenomenological insights? Can we philosophize without actively engaging in laborious research, without employing any tools or techniques of thinking, without having studied the great philosophies of the past and the present? In short, is philosophy merely a question of inspiration? Is existential thinking nothing but a philosophical quietism? It goes without saying that the answer to these questions will entail consequences of the first importance.

IMMANENCY AND TRANSCENDENCY OF THE *Logos*

Let us begin by pointing out that we have already given an implicit answer to these questions in Chapter Four where we first encountered the *logos*. An explicitation of this answer, however, will further our differentiated understanding of the immanency of existential thinking. In Chapter Four we found that the *logos* begins as a *re-flection* on the primary data of philosophy. Philosophy is a re-flection on our pre-reflective and lived experience of being-in-the-world focalized by our primitive cognitive intention towards Being. This implies that the *logos* has two structural elements which are of the greatest importance at this point of our study. Insofar as the *logos* goes back into the *immediately lived data* of our ex-sistence, existential thinking involves the experiential totality of this ex-sistence and is a truly *immanent* way of thinking. Insofar, however, as the *logos* is focalized by the primordial *inspiration* of wonder, existential thinking involves the all-encompassing totality of Being and characterized by a veritable *transcendency*.

Now, it is precisely by overlooking the *immanency* of the *logos* that we arrive at the misconception of existential thinking as a sort of philosophical quietism. It is, therefore, on the *immanency* of existential thinking that we will focus our attention in the present chapter. As we know from Chapter Four, existential thinking is not an acosmic, disembodied and absolutely creative way of thinking. The *logos* is not a system in a vacuum. Existential thinking never starts from zero, but always re-flects upon the immediate data of our lived experience. This is why it is so important that our pre-reflective being-in-the-world, which is sometimes called the "natural world," reveals itself as it *is*, unspoiled by preconceived ideas, uncorrupted by prejudices or uncritically accepted "self-evidences." Philosophy, as we have seen,[125] has to be faithful to its primary data by *accurately describing* their original self-manifestation. In order to do this, we have to remove the screens that "filter" our experience of the "natural world," and to return to the pristine innocence of original perceptions. This return to the original world of unadulterated phenomena is by no means an easy task. On the contrary, it requires a great effort on the part of the philosopher, and a skillful and concentrated use of the techniques of the so-called "phenomenological reduction." Phenomenological reduction is the technique which reduces the phenomena to their original givenness, and removes any foreign elements they might contain.[126]

PHENOMENOLOGICAL REDUCTION

In its *pre-philosophical stage* this "phenomenological reduction" is a *descriptive analysis* of the phenomena under consideration. This descriptive analysis, however, should be sharply contrasted with the reductive analysis of the natural sciences which attempts to dissect its data into elementary parts and to reduce these parts to their merely quantitative aspects. The descriptive analysis of phenomenological reduction, on the other hand, is precisely performed *within* the act of intuiting the whole of the phenomenon and of its manifold relationships. This descriptive analysis aims at revealing the phenomenon in its original "self-givenness," or in the irreducible uniqueness of the totality of its structural characteristics. Although at first blush this may sound surprisingly simple, the truth is that it is surprisingly difficult. Phenomenological description requires painstaking concentration and hard work on the part of the phenomenologist. "Only he," says Herbert Spiegelberg, "who has experienced genuine perplexity and frustration in the face of phenomena when trying to find the proper description for them knows what phenomenological seeing really means."[127] And in his *Being and Time* Martin Heidegger gives us the reason for this perplexity and frustration. " 'Behind' the phenomena of phenomenology," he says, "there is essentially nothing else; on the other hand, what is to become a phenomenon can be hidden. And just because the phenomena are proximally and for the most part *not* given, there is need for phenomenology. Covered-up-ness is the counter-concept to 'phenomenon'."[128]

Now, the descriptive phase of phenomenological reduction gradually unconceals that which at first is concealed, gradually purifies that which at first is invaded by foreign elements, and gradually breaks the charm of uncritically accepted self-evidences by practicing a "special asceticism" (Paul Ricoeur). This aim can, at least partially, be obtained by comparing the phenomenon under consideration with closely related phenomena, by submitting the original phenomenon to a series of "free variations," by comparing the similarities and dissimilarities of their structural elements, and by systematically changing the standpoint from which we scrutinize the phenomenon in question.

AN EXAMPLE: THE PHENOMENON OF BEAUTY

Let us illustrate the phenomenological description by means of a concrete example. For our example we have chosen *the phenomenon of beauty*. It is, of course, impossible to do full justice to such an example within the confines of this study. We, therefore, have to restrict ourselves to a few basic observations concerning the descriptive analysis of the phenomenon of beauty. The phenomenological description of beauty is notoriously difficult. We would not have chosen this example without an important reason for our choice. This reason is twofold. In the first place, the phenomenon of beauty resists the reductive analysis of objectifying thinking, and is inaccessible to the methods of the natural sciences. Secondly, the phenomenon of beauty, as we shall soon discover, cannot remain a "mere example," but reveals itself as *the actual way of access* to phenomenological description. This may come as a shock to those who regard beauty as a property of the object, a merely subjective feeling, a means for relaxation or a delicacy for the connoisseur. We will, therefore, also be confronted with the task of examining if these opinions are not precisely based on prejudices that have to be cleared away in order to encounter the phenomenon of beauty in its original self-givenness.

Phenomenological description does not start from zero. We would, for instance, not even attempt a description of beauty if we had not encountered this phenomenon in the world of our pre-reflective existence. We all know what beauty means if we only stop for a moment to consider our most noteworthy occasions of enjoying the phenomenon of beauty. We may remember the times when we listened to a fine symphony or gazed over a beautiful landscape, when we were deeply moved by a novel, a great painting or an awe-inspiring tragedy. It would have been impossible to mistake these moments of beauty for anything else. Yet, confusion may arise as soon as we ask ourselves the question what beauty *really means*. We don't even have a leitmotiv in the chaos of questions that springs to our mind. Is beauty a property of the object, existing out there in the trees and sunsets, in the paintings and symphonies? Or is beauty rather a matter of feeling, merely subjective and undisputable? Does beauty reside in art or in nature? Does beauty reveal itself in the form or rather in the content of an artwork? Is beauty nourished by reality or rather by illusion? Does beauty originate in technique or in inspiration? Are we free to create beauty, or are we determined by our own culture? Is the joy of beauty sheer sense-pleasure or something that makes us spiritually happy? Does beauty appeal to our intellect or rather to our emotional life? Is beauty a "thing-in-itself" independent of the human beholder or creator? Or, as James Jarrett puts it: "*Was* there beauty before there were men to say 'How beautiful!' . . . . And if the earth grows cold and all life dies, will there be beauty still, a beauty of rocks and ice and thin shadows from the feeble sun—a beauty to be forever unobserved?"[129]

With all these questions, however, we have already overshot the limits of phenomenological description. The question where beauty is "supposed" to be located is not a phenomenological question. It is not a "going to the things themselves," but a question resulting from an uncritically accepted "standpoint-philosophy" that *covers up* the phenomenon of beauty and blocks the self-manifestation of its structural totality. The decisive question is not how to "fit" the phenomenon of beauty in our pre-conceived "world view," but whether and how it is a phenomenon of our actual experience. If the phenomenon of beauty contradicts our world view, then so much the worse for that world view. Here we allow the phenomena to have the first and the last word by suspending our belief in any pre-conceived ideas. The standpoint-philosophy underlying our dichotomizing "either . . . or" questions was clearly inspired by the Cartesian dualism. Dualism forbids us to accept any phenomenon that, as the phenomenon of beauty, insists on belonging to the world of man and the world of things at the same time. The abstractive and atomizing ways of thinking of these *nothing but* philosophies can only survive by systematically "overlooking" everything else. What is not "supposed" to appear is regarded as "irrelevant," is left out of consideration or even explained away. The motto of these thinkers reads: "My mind is already made up. Don't confuse me with the facts."

VARIOUS STANDPOINTS

Now, let us focus the descriptive analysis of the phenomenon of beauty on the example of a blossoming tree. Exploiting the dialectical situation of our pre-reflective existence, we may systematically compare the aesthetic attitude towards the tree with other attitudes and standpoints, and thus bring into focus some structural elements of the aesthetic phenomenon.

In our everyday existence we open our eyes and see the concrete tree. We take it for granted that we see the concrete tree, and no further questions are asked. The farmer and the carpenter also see the concrete tree, but their attitude is practical. They see the tree as a *means* for something else. How many pounds of cherries or how many shelves can I get out of this tree? The tree is bestowed with implemental characteristics, becomes a stimulus for practical action, and raises the question: "what is it good for?" From his standpoint the biologist will try to classify the tree and determine its species. (Let us pass over the classical logician who gets visions about the "Tree of Porphyry"). The standpoint of the physical scientist is abstractive and ob-jectifying. He reduces his data in such a way that they progressively reveal their quantitative face, and become calculable and predictable within a systematic network of mathematical relationships. From the standpoint of the physicist the actual perception of the blossoming tree is replaced by a system of mathematical symbols through which he understands that out there is an unimaginable emptiness interspersed with some tiny electrical charges flying about with great speed.[130] The scientist asks himself experimental questions about the functional "how" of things. The philosopher, on the other hand, asks himself experiential questions about the fundamental "why" of things. These questions, as we know, are always asked within the light of primordial wonder. The philosopher wonders at the being of the blossoming tree, and is carried beyond the mere ocular perception of the tree into the transcendent vision of the mystery of Being. He opens himself to the wonder-ful fact that beings *are,* and tries to com-prehend their fundamental truths. The standpoint of the philosopher is the standpoint of the *logos.*

Everydayness and Beauty

How, then, does the aesthetic attitude towards the blossoming tree compare with the aforementioned standpoints? When I[131] behold the beauty of the blossoming tree, I perceive, as I do in my everyday existence, the tree in its very concreteness. Yet, the matter-of-factness of the everyday perception has lost its obviousness, and a mysterious transparency has taken its place. The tree is no longer a neutral object standing over against me, but the beautiful tree and my intimate self are grasped together in a blissful unity. The everyday concreteness loses its solidity and opens up into a translucent concreteness of inexhaustible depth. Space is no longer divided into "separate places," but it has become something ethereal in which everything is everywhere. Time is no longer "cut up" in separate moments, but it has turned into a "reposeful now" in which everything is simultaneous.

Utility and Beauty

As compared with the practical attitude the aesthetic attitude towards the blossoming tree is non-pragmatic. I experience the beautiful tree as something worthwhile in and for itself, as something to be enjoyed for its own sake. A question such as "what is it good for?" really offends the dignity of this mysterious experience.

Science and Beauty

There is a very great difference between the aesthetic attitude on the one hand, and the scientific attitude on the other. Beholding the beauty of the blossoming tree I do not abstract from my concrete experience of the tree, nor do I classify or quantify the tree, or translate my perception of the tree into a system of concepts or mathematical symbols. On the contrary, beholding the beautiful tree I perceive the tree in the translucent and inexhaustible concreteness of its mysterious being. Instead of objectifying the tree and placing it at a quantifiable distance, I grasp it within the profound intimacy of a "cosmic sympathy." In this "cosmic sympathy" the primordial depth of a cosmic universality and the concrete individuality of the blossoming tree are grasped together. They are grasped together not by my calculative thinking or by any particular theoretical or practical faculty, but rather in the ravishing harmony of all the dimensions of my ex-sistence. My aesthetic experience of the tree does not translate its object into a system of symbols, but the existential harmony of my aesthetic experience *is* a symbol in the deepest sense of the term. In my "grasping-together" of the concreteness of the individual tree and the primordial depth of the cosmic universality the literal meaning of the tree stands for something other than itself. Or, more correctly, the literal meaning does not stand *for* something else; it rather stands *in* something other than itself, and this "otherness" is its own beyond. In its most fundamental meaning a symbol is a "meeting of two worlds," and it is only in a secondary and derivative sense that we can speak of a symbol as a "referential sign."[132] The aesthetic symbol *as* aesthetic does not refer to man's experiences of non-aesthetic objects and events; it is the merging of the world of the usual and the world of the un-usual into one. The so called "absolute" music and "nonobjective" painting are not less beautiful, or for that matter less symbolic, because they do not refer to anything at all! This is in agreement with Susanne Langer's illuminating statement: "The artistic symbol, *qua* artistic, negotiates insight, not reference; it does not rest upon convention, but motivates and dictates convention. It is deeper than any semantic of accepted signs and their referents, more essential than any schema that may be heuristically read."[133] The twofold intentionality of the aesthetic phenomenon "throws together" (*sun*—together; *balloo*—to throw) the clarity of its literal meaning and the mysteriousness of its cosmic meaning. As contrasted with scientific symbolism which opens up my everyday world into an "outward" beyond, the aesthetic symbolism transcends this world rather into an "inward" beyond. The phenomenon of beauty transcends both the workaday world and the world of science, and opens up before my wondering glance the un-usual, fascinating and awe-inspiring depth of the world of aesthetic symbolism.

Philosophy and Beauty

The philosopher also wonders, and is carried beyond the matter-of-factness of his everyday existence. As contrasted with my philosophical attitude, however, in my aesthetic attitude towards the blossoming tree I will never ask myself an explicit question about the fundamental "why" of the tree. In both my aesthetic attitude and my philosophical attitude I remain concerned with wonder. But whereas in philosophy my *explicit* questioning of wonder constitutes my existential thinking, in my aesthetic attitude I allow wonder to remain *implicit* in my beautiful object. In the aesthetic attitude I perceive beauty in its own light, in philosophy in the light of the *logos*.

THE AESTHETIC PHENOMENON AS ART AND AS NATURE

By dialectically comparing the aesthetic attitude with some basic non-aesthetic attitudes we have brought to light some structural characteristics of the aesthetic phenomenon. Our example was taken from the beauty of *nature*. We can ask ourselves if the phenomenological analysis of the beauty of *art* will fundamentally alter the picture. When we compare our particular exemplar with various other experiences of both the beauty of nature and the beauty of art, our phenomenological analysis will reveal fundamentally the same structural characteristics. The deeper "why" of this fact will be discussed in the next chapter.

Whether I am listening to a beautiful symphony, or a grand vista captivates my eye, whether I am watching the sun sink away blood-red into the wide ocean, or find myself standing before a great cathedral, or breathlessly absorbed in a fascinating novel, my phenomenological analysis always reveals the same unitary phenomenon with the same structural characteristics. I always find that the matter-of-factness of everyday perception loses its obviousness and that a mysterious transparency takes its place. The beautiful object and my intimate self are grasped together in a blissful unity. Space becomes something ethereal and time turns into a reposeful now in which everything is simultaneous. I perceive my beautiful object in its concrete uniqueness as an inexhaustible and translucent fullness of existence to be enjoyed for its own sake. All the dimensions of my ex-sistence are involved in a ravishing harmony when I grasp together the symbolic unity of the individuality of my concrete object and the primordial depth of a cosmic universality. A delightful and awe-inspiring ecstasy makes me transcend the boundaries of my everyday perception, and a new world of wonder remains gravitated around the individual concreteness of my beautiful object.

THE DANGER OF NAIVE INTUITIONISM

Now, it is evident that this *differentiated* awareness of the structural characteristics of beauty was not yet given in our immediately lived experience of this phenomenon. It is also evident that this differentiated awareness is not the result of a simple and fortuitous "seeing" or of an uncritical intuitionism, but rather of a concentrated and laborious effort on our part. Phenomenological description arrives at its "intuiting of essences" by means of a careful and accurate comparative description of the phenomena under consideration. Phenomenological description, therefore, is the very opposite of naive seeing or uncritical intuitionism.[134] Such a naive intuitionism, in fact, constitutes an acute danger for phenomenology. For, not only does it cover up the phenomena under consideration, but it also conceals the very nature of phenomenology itself. This is precisely why such an uncritical intuitionism itself is one of the unexamined presuppositions that phenomenological reduction attempts to clear out.

Precisely because the essential characteristics of the phenomena are usually concealed, we are in need of a phenomenological description which is not an easy intuitionism, but rather the arduous road of an *hermeneutic* phenomenology. Hermeneutics (*hermeneuoo*—to interpret) is the un-covering interpretation of meanings and structures that are not immediately given, but lie concealed behind the familiar manifestations of things. Hermeneutics as thus understood is not only characteristic of the pre-philosophical stage of phenomenological description, but as an integral constituent of philosophical phenomenology it remains at the service of existential thinking. We will revert to this in the next chapter.

In the meantime, we should be careful not to make a premature transition from the pre-philosophical phenomenological description to the phenomenological aspect of philosophical thinking. An inadequate or superficial description of the phenomena under consideration will prevent us from seeing the possible participation of the phenomena in the dialogue of the *logos*. We would merely be *applying* some monolithic system to an inadequately perceived phenomenon. And this, of course, would be highly unphilosophical. We therefore have to continue our phenomenological description until we have reached a point where our insight into the phenomenon in question is open, and deep and differentiated enough as to permit its spontaneous participation in the dialectics of existential thinking.

Up to now we have described the aesthetic phenomenon from the viewpoint of the *subject pole* or the intending *act (noesis)* of the beholder. We can continue our phenomenological description by dialectically changing our standpoint. We may, for instance, describe the *same* aesthetic phenomenon from the viewpoint of the *object pole* or the intended *content (noema)*. This leads us to a comparative description of the beauty of *nature* and the beauty of *art*. But works of art differ in kind, and we can attempt a comparison between the so called "fine arts," such as poetry, music, sculpture, architecture and painting. All works of art, however, refer to the creative artist who brought them into existence in the act of artistic creation. Now this dialectical changing of viewpoints has opened up a threefold possibility of descriptive comparisons. We can describe and compare the phenomenon of beauty from the viewpoint of the beholder, from the viewpoint of the work of art and from the viewpoint of the creative activity of the artist.

Rather than ending our phenomenological description here, we should continue by making a descriptive comparison between beauty and ugliness, and between beauty and its related categories such as the sublime, the tragic and the comic. Moreover, these comparative descriptions give us a gradual opportunity to purge the aesthetic phenomenon of pseudo-aesthetic invasions by dilettantism, sentimentalism and narcissism. And, finally, also our phenomenological description of the aesthetic phenomenon is a mode of our being-in-the-world-with-others. Also here we are intersubjective, and do not have to start our comparative analysis from zero. We should enter into a dialogue with others that have described the phenomenon of beauty from various viewpoints, and compare notes with philosophers, historians, art critics, psychologists and anthropologists among others.

AESTHETIC SYMBOLISM

From the foregoing it follows that the phenomenological description of the aesthetic phenomenon is an immense and utterly complex task. It would be beyond the scope of this book to undertake this task which is the proper domain of philosophical aesthetics. Here we merely want to restrict ourselves to a few basic observations concerning one single example which is fundamental, and, therefore, expected to shed light on the very ground of existential thinking. For our example we have chosen a brief descriptive comparison of *aesthetic symbolism* as it reveals or conceals itself in the just mentioned viewpoints. We have already seen how from the viewpoint of the beholder the aesthetic phenomenon *is* a symbol in the etymological sense of a "throwing together" of two worlds: the world of the usual and the primordial world of the un-usual. Or, more accurately, aesthetic symbolism is not a comparison between two meanings that were first given separately, or a "throwing together" of two worlds that first existed in their own right and independently of one another. On the contrary, aesthetic symbolism arises *within* the usual world as "its own beyond," and its symbolic meaning is constituted in and through its literal meaning. Aesthetic symbolism does not reveal itself as a translation of the beautiful object, but rather as its translucency. The aesthetic symbol, *qua* aesthetic, negotiates insight, not reference. All this we have learned from our description of the aesthetic phenomenon from the viewpoint of the beholder.

APPARENT CONTRASTS BETWEEN BEAUTY OF ART AND BEAUTY OF NATURE

Let us now consider aesthetic symbolism from the viewpoint of the *object pole* or the noetic content of the phenomenon of beauty. When we concentrate on beauty from the viewpoint of its noetic content we are confronted with two distinct forms of beauty, namely, beauty of nature and beauty of art. A hasty and superficial comparative description of these forms of beauty would discover symbolism in beauty of art, but not in beauty of nature. Beauty of art is found to be a "product manufactured by man," which is more often than not referring to something other than itself. Art, therefore, usually contains signs that stand for something else or symbols that re-present reality and have real meaning. Beauty of nature, on the other hand, is not man-made, manifests itself in a "natural thing" and is self-contained. Beauty of nature, therefore, does not symbolize anything, does not refer to anything else, is non-representational, and its beauty does not add any real or verifiable meaning to the natural object. In short, beauty of nature is the property of a natural object, whereas beauty of art is the property of a man-made object.

HUMAN INVOLVEMENT IN BEAUTY OF NATURE

Nevertheless, in the light of our previous descriptive analysis of beauty from the viewpoint of the beholder this comparison between beauty of art and beauty of nature strikes us as superficial. We are suspicious of the radical dichotomy between beauty of art and beauty of nature, and of the complete elimination of symbolism from the beauty of nature. Was our comparative description really accurate and unprejudiced? Haven't we found the same structural characteristics in both beauty of art and beauty of nature? Haven't we found aesthetic symbolism in both a beautiful sunset and in the beauty of a great painting? If this phenomenological description was correct, then, indeed our present comparison between both forms of beauty must have gone astray. Was our phenomenological seeing impaired by some unexamined prejudice?

A more careful and unbiased phenomenological description shows that the conception of beauty of nature as a "property of a natural object" can only be maintained on the basis of the unexamined absolutism of objectifying thinking. We need not repeat here our refutations of this absolutism given earlier in this book. But we have to free ourselves from our objectivistic prejudice which causes us to miss the original givenness of beauty of art and of beauty of nature. Once we have cleared out this objectivistic pseudo-philosophy we are able to give a more accurate and unprejudiced comparative description of these forms of beauty.

Phenomenologically beauty of *nature* does *not* reveal itself as the mere property of a natural object, but as an intimate unity between that object and the whole of our *human* ex-sistence. In beauty of nature the object pole and the intimate self of the beholder merge mysteriously into one. In other words, the radical distinction between beauty of art and beauty of nature violates the original givenness of these phenomena. Beauty of nature is not a kind of beauty that manifests itself independently of man as contrasted with beauty of art that needs man for its coming into being. For also the phenomenon of beauty of nature involves *the whole of our human ex-sistence* for its coming into being. Moreover, it is precisely in this mysterious union between the beautiful object and its beholder that aesthetic symbolism reveals itself. The beautiful object, therefore, does not constitute aesthetic symbolism by its power to re-present something other than itself, but rather by its potentiality to reveal *within* its usual meaning the primordial meaning of a cosmic universality. Beauty of nature contains aesthetic symbolism notwithstanding the fact that it does not contain any symbols in the semantic sense of *signs*.

An Unexamined Prejudice

Here we have a clear example of the way in which unexamined prejudices or uncritically accepted philosophies can prevent us from going to the "things themselves" and from seeing the phenomena in their original givenness. The absolutism of objectifying thinking maintains that whatever cannot be the object of exact observation, of scientific analysis, of mathematical measurement and of experimental verification is unknowable or even unreal.[135] Now, beauty is *either* a verifiable property of the object, and as such it is real and meaningful and accessible to genuine referential statements, *or else,* beauty is a property or characteristic of the subject, and as such it is merely subjective and lacks any genuine cognitive content. No genuine statements can be made about it; nothing can be said about it that is either true or false. This radical dichotomy between subjectivity and objectivity may have its validity within the realm of the natural sciences. But the presumption of *scientism* to arrogate to itself the right to pronounce judgment upon all that is makes the conformity between subject and object the ultimate criterion of all truth. According to scientism genuine statements are referential statements, genuine meanings are referential meanings and genuine symbols are referential symbols. Restricting ourselves to symbolism, a typical definition of such a genuine symbol is given by Ernest Nagel. "By a symbol," he says, "I understand any occurrence (or type of occurrence), usually linguistic in status, which is taken to signify something else by way of tacit or explicit conventions or rules of language."[136] If by "symbol" here is merely meant "semantic symbol," we can agree of course. But Nagel's definition implies the scientistic assumption of the philosophical ultimacy of referential symbolism. It implies that a symbol *as symbol* is semantic, and that it is a true and authentic symbol only if it is referential. It is this pseudo-philosophical dogma of scientism that has to be exposed and cleared out before we are able to accept, or even to *see* symbolism which is non-referential and transcends the subject-object dichotomy. We do not deny the legitimacy of referential symbols within the realm of objectifying thinking, but we reject the claim of the absolute priority of referential symbols over fundamental symbols. It is the referential symbol and not the authentic symbol which is a derivative. An authentic symbol is not a natural or conventional *sign* that stands for something else. An authentic symbol supposes a relation of meaning to meaning, and not only of meaning to thing.[137] And this is why it takes a non-linguistic science to elucidate the authentic symbol.[138] An authentic symbol as authentic is fundamental and non-referential. It constitutes a unity not between a meaning and a thing, but between a concrete meaning of the usual world and the cosmic meaning of the primordial world of wonder.

Now, it was precisely the pseudo-philosophical prejudice of scientism that prevented us from discovering authentic symbolism in beauty of nature. Only after having cleared away this prejudice are we able to see that beauty of nature is symbolic in the fundamental sense of the term. And, on the other hand, we discover that beauty of art is symbolic not because of its possible referential characteristics or its semantic symbols either, but for the same reason why beauty of nature is symbolic, namely, because it is the self-contained and non-referential encounter of the usual world and the primordial world of wonder. "The aesthetic object," says Mikel Dufrenne, "is not a sign that refers to something other than itself."[139] Or, as Susanne Langer puts it: "A work of art does not point us to a meaning beyond its own presence."[140] Consequently, also a work of art is symbolic in the fundamental sense, no matter whether it contains symbols in the semantic sense or not. And this is why Langer rightly states: "Representational works, if they are good art, are so for the same reason as non-representational ones."[141] The distinction between beauty of nature and beauty of art, therefore, cannot be pressed so far as to become a complete separation. The tentative separation we first arrived at did not result from true phenomenological description, but from the pseudo-philosophical prejudice of scientism. In addition, the very discovery of authentic symbolism in both beauty of nature and beauty of art gives the lie to the conception of beauty as a mere property of a natural and a man-made object respectively. For the primordial world of wonder is a constituent element for the coming-into-being and the permanence of both forms of beauty. And, finally, the radical opposition between the beauty of natural objects and of man-made objects results from an objectivistic conception of the terms *nature* and *man-made,* and is not warranted by the original givenness of the phenomena. Nature is not merely that which exists independent of man. Both beauty of nature and beauty of art involve the entire *nature* of human ex-sistence, and in this deeper sense beauty of nature is also man-made, and beauty of art also presupposes nature. We will revert to this in Chapter IX.

Fundamental and Semantic Symbolism

Aesthetic symbolism, then, is fundamental or *authentic* symbolism since it retains the cosmic dimension of the primordial depth of wonder. Authentic symbolism, therefore, is experiential, involves the all-encompassing experience of wonder and remains inaccessible to our objectifying and abstractive ways of thinking. The preoccupation of semantics, symbolic logic and analytical philosophy with our abstractive ways of thinking has led them to disregard, or even to miss entirely the phenomenon of authentic symbolism. For these non-experiential modes of thinking, a symbol is identified with a *sign* that stands for or replaces something else, or that re-presents an absent reality. But our phenomenological description has revealed that just as logic is a derivative of the *logos,* so also is a referential symbol a derivative of fundamental symbolism, and not the other way around. Susanne Langer bases her distinction between "art symbols" (our "fundamental symbols") and "symbols in art" (our "semantic symbols") for the most part on genuine phenomenological description. But when it comes to a final interpretation, she cannot overcome the scientistic limitations of semantic thinking.[142] The fact that she is convinced that the office of art symbols is to

"present" experience for contemplation rather than to re-present anything at all, and that a more inclusive definition of "symbol" should be
adopted than the one accepted in current semantics, does not preclude
her from making the following statement: "As a work of art is an
expressive form *somewhat like a symbol,* and has import which is
something like meaning, so it makes a logical abstraction, but not in the
familiar way of genuine symbols—perhaps, indeed, a pseudo-abstrac-
tion. The best way to understand all these pseudo-semantics [*sic!*] is to
consider what a work of art is and does, and then compare it with
language . . . ."[143] Unfortunately, this philosophical, or should we
rather say pseudo-philosophical statement vitiates her many fine phenomenological observations. She probes into the very depth of aesthetic
symbolism, but her semantic background prevents her from accepting
its fundamental relevancy. The conception of aesthetic symbolism as
pseudo-semantics is based on the presumption of objectifying thinking
to arrogate to itself the privilege of philosophical ultimacy. And in this
we recognize scientism, the pseudo-philosophical persuasion today.

IMPLICATIONS OF AUTHENTIC SYMBOLISM

But if we accept and understand the fundamental difference between
semantic and authentic symbolism, then it is possible and interesting to
shed light on *some essential implications of authentic symbolism.* And
this is all the more important to the extent that authentic symbolism
will appear to be a lasting constituent in existential thinking.

Presentation and Re-presentation

In the first place, authentic symbolism is not the re-presentation of an
absent thing, but the "presentation" of original meaning. The literal
meaning does not "point to" an independently given cosmic meaning;
the cosmic meaning is given *in* the literal meaning, and is given in no
other way. Authentic symbolism is not a comparison between a literal
and a figurative meaning given separately. For, as Langer puts it: "It is
a single organic composition, which means that its elements are not
independent constituents, expressive in their own right."[144] This does
not mean that there is no inner tension or polarity between the literal
and figurative meanings, but that in the authentic symbols these meanings merge into a single "harmony of contrasts." Authentic symbolism
does not refer to an already established meaning, but it truly "originates" its very own meaning; it is the matrix of fundamental meaning
and the birthplace of authentic language.

Experiential and Abstractive Symbolism

Secondly, in authentic symbolism the ordinary world and the cosmic universality of primordial wonder merge into one. From this it follows that we cannot objectify an authentic symbol. For instance, it is impossible to understand the aesthetic symbolism of a genuine poem from without or from the standpoint of natural science. Our only possible way of access is the experiential involvement of the whole of our existence. A scientific term is exact and univocal, and has a well-defined meaning, even apart from a particular scientific context. A poetic word, however, is not even poetic apart from the poem. Apart from the poem it is a semantic symbol, referential and abstract. It is the authentic symbolism of the poem itself which gives the word its poetic meaning. This is why poetry is so notoriously untranslatable.

Impossibility of Formalization

Thirdly, since an authentic symbol "does not point us to a meaning beyond its own presence," it is impossible, as Karl Jaspers rightly remarks, "to separate the authentic symbol from that which it symbolizes."[145] In other words, it is impossible to formalize authentic symbolism, and to study or understand the fundamental symbol apart from the immediacy of its concrete content.

Confusion between Sign and Symbol

Fourthly, whereas semantic symbols are abstract, authentic symbols are concrete. A semantic symbol is a referential sign, and does not itself possess the reality of that which it signifies. An authentic symbol, on the other hand, makes a reality of the usual world transparent by opening it up into the primordial world of wonder. An authentic symbol, therefore, is *more* real than the reality it transfigures. This important implication may be difficult for us to see. Our modern emphasis on objectifying thinking and our collective fixation in scientism leads to a spontaneous identification of "symbolic" with "abstract." "For many people," says Paul Tillich, "the very term 'symbolic' carries the connotation of non-real. This is partially the result of confusion between sign and symbol and partially due to the identification of reality with empirical reality, with the entire realm of objective things and events."[146]

Profane and Sacred Symbolism

Fifthly, an authentic symbol is the emergence of primordial wonder in the world of our ordinary existence. It is the opening-up of things usual into the mysterious translucency of Being. Rudolf Otto in his classical study *The Idea of the Holy* calls the moments of "awefulness" and "fascination" in the mystery of Being the "numinous" which is our experience of the holy.[147] Paul Tillich in his important comment on this study shows how Otto's phenomenological description of the holy implies several points. "The holy is the *quality* of that which concerns man ultimately."[148] This ultimate concern of man is the fascinating and awe-inspiring mystery which transcends the subject-object dichotomy and which is ultimate "in the double sense of that which is the abyss and that which is the ground of man's being."[149] Now, this accurately describes the *primordial totality*[150] of the mystery of Being which is non-referential and deserves to be respected for its own sake. The holy, therefore, is the progressive emergence of the primordial twilight of the mystery of Being. In authentic symbolism the primordial luminosity and the primordial obscurity of this twilight are orchestrated into a translucid harmony. Authentic "sym-bolism" is "con-secrated" symbolism. Authentic symbols are "sacred" symbols by virtue of their manifestation of the holy. As contrasted with authentic symbols, semantic symbols are "profane" symbols. The terms "sacred" and "profane" here should not be misunderstood. "Sacred" here does not mean "supernatural," nor does it imply "unworldly" as we will discuss shortly. Profane symbols, on the other hand, are not unholy, irreverent or blasphemous. Their meaning is not pejorative, they do not suggest a contempt for sacred things. "Pro-fane" symbols are symbols that are non-holy, that simply do not belong to what is sacred; they are as the term suggests "outside the realm of the holy" (*pro—fanum,* lit. before, i.e. outside the temple). Profane symbols are functional and referential, and not concerned with the mystery of Being. It is in this light that we should understand the "profane" knowledge and the "sacred" knowledge of respectively the first and the second reflection in the thinking of Gabriel Marcel. Logical thinking uses profane symbols, whereas existential thinking is based on sacred symbolism.

Neither Subjectivism nor Transcendentalism

And, finally, our brief descriptive analysis of authentic symbolism has clearly shown that sacred symbolism does not occur apart from the profane world, and that authentic symbols are neither "abstract" nor "unworldly." Considering our whole discussion about primordial wonder in retrospect we realize that this inner polarity of the world of everyday existence and the primordial world of wonder has been a tacit assumption all along. To be sure the primordial experience of wonder itself is an undifferentiated phenomenon, and a distinction between these worlds manifests itself only upon re-flection. But we have never presented primordial wonder as a separate and acosmic entity hovering over our workaday world.[151] On the contrary, our whole discussion has presupposed their mutual implication. We found wonder to be an *all-*encompassing experience, which may be awakened at the sight of a child's face or while watching a sunset, in moments of boredom or despair, or in the midst of our daily occupations. Re-flecting on wonder we discovered that wonder differentiates into a *unitary* structure in which we-find-ourselves-being-together-with-others-in-the-world. In our discussion of philosophy as a method primordial wonder revealed itself as the "lived horizon" of existential thinking. And describing the activity of the *logos* we found that it is primordial wonder which is the lasting source of both the unity and the openness of philosophical systematization. All this flatly contradicts the conception of wonder as a disembodied being, as a world-less entity hovering over the world of man or as a reality placed beyond this world. But, now, a more accurate understanding of the situation is possible in the light of authentic symbolism. In the primordial experience of wonder and the subsequent act of philosophizing man, as Josef Pieper puts it, "transcends his environment and steps forth into 'the world'."[152] But he immediately subjoins the following warning: "That must not, of course, be understood to mean that there are, as it were, two distinct, separate spheres, and as though man could take leave of one and enter the other."[153] The unusual world of wonder (*the* world) manifests itself *in* the usual world (environment) by reason of its authentic sym-bolism. In other words, *the* world (primordial wonder, Being) and *this* world (environment) are not two worlds given separately, but the environment reveals primordial wonder by transcending itself. This transcendence, however, is not a transcendence in the Kantian sense of passing beyond all limits of possible experience. It is not a transcending of experience in the sense of going outside experience at all. "For beyond all experience," says Gabriel Marcel, "there is nothing, . . . nothing that can be thought, and nothing that can be felt."[154] The transcendence we are speaking of here (L. *trans*—across; *scandere*—to climb; to go beyond) is not a going "outside" experience, but rather an experience of that which transcends, or an experience that transcends. The experience of the surrounding world (environment) transcends itself by opening up into the world of wonder as "its own beyond." The surrounding world widens and deepens its own horizon by meeting the "otherness" of primordial wonder as the translucency of its very own "inwardness."

And primordial wonder does not withdraw from the surrounding world, but it withdraws from the usual meaning attached to it by revealing it in a more fundamental and un-usual perspective. To quote Pieper again, "It is in the things we come across in the experience of everyday life that the unusual emerges, and we no longer take them for granted—and that situation corresponds with the inner experience which has always been regarded as the beginning of philosophy: the act of 'marvelling'."[155] Now, to understand the authentic sym-bolism of primordial wonder is to reject any form of *Seinsmystik* or transcendental-ism. But it also entails a rejection of the "univocal" understanding of the "primary datum" of philosophy, namely the fact that I find-myself-together-with-others-in-the-world. To the extent in which this primary datum has become a commonplace in existential thinking it has ceased to be authentic sym-bolism. It has lost its *essential ambiguity* and its thought-provoking enigma. "Being-in-the-world" is either supposed to mean the everyday world of the human subject, or else it seems to stand for the primordial world of Being. There seems to be no way out of the dilemma between subjectivism and transcendentalism. The way out, however, is a more accurate phenomenological description which shows that our authentic "being-in-the-world" is an authentic sym-bol in which the world of Being is both revealed and concealed *within* the world of our everyday existence. A more accurate description of our primary datum would read as follows: I find-myself-Being (*the* World)-together-with-others-in-*this*-world. The hyphenation indicates that we are dealing with a *unitary* structure, that the world of Being does not reveal itself apart from the world of everyday existence. Although a further re-flection differentiates these worlds, it never separates them. They will always remain within a relationship which is so intimate that the one world cannot truly "be" without the other. Martin Heidegger calls this essential ambivalence of existential thinking "the ontological difference."[156]

The Artwork, The Artist and the Beholder

We now want to continue our descriptive comparison of beauty as aesthetic symbolism. Our brief analysis of authentic symbolism will greatly assist us in our task. When we compare aesthetic symbolism from the respective viewpoints of the beholder, the work of art and the creative artist, the difference seems remarkable. The beholder is a sym-bol perceiver, the work of art a symbol revealer and the creative artist a symbol producer. But in the light of the fact that aesthetic symbolism is authentic symbolism the difference appears not to be fundamental at all. For *each* of these viewpoints "reveals" authentic symbolism. The artist reveals authentic symbolism, since his creation is not the mere manufacture of a product but a technique which is inspired by the cosmic dimension of primordial wonder. The artist expresses himself beyond himself. The beholder reveals authentic symbolism since his perception is not mere ocular perception, but a perception filled with astonishment. He perceives his beautiful object within his ec-static participation in the primordial world of wonder. And the work of art reveals authentic symbolism, not as the mere property of an object, but by "con-taining" authentic "sym-bolism." The work of art con-tains (*cum*—together, *tenere*—to hold) beauty by "holding together" the usual world of our surroundings and the un-usual world of wonder in the aesthetic sym-bol (*syn*—together; *ballein*—to throw).

The Problem of Form and Content

We may notice, in passing, how the fact that art "con-tains" authentic sym-bolism throws a fundamental light on the problem of the "content" of art and its relation to the form. When we ask ourselves what is all-important in art: the *what* or the *how,* the *content* or the *form,* then our knowledge that art contains authentic symbolism gives the decisive answer. In authentic symbolism, as we have seen already, it is impossible in principle to separate the form from the content. Neither of the two can be all-important; both play an essential role. And we can answer the "formalist" that in authentic symbolism the form is an important part of the content. In addition, if the fundamental "content" of art is authentic "sym-bolism," then it is *ipso facto* wrong to try to determine the content of a given work of art on the basis of its referential symbols, or even on the basis of the "knowledge" it affords. For "the whole of our ex-sistence" is involved in authentic symbolism. In other words, the openness of our will and love, our primordial enthusiasm and its embodiment, the primordial experience of wonder, the mystery of Being and fundamental questions all belong to the very "content" of artworks. All are cognitive too, but not in the restricted sense of representational and experimentally verifiable knowledge. "Representational works," we quoted Langer as saying, "if they are good art, are so for the same reason as non-representational ones." Fundamentally speaking, therefore, it matters little whether the "con-tent" of an artwork is given in the verbal symbolism of poetry, the tonal symbolism of music or the plastic symbolism of painting. A further detailed study of the form-content controversy in the light of authentic symbolism would be interesting and important, but is beyond the scope of this book.

The work of art, then, "con-tains" or "holds together" the usual and un-usual worlds of the aesthetic "sym-bol" in their appropriate "di-stance" ("standing apart"). This distance, which is called *aesthetic distance,* is neither a mere spatial, nor a mere temporal distance in the usual sense of the terms, but rather the world of the un-usual insofar as it puts things usual into the aesthetic perspective. This aesthetic distance was first called "psychical distance" and profoundly described by the British psychologist Edward Bullough.[157] We will have ample opportunity to further explore the nature and importance of aesthetic distance, which evidently is the *inner duality* of authentic sym-bolism. But let us first conclude our descriptive comparison of aesthetic symbolism by briefly indicating how it reveals or conceals itself in ugliness and in the pseudo-aesthetic attitudes.

AESTHETIC, PSEUDO-AESTHETIC AND NON-AESTHETIC ATTITUDES
TOWARDS THE PHENOMENON OF BEAUTY

In ugliness the sym-bolic world of beauty is revealed, but some road-blocks are encountered in our aesthetic distance. Sentimentality enjoys a pseudo-aesthetic narcissism in the proximity of beauty. In sentimentality we are "underdistanced" and the sym-bolic world of beauty has shrunken to the vanishing point. And pure representationalism makes us concentrate on the accurate and photographic re-rendering of the "usual" to such a degree that we lose contact with the "un-usual" altogether. We are overdistanced, and the authentic symbolism of beauty does no longer exist. Representational symbolism has taken its place. And finally, within the aesthetic di-stance of the tragic we find that the greatness of man stands in "sym-bolic con-flict" with the transcendent and cosmic greatness of superior powers. Here again we are confronted with authentic symbolism. This is also true for the comic. Within the aesthetic di-stance of the comic the cosmic greatness of man is revealed as "standing in sym-bolic con-flict" with the narrow fixity of his own "typical" smallness.

It goes without saying that the phenomenon of beauty will never manifest itself in its original givenness as long as our phenomenological description is not *at the same time* an attempt to purge out unexamined assumptions resulting from fixations in our non-aesthetic attitudes. For instance, a fixation of the "usual" world of our everyday experience results in the dogmatic belief in the ultimate authority of our "ordinary common sense." Some "realists," for instance, are unable to enjoy a fiction story, because "it never really happened." They cannot appreciate that the authentic symbolism of beautiful fiction is *more real* than the reality of their everyday existence. Others cannot understand why people get so excited about a play, since the actors "are only pretending." Or they evaluate paintings merely on the basis of the skillful accuracy with which reality is re-presented. They are offended by paintings that "do not look real." Their non-aesthetic prejudice prevents them from ever seeing the original givenness and the authentic symbolism of the phenomenon of beauty.

The same could be shown for fixations in other non-aesthetic attitudes. If we do not clear out unexamined prejudices and discard ingrained habits our road to original beauty will be blocked. For the merely practical bent of mind it is extremely difficult to assume the aesthetic attitude. For those that are always asking the question: "What is it good for?" beauty is either a waste of time, or else something to "kill" time. Those who have become fixated in a merely analystic frame of mind dichotomize the world into a host of antithetic opposites. Beauty for them is either objective or a matter of taste, it is either realistic or something fictitious, it is mere sensuality or an experience of the spirit. Dichotomies such as these are utterly unacceptable in the light of the holistic nature of aesthetic symbolism. Bullough, therefore, is right in stating that "personal and impersonal, subjective and objective, idealistic and realistic, sensual and spiritual are terms devised for purposes other than esthetic speculation, and become loose and ambiguous as soon as applied outside the sphere of their special meanings."[158] It is important to keep out meanings and distinctions introduced in connection with standpoints other than the aesthetic. And it is irrelevant to the phenomenological approach whether or not the non-aesthetic standpoints can get along with the perception of the aesthetic. Scientific categories, for instance, are notoriously irreconcilable with the aesthetic categories. But if we *a priori* insist on their "getting along" we overlook the pluralistic nature of our universe and the fundamental difference between referential and authentic symbols, and we are bound to miss the original phenomenon of beauty altogether.

AESTHETIC DISTANCE AND PHENOMENOLOGICAL REDUCTION

Our comparative description of aesthetic symbolism should have made it clear by now that the first and non-philosophical phase of phenomenological reduction has *two aspects,* a negative or "cathartic" aspect, and a positive or "revelatory" aspect. These two aspects of phenomenological reduction are co-original insofar as we do not know what to free our experience *from* unless at the same time we know what to free our experience *for.* The cathartic and the revelatory elements of phenomenological reduction are dialectically related. Now, it is most important to note how Bullough aptly ascribes these two functions to the *aesthetic distance* itself! For here we are about to make the main discovery of this chapter, the discovery that the *original perception* of the "natural world" as it *is,* is given *in the aesthetic distance.* The aesthetic distance, according to Bullough, has "a negative, inhibitory aspect" insofar as it cuts out our non-aesthetic attitude, and "a positive side" insofar as it is "the elaboration of the experience on the new basis created by the inhibitory action of Distance."[159] In short, it is the horizon of the un-usual, of the "wonder-ful" that puts things usual, or things as they are uncritically accepted into the truly aesthetic perspective. If, furthermore, we realize, that the word "aesthetic" is derived from the Greek *aisthanesthai* which means "to perceive," and that its original pre-Socratic and its present existential meaning is not dichotomized into sense perception and intellectual perception, but indicates a perception by the whole of man's ex-sistence, then the following statement by Maurice Merleau-Ponty becomes highly meaningful. In the "Preface" to his *Phenomenology of Perception* he writes: "The best formulation of the [phenomenological] reduction is probably that given by Eugen Fink, Husserl's assistant, when he spoke of 'wonder' in the face of the world."[160] In other words, *the inspiration of wonder is a constituent of the technique of reduction.*

NEITHER QUIETISM NOR ACTIVISM

Now, these scraps of phenomenological description should suffice to answer the question we posed in connection with our discussion of the *logos* as philosophical system. Does the *logos* in a single stroke eliminate all our prejudices and mental constructs? Is existential thinking after all some sort of philosophical quietism? The answer is that the *logos* is always ready for us, but that we are not always ready for the *logos.* We have to prepare ourselves for the *logos* by uncovering the phenomena in their original givenness and by clearing out unexamined assumptions and mental constructs. Our insights into the phenomena have to be sufficiently deep and purified and differentiated to make a spontaneous encounter with the *logos* possible. But all this means that we have to engage in the laborious techniques of phenomenological reduction which require a lifetime of hard work on our part. There is no room for philosophical quietism in existential thinking. On the contrary, phenomenological reduction means, at least partially, great effort on our part, painstaking concentration, careful descriptive comparisons, a great amount of reading and extensive research.

We say, "at least partially," for as we have seen already, phenomenological reduction should not be conceived as a "mere technique." This would amount to a sort of philosophical *activism*. But activism is precisely one of our cultural prejudices that the phenomenological reduction tries to put out of gear. Even in its pre-philosophical stage phenomenological description is not a "mere technique" or a mechanical method that automatically leads up to the desired result. We need a "pre-view" of that which we are freeing our perception *for* in order to know what we have to free it *from*. The cathartic and the revelatory aspects of the phenomenological reduction are dialectically related. We have to be assured to work in the right "perspective," before we can eliminate prejudices and reveal the phenomena in their original givenness. This right perspective is, as we have seen, the overwhelming and inspirational experience of primordial wonder. The *inspiration* of wonder is a constituent of the *technique* of reduction. In the experiential openness of wonder "everything" is allowed to appear, and "everything" is kept in suspense. Wonder creates the optimum di-stance of our "original perception" which is the aesthetic perception in the fundamental sense of experiential openness. Nothing is kept out of sight and nothing is taken for granted. Wonder keeps our "return to the things themselves" at the proper di-stance from both the idealist return to pure consciousness and the empiricist return to mere sense data. Wonder keeps our perception of the world at the proper di-stance from a merely practical involvement in things and the indifferent onlooking of the mere spectator. Wonder keeps our phenomenological description at a proper di-stance from both the rationalist insensitivity to phenomenological descriptions and the hypersensitive descriptions of those who get lost in irrelevant details. Wonder keeps us at the proper di-stance from both the deterministic attachment to our surrounding world and the dogmatic belief in absolute creativity and acosmic freedom. Wonder puts things usual in the primordial perspective of aesthetic perception.

Aesthetic Perception as "Original Perception"

Aesthetic perception, therefore, is our *original perception* which reveals the "natural world" as it truly *is,* i.e. as it essentiates in the primordial presence of wonder or the primordial world of Be-ing. Original perception is always experiential, is always imbued with wonder, and is always sym-bolic in the fundamental sense of the word. Original perception cannot be reduced to mere sense-perception or to the mere apprehension of usual sense-objects, such as stones, tables or trees. For in original perception the world of the usual and the world of the un-

usual are "thrown together" in their "aesthetic di-stance." Original perception far transcends our usual preoccupation with the unified apprehension of immediate sense-objects. Our sense-perception is merely a
derivative form of perception, and not, as empiricism wants us to believe, our human perception *par excellence.* Also those who try to
explain perception exclusively in terms of the consciousness of the human subject are prejudiced. For phenomenological reduction which is
nothing but original perception *in statu nascendi,* is always wonder in
the face of the *world* and never in the face of either the subject or the
object alone.

But, now, aren't we exaggerating the significance of the aesthetic
perception at the expense of ordinary sense-perception and of other
possible ways in which human beings perceive? In fact, aren't we plung-
ing headlong into the whirlpool of subjectivism? The answer, of course,
is that by emphasizing the originality of aesthetic perception we do not
at all imply the denial of the existence or importance of other possible
forms of human perception. All we say is that only experiential perception, perception which is rooted in primordial wonder can be original
and fundamental. All other forms of perception are derivative.[161] Moreover, our foregoing elucidations of the aesthetic phenomenon have
made it abundantly clear that aesthetic perception, since it transcends
the subject-object dichotomy, cannot possibly be subjective in the
pejorative sense of subjectivistic. Original perception implies the all-
encompassing experience of Being which "overwhelms" us. Original
perception comes neither from "without" nor from "within," but it
arises out of our wonder in the face of the world, and is truly originative. Original perception, therefore, is none of the following: an act of
any particular human faculty, an elementary sensation or an "atom
feeling," ordinary sense-perception, ob-servation of scientific facts, an
act of the intellect, a clear and distinct idea, an abstract principle, the
reception of a message by something like a physical apparatus.

ORIGINAL PERCEPTION AS THE BIRTH OF THE "NATURAL LIGHT" OF OUR BEING-IN-THE-WORLD

Original perception is the birth of the *lumen naturale,* the natural
light of Being in man. This is why Maurice Merleau-Ponty in his post-
humous work *Le Visible et l'Invisible* suggests terms such as "Insight"
and *"Aha Erlebnis"* in connection with original perception, and states
that this perception is openness "in its own right."[162] In other words,
original perception is not like an optical instrument which receives its
light rays merely "from without" as they are reflected by objects other

than itself. On the contrary, in original perception we witness the birth of a new light in ourselves which is the self-revelation of the mystery of Being. Now, the all-encompassing mystery of Being, as we have seen, reveals itself only in the act in which it is fully received which is the very openness of the whole of our human ex-sistence, and not in an act of any particular human faculty. Original perception is not the sensation as an elementary unit of experience. The conception of original perception as an elementary unit of experience is the mental construct of the early mechanistic and atomistic psychologists, and has long since been refuted by the Gestalt psychologists as being against the facts. Merleau-Ponty in the opening of his *Phenomenology of Perception* calls such alleged elementary units of experience "atoms of feeling," and says that "authors are agreed on it, that this notion corresponds to nothing in our experience, and that the most rudimentary *factual perceptions* that we are acquainted with, in creatures such as the ape or the hen, have a bearing on relationships and not on any absolute terms."[163] In fact, the mechanistic conception of elementary units of sensation is the very counterpart of our existential conception of original perception, just as mechanistic thinking is the very counterpart of existential thinking. The world created by the ob-jectifying attitude of the mechanist is abstract, quantitative, deterministic and atomistic, and the very opposite of the experiential, sym-bolic, dynamic and unitary world of the existential thinker. It is easy to see that our ordinary sense-perception cannot be called original perception for the simple reason that it pertains to our everyday world and does not reach out into the fundamental world of primordial wonder. Those who mistake the observation of scientific facts for our original perception have fallen victims to what we have found to be the dogmatic belief in the absolute priority of abstractive thinking. Earlier in this book we discovered that our human consciousness is not originally and fundamentally a "knowing" one in the sense of intellectual knowledge, but rather a "being-with," or a "lived experience of presence."[164] From this it follows that acts of the intellect, and *a fortiori* clear and distinct ideas and abstract principles are "second-level constructions of the human mind," and should never be mistaken for original perceptions or primary data. And, finally, it is a common but fundamental mistake to understand original perception in terms of the functioning of a physical receiving apparatus. This physicalistic conception of perception in general and of original perception in particular has been effectively refuted among others by Gabriel Marcel. In his book *The Mystery of Being* he demonstrates how the reduction of perception to a physical process implies tacit assumptions that contradict the very data it tries to explain. "What we really are doing," says Marcel, "is to project, in physical terms, the mysterious relationship which the term *datum* implies."[165]

With this sentence Marcel intimates rather than describes the essence of our whole discussion on original perception: we need original perception to grasp the phenomena in their original "givenness." The phenomenological description of original perception both presupposes and results in the original perception of phenomenological description. It is only in the primordial "gift" (datum) of wonder or in the perceived presence of this primordial "datum" that the phenomena "present themselves" in their original "givenness" (phenomenality). It is only within the primordial horizon of the mystery of Being that the original perception of the *mysterious givenness* of philosophical "data" takes place.

PRIMORDIAL WONDER IN RETROSPECT

Our brief discussion of original perception has further differentiated our insight into wonder as the beginning of philosophy. Wonder as the beginning of philosophy is experienced in an original perception which is neither absolute and mechanistic passivity, nor the absolute creativity of acosmic freedom. In this context the merely physical meaning of terms such as "receiving" and "giving" should be completely transcended. To quote Marcel again: "at this level the contrast between activity and passivity—between reception, say, considered as taking, and reception considered as being given something—loses a great deal of its meaning; in the dimension in which we now find ourselves, we must move beyond such categories."[166] Original perception is the fundamental act in which we "receive" the primordial "gift" of wonder. And the creative receptivity of this original perception constitutes the pre-reflective and experiential awareness of the mystery of our Being-in-the-world and its sym-bolic ambiguity. It is precisely by reason of this inner ambiguity that the fundamental symbol of original perception becomes thought-provoking. It is this inner polarity of primordial wonder which invites us to engage in a multi-dimensional re-flection on its mysterious meaning. It is this inner polarity between "being-container" and "being-contained," between immanency and transcendency, between the world of the usual and the world of the un-usual which is the mainspring of all philosophical thinking, and, for that matter, of all human authenticity.

Existential thinking, as we have seen, does not leave its beginning behind, but rather *is* the differentiated self-questioning of its actual beginning. Existential thinking, therefore, *is* a re-flection on the aesthetic perception in the fundamental sense of original perception, and is constantly guided and nourished by this primordial phenomenon. When we started our brief phenomenological description of the aesthetic phenomenon we intimated that our example would be more than a mere illustration since it would prove to be the actual way of access to existential thinking. Although this intimation might have sounded quite enigmatic at first, we are in a position now to understand its true meaning. Our phenomenological description of the aesthetic phenomenon has revealed that this phenomenon is an authentic symbol which opens up the primordial world of wonder in this world. Now, this we have found to be the primordial datum of philosophical thinking which is the lasting source and guiding light of all our philosophical explorations. In other words, the aesthetic phenomenon cannot remain a mere example of phenomenological description, but an adequate description will soon reveal this phenomenon as that which is the beginning of philosophy, and therefore, as a phenomenon which by its very nature is woven into the texture of existential thinking.

EXISTENTIAL THINKING AND AESTHETICS

All this has one obvious implication. Namely, to the extent in which all philosophical thinking is a re-flection on its own beginning: the aesthetic perception in the fundamental sense of the term, philosophy is inherently "aesthetics." Existential thinking does not merely *apply* itself to the aesthetic phenomenon; it cannot even *be* without this primordial perception. It might be objected, however, that whether or not our conclusion is true depends on how we choose to define the term "aesthetics." And this objection would, indeed, be important enough to justify an expatiation on the usage of the term "aesthetics."

Baumgarten on Aesthetics

It is a matter of common knowledge that the term "aesthetics" was coined by Alexander Baumgarten in his *Reflections on Poetry*.[167] As a disciple of the Wolffian philosophy Baumgarten was a thoroughgoing rationalist and a firm believer in the ultimate criterion of "clear and distinct" concepts. But unlike Wolff, Baumgarten did not omit a philosophical treatment of the beautiful on the ground that the concepts concerned with the enjoyment of beauty are not distinct, and correspond to a lower form of apprehension *(vires inferiores)*. Although the logic and the language of beauty are inferior to those of the mathematical sciences, they are neither illogical nor nonsensical. Beauty, according to Baumgarten, is perfection in the order of sense perception. And "aesthetics" is the science which aims at grasping the perfection of sense perception or beauty as such. Baumgarten, to be sure, is not the first philosopher to have reflected on the nature of art and beauty. Ever since Plato's profound meditations on the subject, philosophers have left us a rich legacy of penetrating and original insights into the problems of beauty and art. But Baumgarten's views, although they are neither original nor penetrating, have exercised an especially great influence on the development of modern aesthetics. This of course is not only due to the fact that he coined the term "aesthetics." More important is the fact that he first established aesthetics as an independent branch of philosophical inquiry, and that he firmly established it within the conceptual framework of Cartesian dualism. For throughout the relatively short history of aesthetics the philosophical scene has been dominated by this Cartesian dualism, or the radical dichotomy between spirit and matter, "inner" and "outer" world, subject and object. This accounts for the constant fluctuation of modern theories of beauty between the subjectivistic interpretation of beauty in terms of experience and the objectivistic theories of beauti-less art. For, indeed, if the Greek *aisthesis* which means "perception" is exclusively translated as "sense" perception, and if beauty is identified with some perfection of this sense perception in the broad sense, then art becomes an "ob-ject" for "aesthetic experience." This results in the well-known dualism in modern aesthetics between the theories of our perception of beauty and the theories of the principles of art. This dualism is as unsolvable as the Cartesian dualism on which it rests. Nevertheless, both the subjectivistic and the objectivistic sides of this dualism in aesthetics have one thing in common: they conceal rather than reveal the fundamental phenomenon of beauty, and fail to recognize its philosophical significance as the revelation of Being in the world. We will return to this shortly.

Kantian Aesthetics

Immanuel Kant uses the term "aesthetics" in the first and in the third of his famous *Critiques* in a somewhat different way. At the beginning of his *Critique of Pure Reason* Kant discusses "The Transcendental Aesthetic." Here he deals with the *a priori* forms or conditions of our sense perception, which according to Kant is the only kind of perception and the ultimate material of all thought in man. In this context the term "aesthetic" is used in the etymological sense of "perception." "Transcendental aesthetic" means the analysis of the *a priori* (pure and not experienced) conditions that make it possible for man to organize his unordered sensations into the sense perception of an external object. Kant discovers that space and time are the *a priori* forms of sense perception. Consequently space and time are neither objects themselves or characteristics of objects, nor are they mere illusions. They are the pure or *a priori* forms that make all sense perception possible. We have already seen in our foregoing elucidations of original perception, that sense perception is not the only kind nor the most fundamental kind of perception. Moreover, perception as a "lived experience of presence" precedes phenomenologically any form of "knowing" in the sense of knowing "objects" or having "concepts." The possibility of a fundamental understanding of sense perception depends on our understanding of the Being of perception. An initial investigation has been carried out in the foregoing descriptive analysis of the original perception. Here we found that the Being of perception is to be understood as the perception of Being in the original perception. In original perception sense perception is transcended not by transcending experience, but by the experience of transcending the usual world of sense perceptions into its own beyond, the primordial world of wonder. Sense perception is not fundamentally given until it reveals itself within the original perception, i.e., within our wondering Being-in-the-world. The original perception, therefore, transcends the subject-object dichotomy and refutes the Cartesian dualism as the basic framework within which the essence of perception can be discussed. At first glance Kant may seem to have overcome the Cartesian dualism. On closer examination, however, this appears to be untrue. For instance, in the Preface to the second edition of his *Critique of Pure Reason* Kant writes: "it remains a scandal to philosophy, and to human reason in general, that we should have to accept the existence of things without us . . . . on faith only, unable to meet with any satisfactory proof an opponent, who is pleased to doubt it."[168] The very fact that Kant requires any proof at all for the existence of things in the "external" world demonstrates that he takes the "inner" world of the *human subject* rather than our *"Being-in-the-world"* as his radical point of departure. In his comment on this same Kantian text Martin Heidegger makes the following well-known and well-founded remark: "The 'scandal of philosophy' is not that this proof has yet to be given, but that *such proofs are expected and attempted again and again.*"[169] Even in his *Critique of Judgment* where he applied the transcendental method to the problems of "aesthetics" in the sense of "beauty" Kant remained within the framework of dualistic inspiration. What are the *a priori* conditions which give validity to our aesthetic judgments? In an attempt to answer this question Kant sought to bridge the gap between his first two *Critiques,* between the phenomenal world of understanding and nature and the noumenal world of will and freedom. Now, it is the "aesthetic judgment" as analyzed in the first part of the *Critique of Judgment* which furnishes the connecting link. The "aesthetic judgment" is based on the power of feeling entirely disinterested pleasure or displeasure, as directly related to the representation of an object. Although in Kant's view the ground of this judgment is subjective, incapable of demonstration, and entirely rooted in sensuous and non-conceptual phenomena, it is, nevertheless, not without a certain universal validity and revelatory power. Kant was highly original in the way in which he integrated the "aesthetic judgment" in the philosophy of his *Critiques*. In his actual analysis of beauty, however, he merely followed the lead of the aestheticians of his time.[170]

Modern Views

Thus, traditionally, "aesthetics" has become the study of aesthetic experience rather than of art. And although modern aesthetics has become more differentiated, and has added empirical studies in the psychology and sociology of artistic creation and appreciation, its basic inspiration has remained the same. Many of its antinomies, such as its traditional wavering between subjectivistic and objectivistic interpretations, between theories of art and theories of beauty, between aesthetics as philosophy and aesthetics as science, result from its failure to re-establish contact with its own ontological roots. If, indeed, beauty is essentially "nothing but" some sort of glorified sense perception and its concomitant sensuous satisfaction, then "aesthetics" becomes "the logic of sensuous delight" rather than "the *logos* of original perception." If, indeed, beauty is nothing but a titillation of the senses, then John Locke is right when he states that ". . . it is very seldom seen, that any one discovers Mines of Gold or Silver in Parnassus. 'Tis a pleasant Air, but a barren Soil . . ."[171] If beauty is nothing but a means to please the artistic palate of the connoisseur or aesthete, then it is only to the credit of modern art that it has broken through the pleasure barrier. If beauty is nothing but a narcissistic pastime or a means to bolster up morality or patriotism, then it comes as no surprise that modern theories of art are less devoted to the task of defining beauty, and that artists are more and more inclined to aim at artistic values other than beauty. If beauty is nothing but a subjectivistic phenomenon, then aesthetics as the logic of beauty conceals rather than reveals authentic beauty and its ontological significance; here the "aesthetic" becomes an effective "anaesthetic" producing the ontological anaesthesia of *aestheticism*. If beauty is reduced to nothing but sense perception in the broad sense, then art is reduced to an "ob-ject" for aesthetic experience. Both beauty and art are placed on the level of ob-jectifying thinking and action, and turn into *controllable things*. Art becomes a useful instrument when controlled by governments, political parties, business interests or propaganda. And the feeling of beauty is in danger of being explained away and of becoming something else in disguise, when it is subjected to the exact methods of observation and reductive analyses of the natural sciences. If beauty is nothing but a refined enjoyment, then aesthetics becomes aestheticism which is nothing but a refined hedonism, or a dreamy and narcissistic pseudo-philosophical cult of the absolute primacy of beauty in its sensuous forms. It was this pseudo-philosophical conception of the aesthetic that came under severe attack by the Danish philosopher Søren Kierkegaard. According to Kierkegaard the dialectics of the aesthetic point of view is the dialectics of death.

Lacking the all-encompassing and creative experience of primordial wonder, the aesthete has to satisfy himself with the passing thrill of a momentary pleasure. For him the immediacy of the present moment is all-important. *"Carpe diem"* (lit. seize the day) is his slogan, "enjoy the present moment," for "tomorrow" may never come, or it may come with pain and suffering. The aesthete, therefore, wants to absolutize the present moment. But this also entails his destruction. For he can only absolutize the present moment by eliminating the possibility of tomorrow's sufferings, but this he can only achieve by eliminating tomorrow itself and committing suicide. Moreover, by absolutizing the present moment he reduces it to an "atom of time" in which there is only room for an "atom of feeling" which means, as we have seen, nothing at all. In his passionate attempt to absolutize the passing moments he loses himself in a blind succession of ever vanishing "now-points," he reduces his life to the hope-less sufferings of boredom and despair. The aesthete, therefore, moves away from the existential unity of self-fulfillment into a life of "dis-traction" (Pascal) in which he finds himself to be a "useless passion" (Sartre) making "chaotic, jerky movements, like a galvanized frog" (Kierkegaard). He pines away in melancholy nostalgia, for unable to change the course of time, he can only re-capture his moments of delight as "things of the past." The life of the aesthete has a taste of death. "Time" is his archenemy, and this is why he "spends" his life "killing time." "Then it appears to him," says Kierkegaard, "that time, that the temporal, is his ruin; he demands a more perfect form of existence, and at this point there comes to evidence a fatigue, an apathy, which resembles the languor which is the attendant of pleasure. This apathy may rest so broodingly upon a man that suicide appears to him the only way of escape. . . . He has not chosen himself, like Narcissus he has fallen in love with himself. Such a situation has certainly ended not infrequently in suicide."[172]

Various Meanings of Aesthetics

This elaboration of the term "aesthetics" does not make any claim to being complete, but it suffices to demonstrate that the term is used in at least four different meanings, and to single out the exact meaning we had in mind when we stated that philosophy as a re-flection on original perception is inherently "aesthetics." We like to give each different meaning a different name in order to avoid confusion. Thus we distinguish between "empirical aesthetics," "philosophical aesthetics," "fundamental aesthetics" and "aestheticism."

That authentic philosophy cannot be "aestheticism" is self-evident in the light of the foregoing elucidations. This narcissistic pseudo-philosophy obstructs rather than promotes fundamental thinking. Then, there is "empirical aesthetics" in the modern and broad sense of the term. Empirical aesthetics is a large and diversified science which studies the phenomena of art, of artistic creation and of the appreciation of art and beauty. It employs all methods at its disposal, such as scientific observation, introspection, and, nowadays, phenomenological description. Empirical aesthetics does not expect to arrive at the exactness of the natural sciences, since its essential phenomena are wholly inaccessible to mathematical measurement. Yet, it attempts to achieve a scientific status comparable to that of modern psychology. It collects information from many sources, such as history, sociology, anthropology, psychology, archeology and art criticism. Although modern empirical aesthetics (or should we rather say: "experiential" aesthetics?) usually retains its interest in the traditional philosophy of beauty and art, it is gradually developing into an independent science with many ramifications and specializations. Now, it goes without saying that empirical aesthetics is a *non-philosophical* science insofar as its methods are strictly non-philosophical.

Within the realm of philosophical thinking there are two distinct and meaningful usages of the term "aesthetics." In the first place, our fundamental or philosophical thinking is a re-flection on the primordial experience of wonder or the primordial self-manifestation of Being in the world. Now, our phenomenological description of the "aesthetic phenomenon" has shown that this phenomenon is our original perception of the primordial self-manifestation of Being in the world. Its ontological significance, therefore, is manifest. It is on the "aesthetic phenomenon" in the etymological sense of original "perception" and in the fundamental sense of beauty as the self-manifestation of Being in the world that all authentic philosophy re-flects. It is in the "aesthetic phenomenon" in this fundamental sense of the term that all existential thinking finds its starting point and the lasting source of its philosophical inspiration. It is in this fundamental sense, and *only* in this fundamental sense that the term "fundamental aesthetics" can be applied to all philosophical thinking.[173] For we immediately subjoin the following remarks. The philosopher *as philosopher* needs not to have an ecumenic familiarity with the various arts and with the intricacies of empirical aesthetics. His re-flections on the "aesthetic phenomenon" remain completely oriented towards the fundamental task of answering the primordial question of Being. Fundamental aesthetics, therefore, does *not* attempt to develop a philosophy of art and beauty, but it provides any such attempt with its necessary foundations. In other words, "philosophical aesthetics" which attempts to arrive at an ontological understanding of the specific phenomena of art, artistic creation and appreciation, is a *special* branch of philosophy, it is a regional ontology and not convertible with existential thinking.[174] "Philosophical aesthetics" is a dialogue between "fundamental aesthetics" and "empirical aesthetics." The philosopher who concentrates on philosophical aesthetics must also be conversant with the manifold data and problems of empirical aesthetics. But one does not have to concentrate on philosophical aesthetics in order to be a good philosopher. Without fundamental aesthetics, however, both existential thinking and philosophical aesthetics are unthinkable. This, in our opinion, has sufficiently answered the possible objections of those who might have accused us of "aestheticism."

TOWARDS TRANSCENDENCY

At the beginning of this chapter we have asked ourselves the question: "Is existential thinking merely a question of inspiration?" And we have now found that the answer is in the negative. Our existential thinking goes back into the immediately lived data of our existence, and we have to engage in laborious research, in difficult techniques of phenomenological reduction and in a lifetime of hard work in order to arrive at an original perception of the phenomena. Existential thinking, therefore, cannot be equated with some sort of philosophical quietism. In this pre-philosophical stage of phenomenological reduction we are wholly immanent, we are totally involved with the whole of our existence. But this chapter has also intimated something else. The *inspi-*

ration of wonder is a constituent of the technique of reduction. *Logos*-thinking is focalized by the "overwhelming" and "all-encompassing" inspiration of wonder. The "sym-bolic" meaning of the original perception is thought-provoking and invites us to transcend this world into the comprehensive universality of Being. In other words, already the immanency of existential thinking points towards its transcendency, its ontic structure is ontological. The next question, which we shall consider in the following chapter is: Is existential thinking some sort of *activism?* The answer to this question will be sought in a discussion of the transcendency of existential thinking. This discussion will at the same time mark the passage from the pre-philosophical stage of phenomenological reduction to philosophical phenomeno-logy.

CHAPTER VIII

THE TRANSCENDENCY OF EXISTENTIAL THINKING

Existential thinking, as we have seen in the previous chapters, is "immanent" thinking insofar as it involves our human ex-sistence in its entirety. For existential thinking is *logos*-thinking which is the dialectical self-manifestation of primordial wonder in man. Now, primordial wonder is only given in the act by which it is fully received, namely by the total openness and involvement of man's whole personality. And since primordial wonder is the lasting source, the immanent origin and indwelling principle of existential thinking, it follows that existential thinking is always immanent, that it always involves the whole of our human ex-sistence. As contrasted with the abstractive thinking of the natural sciences existential thinking never detaches itself from the experiential world of the thinker. Moreover, *logos*-thinking begins as a reflection on the immediate data of our lived experience. This is why we have found it to be so important to arrive at a perception of our pre-reflective "Being-in-the-world" as it *is,* uncorrupted by prejudices, mental constructs or preconceived ideas. We have also found, however, that this return to the pristine innocence of original perception is extremely difficult, and requires a laborious and total involvement on the part of the thinker. It is only by means of a skillful and concentrated use of the "phenomenological reduction" that the existential thinker arrives at an original perception of the "natural" world in its primordial givenness.

Yet, we discovered that even in its pre-philosophical phase the phenomenological reduction is not only immanent. For the very technique of reduction implies the overwhelming, inspirational and all-encompassing experience of wonder. In other words, the phenomenological reduction itself contains an element of transcendency and involves the passage beyond the world of beings into the World of Being. And if it is true that the phenomenological reduction contains an element of transcendency in its ontic or pre-philosophical phase, then this must be *a fortiori* true for its philosophical phase where phenomenology becomes an integral part of the *logos,* co-original with ontology and dialectics. In this chapter we shall concentrate on the philosophical significance of the *transcendency* of existential thinking both in its ontic and its ontological phases. We then shall raise our "example" of the "aesthetic phenomenon" to the philosophical level with a view to further articulating our understanding of existential thinking.

MISCONCEPTIONS AND OMISSIONS

As we have seen, phenomenological reduction as "wonder in the face of the world" is never merely a technical procedure and hard work, but always *at the same time,* and even more fundamentally, a genuine *inspiration.* As an inspiration the phenomenological reduction *transcends* the world of work into the world of wonder. But before we proceed to further clarify the ontological significance of this transcendency, we must prevent some common misconceptions concerning "inspiration" and "transcendency" from obstructing our phenomenological vision.

Our previous chapter[175] has already shown that in the context of existential thinking the term "transcendency," which etymologically means "a going beyond," cannot be understood in the physical sense of "going outside." Our original perception reveals that "transcendency" is not a physical distance between two separate things, but rather the inner polarity of an encounter between two worlds within the "aesthetic di-stance" of authentic sym-bolism. In fact, transcendency is the very dynamism which constitutes the primordial openness of our authentic existence *as ex-sistence.* Consequently, transcendency here cannot be taken in the sense of the Cartesian dualism where it indicates the passage of a conscious subject beyond itself to an objective reality "outside" itself. Transcendency is not primarily found within the subject-object relationship at all, but rather in that which renders such a relationship possible: the very openness of our ex-sistence as "Being-in-the-world." It is this "Being-in-the-world" which creates an open domain within which it becomes possible for a subject to establish contact with an object, and which is prior to the emergence of any particular encounter. It is this unitary phenomenon of "Being-in-the-world" which shows that we are essentially always already "outside" *as "ex-sistence,"* and that the misconception of transcendency as a radical passage from an "inside" to an "outside" results from a failure to grasp the primary data of human ex-sistence. Moreover, as we noted in the last chapter, "transcendency" in the Kantian sense of "a passage beyond all limits of possible experience," or of "a passage to whatever is prior to all experience *(a priori)*" is equally unacceptable. For, we have no experience of that which transcends experience, but we do have the "transcending experience" of "Being-in-the-world" which is *a priori* in the sense that it is *prior to* the emergence of any form of knowledge or experience, to any sort of relationship, to any kind of encounter.

When we consult the history of philosophy or even the history of aesthetics we discover that the term "inspiration" is conspicuous by its absence. Even the few passing remarks we find from Plato to Bergson only serve to emphasize this fact. Apart from theology where the problem of "divine inspiration" has been a perennial topic of discussion, most sciences seem to be eager to dodge the issue and to provide the problem of inspiration with a premature epitaph, such as: too difficult; irrationality; subjectivism; sweet ecstacy or even sheer madness. There are various possible explanations for this strange omission. Among others, we can point to the fact that the question of inspiration is very difficult and complex indeed. Moreover, it is impossible for the merely objectifying frame of mind to regard the experiential phenomenon of inspiration as meaningful. This would be subjectivism or irrationalism. For others the term "inspiration" may be too closely associated with "aestheticism" where it does not mean much more than "a sweet ecstacy." Another possible factor is the fact that Western philosophy since Plato has always had the "optic" approach in thinking, has always emphasized the metaphor of "seeing" (Gr. *idein*—to see). Beings are known when their what-ness (idea) is visible to our view. Essences, therefore, are always thought of as being "in front of us," whereas it is characteristic of inspiration that it approaches us "from behind" so to speak. In philosophy terms such as "intuition," "vision" and "view" have always overshadowed the term "inspiration." Nevertheless, to the extent in which we have lost contact with our *primordial inspiration of wonder,* we have lost contact with our strictly philosophical inspiration. Primordial wonder is the "overwhelming" and "inspirational" experience of Being which is the most fundamental "datum" of existential thinking. It is the primordial "gift" which constitutes the philosopher. In fact, it is the inspiration we *are.* In our earlier chapters it has become abundantly clear that the primordial inspiration of wonder is neither subjective nor irrational. And in the previous chapter we found that this primordial inspiration is neither a "sweet ecstacy" nor an "easy intuitionism," but a primordial experience involving existential awe and anxiety, involving the primordial con-flict of two worlds, involving the whole of our ex-sistence including painful purifications and hard work. Whatever the explanation for the omission of inspiration in philosophy may be, one thing is clear, namely that a rejection of the primordial inspiration of wonder is tantamount to a rejection of the transcendency of philosophical thinking. And a failure to understand the ontological significance of transcendency results in an atrophy of the Being-dimension, and, therefore, of the philosophical authenticity of fundamental thinking.

REDUCTION AT THE SERVICE OF PRIMORDIAL INSPIRATION

We are now prepared to begin our elucidation of the ontological significance of the transcendency of existential thinking. As we have seen, phenomenological reduction as "wonder" in the face of the world is not merely hard work, but also primordial *inspiration*. As an inspiration the phenomenological reduction *transcends* the world of work into the world of wonder, and this transcendency is the original "ec-stacy" of our primordial inspiration. Consequently, the phenomenological reduction does *not* put everything out of play. It merely eliminates both our prejudices and our familiar acceptance of things (its negative aspect) in the light of the primordial inspiration of wonder (its positive aspect). "The most important lesson," says Merleau-Ponty, "which the reduction teaches us is the impossibility of a complete reduction."[176] The primordial inspiration of wonder is a constitutive element of the phenomenological reduction. And wonder originates "the unmotivated upsurge of the world,"[177] con-stitutes the world as fundamental paradox, reveals the world as primordial sym-bol in which everything is given and everything remains in suspense. Wonder places the phenomenological techniques in the truly phenomeno-logical perspective. This perspective is not a merely technological perspective, or the perspective of the craftsman, but more fundamentally that of a "respectful di-stance." This respectful distance of the phenomenological attitude is not the quantitative di-stance of an ob-jective "spectacle," standing over against a merely "onlooking" subject (*spicere*—to look at). The "re-spect-ful di-stance" brings back what is looked at (*re*-back; and *spicere*) into the per-spective (*per*—through; and *spicere*) of the awe-inspiring and fascinating transparency of the primordial depth of wonder. In other words, the "respectful distance" of phenomenological reduction is the "aesthetic distance" of our *original perception*. The perception of phenomena in their original givenness presupposes the primordial transcendency of wonder.

The true phenomenologist practices his technical skills *within* the primordial inspiration of wonder. Thus the phenomenological reduction closely resembles the creative activity of the artist. Just as the artist in one differentiated but undivided act mobilizes his tools and techniques, and allows his inspiration to execute the work of art through them, so also the phenomenologist employs his techniques of comparative description allowing the primordial inspiration of wonder to reveal itself through them as the world of original phenomena. The techniques of the artist will produce art only when they are put at the service of his artistic inspiration. The techniques of phenomenological reduction will reveal original phenomena only when put at the service of the primordial inspiration of wonder. The phenomenologist "re-collects" or "gathers together again" the "data" of the visible world in the presence of the primordial "gift" of the invisible world of wonder. The artist does not have a complete idea of his work of art before he brings it into being, but he discovers his creation in the very act of creating it. "From the moment," says Henri Bergson, "that the musician has the precise and complete idea of the symphony he means to compose, the symphony is done."[178] The work (the technical arrangement) and the art (the beautiful arrangement) are created at one single stroke into the unique and original whole of the artwork. The new arrangement is not merely a re-arrangement of pre-existing elements, but it results from a sym-bolic encounter between two worlds. We could compare the inspired technique of the artist with the activity of an invisible magnet which re-arranges in a single stroke a heap of iron filings in such a way that all filings show the lines of force of the magnetic field. Likewise the phenomenological reduction is not merely a "descriptive technique" on the level of essences, but it is at the same time a complex though indivisible act which in one single stroke perceives the essences as presences within the mysterious inspiration of the primordial world of wonder.

RIGOROUS SCIENCE?

But what is left of philosophy as a "rigorous science" when the pre-philosophical world on which it re-flects resembles so closely the world of the creative artist? Is it not the task of philosophy to re-flect on reality as it *is*, rather than on reality as it has been changed by man? The answer, of course, is that this is true, but also that once again we have been deceived by our scientistic prejudices. It is precisely *because* philosophy re-flects on reality as it *is*, that phenomenological reduction and artistic creativity are alike. For, as we have shown, both the phenomenologist and the artist grasp the natural world as it *is* within the primordial inspiration of wonder or within the "aesthetic di-stance" of the original perceptions. It is the natural scientist and not the phenomenologist or the artist who really changes reality. It is the scientist who ob-jectifies his data, places them at a controllable di-stance and translates them into a system of univocal concepts and mathematical symbols. The artist and the phenomenologist, on the other hand, are not interested in the quantifying viewpoint which places its data at a "controllable" distance. Their primordial inspiration induces them to view their data from the "respectful" distance of original perception, and this permits them to grasp the phenomena as they *are,* as they reveal themselves in their "original givenness" in the light of the primordial "gift" of wonder. For instance, the artist perceives the blossoming tree in its inexhaustible concreteness, whereas the scientist is merely aware of some electrical charges flying about at high speed.

Both the artist and the phenomenologist are profoundly *moved* by the primordial inspiration of wonder which induces them to "orientate" their world towards this primordial "datum." This "movement" of the progressive self-orientation of the artwork or the phenomenal world is at least as rigorous as the strictness of the exact sciences. This implies for the phenomenological reduction that it begins as a "movement" before it begins as a philosophy. All this has been succinctly stated by Maurice Merleau-Ponty. "If phenomenology," he says, "was a movement before becoming a doctrine or a philosophical system, this was attributable neither to accident, nor to fraudulent intent. It is as painstaking as the works of Balzac, Proust, Valéry or Cézanne—by reason of the same kind of attentiveness and wonder, the same demand for awareness, the same will to seize the meaning of the world. . . . as that meaning comes into being."[179] We find the same insights expressed by Gabriel Marcel where he writes: "I think we ought to aim at a restoration of that unity of poetic vision and philosophic creativity of which the great pre-Socratic philosophers offer us one of the first examples."[180]

EXISTENTIAL THINKING AND HOLISTIC PSYCHOLOGY

It is interesting to note in passing that the same concern to recover the original and holistic perception on the pre-philosophical level of the *Lebenswelt* (the "life-world") is also found among many contemporary psychologists and psychiatrists. Especially noteworthy in this connection are various modern movements, such as existential psychology, humanistic psychology, personalistic psychology, Self-psychology, phenomenological psychology, non-directive psychology, neo-freudian psychology among others. Every psychological theory has among its often unexamined presuppositions at least an implicit philosophy of man, whether the psychologist is aware of it or not.[181] The relatively short history of psychology has been dominated by the *Cartesian dualism,* or the radical split between spirit and matter, "inner" and "outer" world, self and non-self, subject and object. "Virtually all modern psychological theories," says Gordon Allport, "seem oriented toward one of [these] two polar conceptions," which he respectively calls the "Leibnitzian" and the "Lockean" traditions.[182] These two opposite traditions result in mental constructs that block our original perception of human ex-sistence and of reality as a whole. We no longer grasp the *whole* man and his relation to the *whole* of Being; what we perceive is rather a "detotalized" man (Le Senne) and his relation to a truncated reality. What the above mentioned psychological movements have in common with the phenomenological movement in philosophy is precisely their profound interest in restoring the original and holistic perception of man and his world of which the great pre-Socratic philosophers offer us one of the first examples (Marcel). We are witnessing today a necessary and long overdue rapprochement between philosophy and psychology. This common interest in original and authentic perception has been their "missing link" in the past, and constitutes the "common ground" for a fruitful dialogue today. When we speak of "dialogue," of course, we not only imply a certain unity, but also an essential difference. We will revert to this later on.

Both the phenomenological philosopher and psychologist are one in their concern for re-achieving an original and experiential contact with the *life-world.* Both the phenomenological reduction and the "holistic analysis"[183] gradually eliminate the merely "re-presentational" type of knowledge and return to our knowledge which immediately attains the "things themselves" (Husserl). Instead of merely thinking in terms of the subject-object relationship, the perceiver gathers himself into a primordial compenetration of perceiver and *world* in which the originality of perception is not guaranteed by the mere "intuiting" of an isolated essence, but by dis-covering its presence in the primordial context of *the* world *(Ur-gestalt).* It should be emphasized, however, that in the implicit and undifferentiated experience of primordial wonder the world is not known yet *as* world, nor does the original perception reveal itself *as* perception, or for that matter as distinct from any other fundamental phenomenon. The primordial inspiration of wonder is an immediately lived and pre-reflective, exclamatory awareness which constitutes the very openness of our authentic ex-sistence. Consequently, the original perception of the primordial inspiration does not only involve the whole of our ex-sistence, but we also bring ourselves into "ex-sistence" through this perception. It is, therefore, not a fortuitous coincidence that Carl Rogers, discussing one of his pivotal insights: "the openness to experience," quotes Maslow on "wonder." "Maslow" he writes, "might be speaking of clients I have known when he says, 'self-actualized people have a wonderful capacity to appreciate again and again, freshly and naively, the basic goods of life with awe, pleasure, wonder, and even ecstacy, however stale these experiences may be for other people'."[184] For Maslow the "oceanic feeling" is a characteristic of self-actualizing people,[185] and phenomena such as "wonder," "awe," "reverence," "surrender before experience as before something great" and "being overwhelmed" permeate all our "peak-experiences."[186] Especially in the peak-experiences of love and beauty he finds that "one small part of the world is perceived as if it were for the moment all of the world."[187] It is evident that these psychologists are discussing the same original perception of the same experiential world as we are, and that their "holistic analyses" are only meaningful in the light of this primordial inspiration.

But there is also an essential *difference* between the holistic analyses of the experiential psychologist on the one hand, and the philosophical re-flections on these data by the existential thinker on the other. Whereas the holistic analyses of the psychologist remain *within* the *ontic* experience of the *life-world (Lebenswelt),* for the philosopher they serve as a gateway to his *ontological* reflections on our human ex-sistence. The experiential psychologist wants to know what the *life-world* of the child or the adolescent, the male or the female, the healthy or psychotic personality looks like. The philosopher, on the other hand, wants to understand what phenomena such as wonder, man, world etc. *fundamentally are,* or, in other words, he wants to "com-prehend" them in the primordial light of the *logos.*

From Ontic to Ontological Phenomenology

It is evident that we will find an analogous difference between the pre-philosophical phase of phenomenological reduction on the one hand, and the truly philosophical phenomeno-logy on the other. And this brings us to the second part of this chapter where we will make the actual transition from pre-philosophical phenomenology to phenomenology as an integral aspect of *logos*-thinking, or from the *ontic imma-nency* of descriptive analyses to the authentic *transcendency* of the *ontological* dimension of existential thinking. For the *logos*-thinker the phenomenological reduction and the ontic immanency of his original perceptions serve as a gateway to his "onto-logical" re-flections on these primary phenomena.[188] And since onto-logical re-flection does not leave its starting point behind but rather goes back into it, it follows that the immanency of phenomenological reduction and its techniques, and of original perception and its primordial inspiration remains present in the authentic transcendency of existential thinking. And this entails, paradoxically, that since the beginning becomes more beginning, the immanency becomes more immanent to the extent in which it is transcended by the interiorizing self-transcendency of the onto-logical dimension.

It is only in the light of the *logos* that the ontic world of original perceptions (phenomena) reveals its implicit ontological character. It is only in the light of the *logos* that we understand the pre-philosophical phase of phenomenological description as an *implicit logos*. The pre-philosophical laborious analysis of our *life-world* is a "dialectical" comparison of original "phenomena" within the primordial inspiration of "Being." Although the ontological, the phenomenological and the dialectical aspects of the *logos* are implicitly present and implicitly grasped in the ontic phase of the phenomenological reduction, they are not yet known *as such,* they are not yet known explicitly, and as co-original aspects of the *logos* they remain concealed. It is only in the transcendency of the ontological stage where we wonder at primordial wonder, and where we re-flect on the original perception of our primary data, that the *logos* becomes *explicitly logos,* and manifests itself as the dialectical self-manifestation of primordial Being. It is on this level of transcendency that the *logos* in a sudden, spontaneous and inspired convergence of its ontological, phenomenological and dialectical aspects "sets apart" the original "phenomena" in their primordial collectedness of "Being."

Primordial or implicit wonder is given to put the familiar phenomena in the unfamiliar perspective of the "aesthetic" perception of their *ontic* originality. The *logos* as explicit wonder is given to provide this ontic perspective with its *onto-logical* depth, differentiation and significance. The pre-philosophical reduction eliminates the obviousness from the usual world. The philosophical reduction eliminates the unreflectedness from the un-usual world of the pre-philosophical reduction. The philosophical phase "transcends" the pre-philosophical phase of phenomenological reduction, but not in the sense that it takes leave of it. On the contrary, as co-original with the ontological and dialectical aspects of the *logos* the philosophical phase of phenomenology is a re-flection on the pre-philosophical reduction and its strange blend of laborious and inspirational elements. *Philosophy remains essentially a mysterious unity between hard work and primordial inspiration.*

ARTISTIC AND PHILOSOPHICAL INSPIRATION

At this point we must note the striking analogy between philosophical inspiration on the one hand, the artistic inspiration on the other. And this strong resemblance between the creative process in art and philosophy should not surprise us, for both the philosopher and the artist are concerned with primordial wonder, both the philosopher and the artist reveal Being in the world and aim at the originality of "aesthetic" perception. We want to draw the reader's attention to a few common structural characteristics of the creative processes of the philosopher and the artist with a view to elucidating the inspirational nature of existential thinking as fundamental aesthetics. We do not intend to give a philosophy of artistic creativity since philosophical aesthetics is beyond the scope of this book. We merely want to restrict ourselves to a few fundamental observations concerning some structural characteristics of the phenomenon of inspiration. This will not only further our understanding of the transcendency of existential thinking, but also demonstrate how fundamental aesthetics provides philosophical aesthetics with its necessary foundations.

The Fact of Inspiration

In their descriptive analyses of their creative activities many of the greatest thinkers and artists have given us a vivid and detailed account of "the phenomenon of inspiration."[189] In spite of many variations on the theme the same characteristic features recur again and again in the descriptions of the creative process. In the first place, it is generally agreed that the creative process is an "inspired" process, but also that normally this inspiration will evaporate if it is not "worked out," if it is not incarnated in some medium in which the artist or thinker has his expert knowledge or skills. Edmund Sinnot sums up the thinking on this point in his following statement: ". . . inspirations, it is well recognized, rarely come unless an individual has immersed himself in a subject. He must have a rich background of knowledge and experience in it."[190] This paradoxical unity between hard work and primordial inspiration is also characteristic of philosophical thinking, and, fundamentally, for the same reasons. Although the *fact* of inspiration has seldom been a point of discussion, its *role* in the creative process has been both exalted and minimized or even disregarded altogether. Whether the creator interprets his creative activity in terms of "sheer inspiration" or in terms of "hard work" often depends on what psychologically has impressed him most, or also on his philosophical pre-conceptions of the nature of transcendency. But, as we have seen already, a true understanding of inspiration as transcendency implies our openness to the primordial gift of wonder and at the same time the involvement of the whole of our ex-sistence through conscious efforts, cultivation of sensitivity, development of skills and techniques, gathering of data, multidimensional explorations etc. It is true what Dostoevski wrote to his brother: "Without inspiration one can't of course begin anything."[191] There is also truth in the well-known saying of Edison: "Genius is one per cent inspiration and ninety-nine per cent perspiration." But the full meaning of both statements is only found in their togetherness. Or as Henry Bugbee, Jr. puts it: "Insight," he says, "is earned to be sure, but it is not steered, and it must find its own articulate form. If it is to become more than sporadic and utterly ephemeral, one must pay attention to it, it must be *worked out*."[192]

Suddenness and Unexpectedness

Another structural characteristic of authentic inspiration is its "suddenness" and "unexpectedness." Every creative artist and thinker could have made the following words of Tchaikowsky his own: "Generally speaking, the germ of a future composition comes suddenly and unexpectedly."[193] And, speaking of the *primordial* inspiration of wonder in chapter three, we cited a text of Maritain where he quotes a close acquaintance of his as saying: ". . . it often happened that by a sudden intuition I experienced the reality of my own being, of the deepest, first principle that placed me outside nothingness."[194] Moments when insights worth considering or germs to be developed occur to artists and thinkers have always impressed them by their suddenness and unexpected spontaneity. Now, authentic inspiration is sudden and unexpected by reason of the nature of that which manifests itself in it, namely the primordial gift of wonder or the *all-encompassing* experience of Being. This primordial world of wonder, as we have often seen, "transcends" the usual world of particular beings or groups of beings, and of any particular standpoints or perceptions. The primordial gift of inspiration, therefore, manifests itself "at one stroke" in an undivided and indivisible act of creation, and cannot be conceived as a succession of "separate" parts or "discrete" moments. The primordial gift of inspiration is sudden and unexpected. This, of course, is not to say that the creative process immediately results in a final product. On the contrary, normally the beginning inspiration is only a germinal insight, a theme, a glimpse, a hunch or a rudimentary awareness of something original announcing itself. This nascent inspiration has to "grow," has to be "worked out," reaches its maturity only through various phases of a creative process. The artist does not even fully understand his inspiration until its expression has reached its final completion, and the philosopher who re-flects on the inexhaustibility of primordial inspiration never even reaches such a point. By calling authentic inspiration sudden and unexpected we do not contradict the fact that the creative act is a differentiated process in which various steps and phases can be distinguished. The suddenness and unexpectedness of authentic inspiration result from its revelation of wonder which constitutes the creative process as a *unitary* structure and the creative act as an *indivisible* act and a *unique* and *irreducible* experience.

Being Possessed

The structural characteristics of fundamental phenomena are, of course, always interwoven and interlocking characteristics; they are never separate or isolated features. In other words, when we say that the sense of "being possessed" is "another" structural characteristic of inspiration, we do not mean this in an additive sense. The very suddenness and unexpectedness of inspiration, for instance, already implies that we do not have direct control over inspiration, and that inspiration, as the word itself indicates, is an "overwhelming" experience (*in* and *spirare*—to breathe into, to infuse by breathing). Inspiration does not occur by command. It is generally agreed that inspiration escapes our control, and that no one can say "now I will be inspired." Creative artists and writers often regard themselves as a mere "instrument," as a "medium" or a "mouthpiece," and they "are often surprised to astonishment at the results of their work which seems to have been in some way 'given' to them."[195] And this feature has been known to the western world ever since Plato put the following words into the mouth of Socrates: "all good poets, epic as well as lyric, compose their beautiful poems not by art, but because they are inspired and possessed."[196] But whereas this characteristic of inspiration has been readily accepted in the history of art and literature, it has seldom been recognized as an essential constituent of philosophical thought. We have seen that philosophers have often minimized and disregarded the role of inspiration in philosophy for fear of subjectivism. But as early as in Chapter Three, where we first discovered the inspirational characteristics of primordial wonder, the conception of primordial inspiration as subjectivism was refuted.[197] Paradoxically, the danger of subjectivism is especially great for those who have fallen victims to what Bugbee aptly calls "the dogma of the ultimacy of a merely *optical* mode of thought."[198] For they fail to "transcend" the subject-object dichotomy, they do not grasp the all-encompassing universality of primordial wonder and allow this original principle of all philosophical inspiration to atrophy. They think that their primary responsibility is to the "ob-jects" as standing over against themselves as subjects, whereas the fundamental responsibility of the authentic philosopher is to primordial wonder which "transcends" the objectivity of all objects and the subjectivity of all subjects. And the term "responsibility" here is used in both the etymological and the ontological sense of "capacity to respond to the primordial inspiration of Being."

An Overwhelming Phenomenon

In other words, existential thinking, insofar as it is *inspirational,* is not entirely "ours." Nor is it within our power to, strictly speaking, "control" its emergence. And to the extent in which existential thinking "transcends" our "controlling" way of thinking it is truly "meta-technical," and transcends all modes of expert or professional thinking. Existential thinking "transpires" beyond controllable conditions, and can hardly be defined in terms of "correct rules to be followed." The existential thinker is as such never an "expert" in existential thinking. We are experts or professionals insofar as we have special skill or knowledge, insofar as we *control* our special field of occupation. To the extent to which the existential thinker is involved in the *all-encompassing* and *overwhelming* inspiration of primordial wonder his thinking transcends the merely specialized thinking of the expert. In the absence of this primordial inspiration both philosophical and artistic techniques would become meaningless, since they would lead to a merely mechanical repetition of the same. Both the existential thinker and the artist, while drawing upon all resources of technique and materials, allow the primordial gift of inspiration to create their fundamental insights and works of art in and through them. Thus all the parts of an artwork or of a philosophical insight are created within the light of original inspiration, and co-originate with the emergence of the whole.

Importance of the Dream-like Consciousness

Another structural characteristic of the creative process is the dream-like consciousness of the creator. Creative thinkers and artists have always been called "dreamers." To those accustomed to regarding this as a derogatory qualification, it comes as something of a surprise to learn of the fundamental importance attached to the dream-like states of consciousness on the part of those who describe the creative activity. We, for our part, regard this dream-like consciousness as another structural characteristic of the creative process, co-original with the aforementioned characteristics.

This dream-like consciousness is our existential readiness to "receive" the primordial gift of inspiration and to be overwhelmed or possessed by that which "transcends." It is our fundamental willingness to surrender to the "oceanic feeling" of wonder, to inhibit all our individual urgencies, and to disengage from any theoretical or practical concerns that hold us down on the level of our unauthentic existence. It is, of course, this reductive asceticism, this struggle between the original exigency of inspiration and the individual urgencies of the creator that often turns the creative process into a restless experience and a painful effort. Speaking of the dream-like characteristic of creative thinking, Dr. Harding presents us with the following relevant statement: "Having learned to dream over the subject the thinker must learn not to obtrude his own personal wishes but to follow where the truth leads him. He who wishes to express *himself* is on the wrong track: his aim should be to express beyond himself. In fact the procedure bears an analogy to the mystic way. The sinking of the personality; the retirement for the time-being of the intellect from everything irrelevant; holding the intellect by the will so that it watches, but does not disturb, the natural development of the idea; merging himself into the great sea of life beyond himself in order that he may become one with it: these are the characteristics alike of mystic, seer, and thinker."[199]

To the technocrat, of course, this dream-like consciousness is merely an idle and meaningless musing, a typical weakness of irrationality. To the artist and the existential thinker, however, this dream-like consciousness is a structural characteristic of their creative activity. For it keeps them in touch with the oceanic consciousness of primordial inspiration. And this consciousness is dream-like because it both "transcends" the activities of our everyday world and "presents" us with the chiaroscuro of the mystery of Being. Creativity is always emergence out of the unknown and is constantly nourished by its "ab-sence" from every-thing in particular. It is this ec-static absent-mindedness that constitutes the dream-like state of consciousness in which every-thing is in suspense, in which the artist is "both asleep and awake." It is this ec-static absent-mindedness which keeps the artist at an aesthetic distance from any preoccupation with particulars, and which constitutes his creative fidelity to the spontaneous depths of primordial inspiration. It is the same ec-static absent-mindedness which allows the existential thinker to "transcend" the activism of his workaday world, and to "listen to the voice of Being." In this existential "listening" (Heidegger) or "availability" (Marcel) the existential thinker "wanders away" from his involvement in the immediate situation and becomes rooted in the primordial situation which antecedes both all theoretical thinking and all practical activity. This absent-mindedness, therefore, has nothing in common with the "abstractiveness" of the objectifying frame of mind. On the contrary, this absent-mindedness is rather the present-mindedness of the artist and the existential thinker in the concrete and all-encompassing transcendency of the primordial world of wonder.[200]

Creative Receptivity

Those who mistake this dream-like consciousness for a state of pure passivity fail to understand the true nature of transcendency. They use the mechanical system of a physical receiving apparatus as the model for an understanding of our receptive openness to primordial Being. But the model of a physical receiving apparatus belongs to the context of objectifying thinking which conceals rather than reveals the way in which authentic ex-sistence "receives" its primordial inspiration. The receptivity of the creative process cannot be reduced to the mechanical receptivity of a physical process. The authentic reception of primordial Being is neither a purely passive nor a purely active receptivity, but rather a mixture, or, more correctly, a compound of both.[201] Or, as Gabriel Marcel puts it: "at this level the contrast between activity and passivity—between reception, say, considered as taking, and reception considered as being given something—loses a great deal of its meaning; in the dimension in which we now find ourselves, we must move beyond such categories."[202] For, fundamentally speaking, all human creativity is *given creativity,* all human creativity is the reception of the primordial gift of inspiration. As Martin Heidegger states it: "All projection—and, consequently, even man's 'creative' activity—is *thrown*."[203]

A gift becomes a gift only to the extent in which it is "received." Thus the very reception of the primordial gift of inspiration is a constituent of this gift. Hence it is a mistake to visualize our reception of inspiration as the act by which one entity, called the human subject, attempts to "grasp" another entity, called primordial inspiration. As we have seen already, it is precisely man's essence to "ex-sist," i.e., to pass beyond himself as a mere entity to the primordial openness of Being. This self-transcendency constitutes his authentic ex-sistence and makes him essentially more than he is. In other words, man and inspiration are not two separate and independent entities, but the inspired man is authentic ex-sistence as "Being-in-the-world" which is a *unitary* phenomenon. Inspiration cannot manifest itself fully independent of man's willingness to let it "happen." We cannot have access to the self-revelation of inspiration without "welcoming" it with the "responsiveness" of our entire ex-sistence. In short, the primordial gift of inspiration is a paradoxical union between activity and passivity, between creativity and receptivity or between spontaneity and responsiveness. The phenomenon of primordial inspiration constitutes the element of transcendency in both artistic creativity and existential thinking. And it is this transcendency of inspiration which cuts across the traditional opposition between empiricism and idealism. For our original perception is neither given in the pure passivity of the self-less world of empiricism nor constituted by the pure creativity of the world-less self of idealism. Our original perception reveals itself in the *creative receptivity* of our inspired ex-sistence which both "takes" part and "has" part in the primordial World of Being.

Primordial Enthusiasm

And this brings us to a last structural characteristic of the phenomenon of inspiration. To say that the inspired person "transcends" the established order of our everyday existence is to say that inspiration constitutes an experience of *ecstacy*. Authentic inspiration is "ec-static" by reason of the fact that through inspiration man passes "beyond" himself by allowing himself to be "overwhelmed" by the transcendency of the primordial world of wonder. This primordial gift of inspiration *is* our authentic ex-sistence as *ec-stacy* (*ek*—out; and *histanai*—to place: to stand out, to be beyond oneself). Etymologically the word *ecstacy* means "trans-scendency" (a going beyond), but it generally connotes emotional involvement of a trance-like nature, or a state of being over-whelmed with a delightful and awe-inspiring experience. Now, as we have seen already, our human consciousness is not originally a "knowing" one in the intellectualist sense of the term, but rather a "being-with," an existential involvement or a lived experience of presence.[204] To put it differently, our original way of access to Being is given in our "experiential attunement" to this primordial phenomenon. And this "experiential attunement" to primordial Being is our very experience of primordial wonder. Primordial wonder is the ontological "mood" in which we first discover our being-attuned to primordial Being. Although we have implied it all along, we have had to wait until our present discussion on transcendence as ecstacy in order to discover primordial wonder *as primordial mood*. This "primordial mood" is *ontological,* more fundamental than, and, as Heidegger correctly says, "prior to all psychology of moods."[205] The term "primordial mood," however, might still be too suggestive of passivity, immanency and subjectivism. This is why we prefer Eugen Fink's expression: *primordial enthusiasm (en* and *theos:* 'being possessed' by a supreme Being).[206] The term "enthusiasm" signifies more explicitly the inspirational dynamism, the all-encompassing experience and the ec-static transcendency of our primordial mood. Primordial enthusiasm is the ec-static and rapturous mood of the sudden experience of primordial wonder. Primordial enthusiasm is the ec-static attunement of authentic ex-sistence to wonder as our primordial inspiration. Primordial enthusiasm is the ec-static indwelling in the mystery of Being with its fascinating and awe-inspiring moods as the first differentiations of our primordial mood of wonder. Primordial enthusiasm is a structural characteristic of the inspiration of both the creative artist and the existential thinker which makes them express themselves "beyond" themselves.

Neither Subjectivism nor Sentimentalism

Both philosophical insights and works of art come out of the attunement to the dimension of enthusiastic inspiration. Because of this all philosophical and artistic creativity overpasses the established order of our customary and mediocre dailiness. No wonder that those who are exclusively centered upon this order regard all creative activity as "eccentricity," and consider "out of order" everyone who transcends the established world, who yields to the "oceanic consciousness," or who allows himself to be attuned to the primordial ecstacy of enthusiasm. It goes without saying that the claim that fundamental thinking finds its permanent source in enthusiasm is also unacceptable to those whose thinking is centered upon the exclusive use of controlling and objectifying methods. To them the creative and reverent receptivity of our primordial enthusiasm is sheer subjectivism. Earlier in this book we have shown again and again that this absolutism of objectifying thinking itself is a subjectivistic and self-contradictory dogma, that the experience of primordial wonder transcends the dichotomy between subject and object, and that fundamental thinking takes place in the region where man is attuned to primordial Being. There is no need to repeat our argumentations. But it is important, here, to understand our earlier findings more explicitly in the light of transcendency. Fundamental thinking as attuned to primordial Being is the ecstatic indwelling in the primordial truth of wonder. And, once again, we discover that fundamental thinking is truly "ex-sistential" thinking, for its essence lies in the "ec-static" standing out into the enthusiastic transcendency of wonder. In addition, wonder is not only the beginning, but also the *lasting* source and inspiration of all philosophical thinking. The existential thinker, therefore, must at all times maintain his attunement with primordial enthusiasm. And this is the insight that Plato expressed when he stated that "wonder is the basic mood of a philosopher."[207]

Those who understand our emphasis on the role of primordial enthusiasm in existential thinking to mean that this thinking is a philosophy of sentiment, or worse, a sentimental philosophy are completely mistaken. For, the very fact that primordial enthusiasm is an essential, irreducible and lasting component of the luminosity of "ex-sistential" thinking differentiates it from any "particular" sentiment, mood, affection or emotion in the ordinary or psychological sense of the word. Primordial enthusiasm originates as an "all-encompassing" involvement, and never as an affective coloring of a "particular" event. The primordial mood is not some sort of subjective or "internal" commentary on an "external" situation, but rather the affective and ex-sistential disclosure of our "primordial" situation. As the disclosure of our original Being-conscious-in-the-world primordial mood is our *ontological disposition* (*dis*—apart; *ponere*—to place). The term "disposition" here is taken in its full etymological sense and at the same time with its connotation of "affectivity." Primordial enthusiasm discloses our original situation as the "attunement" of our original "givenness" ("positivity"—*ponere*) to the primordial "openness" *(dis)* of the World of Being. This inspirational and all-encompassing nature of primordial mood is well expressed by Martin Heidegger where, speaking of ontological mood, he makes the following concise statement: "A mood assails us. It comes neither from 'outside' nor from 'inside', but arises out of Being-in-the-world, as a way of such Being."[208]

In sum, to the extent to which the *logos* is a primordial inspiration existential thinking is transcendency and characterized by its suddenness and unexpected spontaneity, by its openness to the primordial gift of wonder and its listening to that which overwhelms, and by the ecstacy of its primordial enthusiasm. These insights provide us with the necessary ontological foundations for a philosophical aesthetics. We will revert to this in the final section of this chapter. What interests us most at the moment is the fact that we have found the answer to the question we raised at the beginning of Chapter Seven and to some related questions.

Interplay of Work and Inspiration

In previous chapters we have found that the *logos* sets the multiplicity of philosophical phenomena together in their primordial unity of wonder and thus con-stitutes philosophy as a sys-tem. Chapter Seven raised the question of philosophical quietism. Does the *logos* reveal in a single stroke the whole philosophical system and the essence of all entities? Don't we have to do anything on our part? Don't we have to work and to concentrate, to employ tools and technical skills, and to engage in laborious research? In short, is *logos*-thinking merely hard work or sheer inspiration? Is existential thinking a matter of activism or of quietism?[209]

Our explorations of the immanency of existential thinking in chapter seven have answered this question in part. Here we found that the *logos* is always ready for us, but that we are not always ready for the *logos*. We have to prepare ourselves for the *logos* by engaging in laborious techniques of phenomenological reduction that reduce the phenomena to their original givenness. Although the inspiration of wonder is a constituent of the technique of reduction, this technique also implies the involvement of the whole of our ex-sistence. The ex-sistential thinker thinks with his mind, his heart and his hands. Existential thinking involves all our potentialities such as: sensitivity, technical skills, hard work, discipline, laborious research, profound concentration, intersubjective dialogues, love, humility, respect, asceticism and wonder. Existential thinking, therefore, cannot be equated with sheer inspiration. The conception of existential thinking as some sort of quietist philosophy has to be rejected.

But, on the other hand, is existential thinking only a matter of hard work and activism? In answer to this question we have to remind the reader that chapter seven has shown that the pre-philosophical reduction involves the primordial experience of wonder. The immanency of existential thinking points towards its transcendency. The ontic immanency of existential thinking provokes ontological transcendency, the technique of reduction makes the passage beyond the world of beings into the World of Being or into the primordial inspiration of wonder. And if this is true for the pre-philosophical level of philosophy, then it must *a fortiori* be true for the philosophical phase where phenomenology becomes an integral aspect of the *logos* as the dialectical self-manifestation of Being in man. It is in the present chapter that we have made this passage from the pre-philosophical stage of phenomenological reduction to *philosophical phenomenology,* or to the transcendency of the ontological dimension of existential thinking. Now it is on this level of transcendency that the *logos* in a sudden, spontaneous and inspired convergence of its ontological, phenomenological and dialectical aspects "sets apart" the original "phenomena" in their primordial collectedness of "Being."[210] In other words, the co-originality of the phenomenological and the dialectical aspects of the philosophical method with the primordial inspiration of existential thinking (the ontological aspect) con-stitutes in a single stroke the whole of the philosophical sys-tem. It is precisely the transcendency of existential thinking which provides it with its primordial inspiration and explains the suddenness and unexpected spontaneity of its appearance. Phenomena are perceived in their *onto-logical* givenness only when they are com-prehended *in one single stroke* within the irreducible totality emerging from this primordial inspiration. The *logos* does not "con-struct" (*cum*—together; *struere*—to pile up) this primordial totality from "isolated" phenomena, but it "con-stitutes" the philosophical system *at once* as a unitary and irreducible phenomenon within the primordial inspiration of wonder. Consequently, we have also to *reject* the conception of existential thinking as *activism*. When we are prepared to co-operate with the primordial inspiration, then, suddenly and unexpectedly, the phenomena begin to "fall" into place and converge into a unique context of meaning.

A STATIC AND CLOSED PHILOSOPHY?

But doesn't this sudden and unexpected "falling into place" of the phenomena result in a static and closed philosophy where everything is "in perfect order"? Doesn't this converging into a unique context of meaning result into a fixed realm of static essences? The answer is evidently: no! by reason of the fact that philosophy is a mysterious fusion between hard work and primordial inspiration. Existential thinking as a re-flection on phenomenological reduction in wonder remains openness as primordial inspiration, and remains hermeneutics also on the philosophical level. In a never ending spiral movement the *logos* as phenomenological reduction puts itself at the service of the *logos* as inspiration. Philosophy is always a beginning. In contrast with the fixity of a closed system, the *logos* as system is the lasting *source* and *inspiration* of our philosophical explorations, rather than arrival at the terminus of philosophical thought. Philosophy never coagulates into the finished product of a closed system. The *logos* as the matrix of fundamental meaning is not a realm of static essences, but rather the ontological World of dynamic presences. These onto-logical presences become more and more *given,* more and more *self-evident* to the extent to which our reductive techniques succeed in "com-prehending" them in the light of our primordial inspiration.

Moreover, even the *techniques* of phenomenological reduction are never static devices either. They are never ready-made or mechanical procedures that automatically lead up to certain desired results. Philosophical techniques are never "mere" work in the sense of mere "manufacture" (hand-work) of "products" by means of a merely mechanical re-arrangement of pre-existing parts. For, as we have seen in Chapter Seven, the inspiration of wonder itself is a constituent of the techniques of phenomenological reduction. In existential thinking the philosophical techniques are put at the service of the primordial inspiration of wonder. Due to this ontic osmosis philosophical techniques are inspired techniques. They participate in the creative openness and the dynamic originality of the inspirational transcendency of the *logos*.

The Dilemma between Absolutism and Relativism

But, now, an even more disturbing question forces itself upon us. How to account for the great *variety* of philosophical systems if the *logos* constitutes in one single stroke the whole of the philosophical system? Does not existential thinking after all, in spite of its openness and dynamism, result in the absolutism of a *monolithic* system? Is not philosophy a bowling game in which the *logos* is the ball that is supposed to knock down the pins placed upright by any other philosophical thinker? Did not we say with Hegel that "the truth is in the whole," and is not the *logos* this whole, and, therefore, *the* truth? Are not we confronted with a dilemma between the absolutism of the *logos* or the relativism of a plurality of systems?

Indeed, we must sail between the Scylla of absolutism and the Charybdis of relativism with suspicion and great caution. From the standpoint of the natural scientist the actual diversity of philosophical systems seems utterly irresponsible, if not downright scandalous. To the "sound common sense" the unity of the *logos* seems to be a merely arbitrary invention hovering over the real world of man. Even many philosophers look upon this plurality of systems with suspicion, and regard it as the result of a failure to think philosophically. However, in the light of our foregoing elucidations of the immanency and transcendency of existential thinking an implicit answer to this disturbing question has been given. It is our present task to make this answer explicit.

Existential Thinking as "Morpho-logy"

It is true that the inspiration (transcendency) of the *logos* constitutes in one single stroke the whole of the philosophical system. It is true that the *logos* in a sudden, spontaneous and inspired convergence of its ontological, phenomenological and dialectical aspects "sets apart" the original phenomena in their primordial "collectedness" of Being. But it is also true that the *logos* does not do this in a world-less or disembodied manner. The *logos* does not reveal itself as an acosmic entity hovering over the ordinary world of man. The transcendency of the *logos* does not function apart from its immanency. On the contrary, the *logos* as a re-flection on our original perception of the aesthetic sym-bol con-tains (holds together) the pre-reflective experience of our ordinary world and the extra-ordinary world of wonder. *Logos*-thinking involves man's ex-sistence *in its entirety*. The primordial gift of inspiration is only received by those who are willing to receive it with the whole of their personality, and who at the same time are prepared to engage in hard work, painstaking concentration and laborious research. Strictly speaking, we do not *have* philosophies, but we *are* philosophers. Consequently, the incarnation of the *logos* takes on different forms, different structures and different embodiments in different thinkers, in different times and in different cultures. The *logos* as the differentiated self-manifestation of Being embodied in the thinker has always already set itself into *morphe* (form). No meaningful manifestation of Being is possible without taking on some form in some language. Existential thinking is "morpho-logy" in the most original sense of this term.[211]

The "Ex-sistential Way" out of the Dilemma between Absolutism and Relativism

It is precisely because of this immanency, because of this variegated embodiment that the *logos* cannot present itself as a static and universally valid "ob-ject" to a community of impersonal ob-servers. And it is for the same reason that the *logos* does not manifest itself as a timeless entity, value or idea hovering over the ordinary world of man. On the contrary, the *logos* is not given to the thinker as a separate entity, but as that which not only transcends but also permeates the whole of his personality. The *logos* is embodied in the entire ex-sistence of the existential thinker. The *logos* is incarnated in his background, his historical and cultural milieu, his personal interests and problems, in the sedimentation of his previous experiences, in his work, his research, his language, his encounters, etc. And it is precisely out of the difference of experience, out of the difference of presence to reality, out of the difference of form *(morphe)* that a different style of *logos*, a different incarnation of Being, a different philosophical system is born. And as a different form of the same *logos,* no authentic system is complete or definitive, no authentic system is closed either to itself or to any other authentic system. Consequently, the plurality of philosophical systems does not as such result from a failure to think philosophically. On the contrary, it is the absolutism of any single system that results from such a failure. And this failure may consist either in hypostatizing the *logos* and isolating it from its historical manifestations, or in mistaking a particular historical manifestation for *the* expression of the ever enduring and unchanging validity of the *logos.* Divergent systems, therefore, do not have to be contradictory, they do not have to exclude one another in the logical sense of the term. Here we are beyond the univocity of the merely logical frame of mind. Here we find ourselves within the history of the *logos* which manifests itself through the embodiment in a great variety of dialectically related fundamental thinkers. No single authentic embodiment of the *logos* into a particular philosophical system can monopolize the history of philosophy. No single authentic system can refute or even replace another authentic system. But one authentic thinker can inspire, enrich and complement another thinker in their dialectical relationship of unity-in-opposition.

In existential thinking, then, there is no room for the absolutism of a monolithic system. The *logos,* to be sure, is the whole. But this whole manifests itself through a great diversity of concrete historical embodiments. On the other hand, in existential thinking there is no room for sceptical relativism either. For, the historical diversity of embodiments is not a diversity of unrelated truths. On the contrary, the plurality of systems is the necessary diversity of "styles" in which the *same* Being dialectically manifests itself. The plurality of systems is the necessary diversity of embodiments of the same *logos,* and, therefore, of the same fundamental unconcealment of Being, or the same truth as *aletheia.* Consequently, we have to reject either horn of the dilemma between absolutism and relativism.

At times we are all baffled by the great diversity of philosophical systems. But those who ask themselves in this predicament the question "What system should we follow or study?" ask themselves a very unphilosophical question. Philosophizing is never merely a matter of learning or following a system. A philosophical system is never the end-product of the thinking of the philosopher that exists independent of its creator. For a system is philosophical only to the extent to which it originates from a concrete encounter between the *logos* and the *total experiential involvement* of the existential thinker. Employing the terminology of Gabriel Marcel we could say that a philosophical system is never the mere result of *"la pensée pensée"* (finished thought), but that a system in order to be truly philosophical has to be *"la pensée pensante"* (thinking thought). The natural scientist can to a certain degree start from the achievements of his predecessors and begin where they left off. The philosopher, however, can never do this, since it would involve him in an illegitimate hypostatization of the system, the method and the "results." The philosopher never arrives at "results" in the sense of the finished product of a closed system that can be handed down from generation to generation. Every true philosopher, every existential thinker makes in the truest sense of the term a new and irreplaceable beginning in the history of philosophy. In every response to the call of the *logos* the entire personality of the existential thinker is at stake.[212] All this is succinctly summarized by the following words of Eugen Fink: "All manifestations of authentic thinking are transitory, but the "Logos" itself is the ever-living fire, the *'pur aeizooon'* of Heracleitos."[213]

IMPLICATIONS FOR EPISTEMOLOGY

Before bringing this chapter to a conclusion we want to take the opportunity to reflect on some basic issues of *epistemology* for which the foregoing elucidations of existential thinking have us fully prepared. During the past few centuries epistemology has often been presented as the supreme court of justice in matters of philosophy. How can we legitimately philosophize, so it was argued, before we have ascertained the validity of our philosophical knowledge? Don't we have to settle the problem of knowledge once and for all, don't we have to verify its possibility and to establish its method before we can securely engage in philosophizing? We have to get our tools ready before we can get to work. All this sounds very logical. It should be remembered, however, that we are not concerned here with logical thinking but rather with the fundamental thinking of the *logos*. Although at first blush the arguments may look very plausible, a closer examination reveals that they flatly contradict our phenomenological findings concerning existential thinking.

Existential thinking, as we have seen, does not "have" a method, but it rather *is* a method. It is a method in which primordial Being dialectically manifests itself. This dialectical self-manifestation of Being as *logos* is co-originally ontology, phenomenology and dialectics. These three "aspects" of existential thinking, therefore, are not three different methods, but rather three interdependent constituents of a single and undivided method. Existential thinking originates in a re-flection on the primary data of philosophy where we-find-ourselves-Being-together-with-others-in-the-world. And this world in which we find ourselves is a mysterious and sym-bolic fusion of the experiential immanency of the world of the thinker and the inspirational transcendency of the world of the *logos*.

Equiprimordiality of Epistemology and Existential Thinking

Now, in the light of these and previous findings concerning existential thinking it becomes evident that we cannot possibly settle the problems of philosophical knowledge and method prior to or apart from philosophical thinking itself. Any attempt to verify the possibility or validity of philosophical thinking as a preliminary to philosophy itself would fail, for such an attempt would violate the very nature of philosophical thinking and contradict its structural phenomena. We propose to clarify this in a few points.

The view that the problem of philosophical knowledge should be settled "before" the actual beginning of philosophy flatly contradicts our findings in the chapter on "Wonder and Philosophical Authenticity." Here we discovered that "the actual beginning of philosophy is the criterion of philosophical authenticity," and "of all 'true' philosophizing."[214] Consequently, those who try to ascertain the validity of philosophical thinking "before" the actual beginning of philosophy are looking for a criterion "outside" the region where this criterion is actually found, namely not "before" but "in" the actual beginning of philosophical thinking.

Ontology as Criteriology

As we have seen,[215] philosophy itself is essentially "a critical way of thinking." For the actual beginning of philosophy as the criterion of philosophical authenticity is that which "decides upon" or "ascertains" the philosophical truth. And philosophy is essentially a re-flection on its actual beginning, and, therefore, a going back into its own criterion. Philosophy *is* this self-questioning fundamental criterion, and all fundamental thinking is self-critical. In other words, onto-logy is inherently criterio-logical. Epistemology is an integral constituent of existential thinking.

Epistemology as a Never-ending Task

It is not only impossible to settle the epistemological problem prior to philosophy, it is also contrary to its philosophical nature to settle it "once and for all." As an integral constituent of philosophical thinking epistemology can never settle any question once and for all, and the verification of philosophical thinking remains *a never-ending philosophical task*. The verification of philosophical thinking, as we have seen,[216] cannot result from non-philosophical or logical demonstration *(beweisen)*, but it *is* as the dialectical self-manifestation of Being a progressive *self-demonstration (aufweisen)*. The verification of philosophical thinking never presents itself in the form of "an accomplished fact," but rather as the progressive *self-verification* of existential thinking which makes the truth of its beginning more and more true or trustworthy in the never-ending adventure of its interiorizing self-transcendency.

Hypostatization of Epistemology leads to Antinomies

The attempt to settle the epistemological problem once and for all prior to our actual philosophical thinking amounts to a truncation of the primary data of *logos*-thinking or to a "detotalization" of the original totality of our human ex-sistence. It goes without saying that such a truncation causes philosophical thinking to disintegrate into unsolvable paralogisms, dualisms and antinomies. This, for instance, is what happened to René Descartes who established his criterion of philosophical truth on the basis of his firm belief in the universal validity of a *mathesis universalis*. It was this pre-philosophical criterion of truth, namely the clarity and distinctness of ideas *(idées claires et distinctes)* which necessitated the Cartesian dualism between mind and matter, soul and body, inner and outer world. Another example is the famous philosopher of Königsberg, Immanuel Kant, who attempted a critical investigation of the "pure reason" as a preliminary to any possible metaphysics. The outcome is well-known. Kant exposed the paralogisms and antinomies resulting from our attempt to use the pure reason, and established the speculative impotency of metaphysical thinking. Hegel rightly criticized Kant for trying to construct a critical method of investigation prior to metaphysics.

Neither Phenomenology nor Dialectics alone can constitute an Epistemology

It should be clear that also those who regard either phenomenology or dialectics as the only and absolute method and criterion of philosophical thinking truncate the primary data of *logos*-thinking. For, *logos*-thinking, as we have seen,[217] begins as a multi-dimensional dialogue between the Being of phenomena and the phenomenon of Being. Ontology, phenomenology and dialectics are from the beginning co-original aspects of existential thinking. Authentic philosophy, therefore, cannot possibly be constructed in such a way that phenomenology flows out of dialectics, or that dialectics proceeds from phenomenology, or that either phenomenology or dialectics is an established method "to be applied" to ontological research. The co-originality and the interpenetration of ontology, phenomenology and dialectics demonstrate that these "aspects" of philosophical thinking cannot function apart from one another, and that both phenomenology and dialectics are *constituents of our actual way of access to Being.* A hypostatization of either phenomenology or dialectics would not only entail an impossible formalization of philosophical method,[218] but also contradict the fact that phenomenology and dialectics are integral components of the *logos.* It should be emphasized, however, that this insight does not entail the rejection of any *pre-philosophical* "theory of knowledge." On the contrary, such theories are necessary and of essential importance. The psychology of the cognitive processes, for instance, which examines features such as perception, imagination, memory, reasoning etc. presents us with indispensable data for an epistemological interpretation of the principal kinds of human knowledge.[219] On the other hand, philosophical epistemology can be of interest to psychologists and may often prove psychologically suggestive. It should be realized, however, that the interest of philosophical and fundamental epistemology here can never be direct, as though a simple translation into operational concepts would produce a working framework for psychological research.[220]

Epistemology as an Integral Constituent of Existential Thinking

Fundamental epistemology, as an integral constituent of existential thinking is *ipso facto* a constituent of our philosophical way of access to the original perception of Being. It is this original perception of Being, as we have seen,[221] which makes us transcend the subject-object dichotomy and which makes us ex-sist authentically. It is in the original perception of Being that we have our experiential encounter with the sym-bolic union between the ordinary world of things *(res)* and the extra-ordinary World of Being. As an integral constituent of philosophical thinking fundamental epistemology begins not "before" but "at" the beginning of philosophy as the critical element of our re-flection on the encounter between beings and Being. In other words, from its very beginning fundamental epistemology is a "critical presence" to the dialogue between the World of Being and the world of entities. Epistemology, therefore, does not have its beginning in either the "external" or the "inner" world, but it arises as a critical re-flection of our Being-in-the-world. Consequently, we have to reject the following traditional questions as contradictory to the primary data of epistemology: "Can the existence of anything outside the subject be asserted?" "Can we prove the existence of an 'external' world?" "Can we know the 'Thing-in-itself'?" "Can we bridge the gap between our consciousness and reality?" Questions such as these are epistemological pseudo-problems. Whether or not we can "arrive at" a knowledge of Being or reality is not an epistemological question, precisely because epistemology originates as a critical re-flection on the ever-deepening dialogue between reality and Being. As we have seen with Heidegger, the "scandal of philosophy" is not that these questions have not been answered yet, but rather that they are still being asked.

The Inadequacy of Exclusively Epistemological Questions

The foregoing points have made it clear that the question of fundamental truth is *not exclusively* an epistemological question, but more basically a question of the ontological dimension of existential thinking. Even the question what "truth" or for that matter what "epistemology" fundamentally are presupposes *that we know* their "Being," what their "ontological" dimension is. As we have seen over and again, it is the "ontological" dimension which authenticates philosophical thinking. And it is for this reason that we discovered in our Chapter on "Logic and *Logos*" that both traditional theories of the nature of the truth are insufficiently fundamental. Both the correspondence theory and the coherence theory result from questions that are *too exclusively* epistemological. Let us quote our finding in the just-mentioned chapter: "Neither the truth as correspondence nor the truth as coherency are as such sufficiently fundamental to constitute the truth of a philosophical system. A philosophical system is true when its coherency corresponds to the *dialectical unconcealment of primordial wonder* as the truth *(aletheia)* of the *logos*."[222]

Rejection of the Absolute Primacy of Epistemology

That we have to verify philosophical thinking, therefore, cannot mean that "before" philosophizing can begin, there must be a preliminary discipline that settles the problems of philosophical knowledge and method once and for all. Nor does it mean that we establish the possibility, the limits and the origin of philosophical thinking "apart" from this integral thinking itself. In other words, *we have to reject the idea of the absolute primacy of epistemology* in any sense of the term. As a pre-philosophical theory of knowledge epistemology cannot be the final court of appeal in matters of philosophical thinking. There can be no valid criterion or verification of philosophy outside philosophical thinking itself. And as an integral constituent of philosophical thinking fundamental epistemology remains subject to the triarchy of onto-logy, phenomeno-logy and dia-lectics. To commit oneself to a verification principle or to a pre-established methodology of philosophical thinking "before" the actual and integral beginning of philosophy entails a contradiction of the primary data of existential thinking. If existential thinking is to be verified, it must be verified by existential thinking itself. This self-verification, as we have seen,[223] is not a vicious circle, but it corresponds to the circular movement of fundamental thinking which is a re-flection on its own beginning. Existential thinking is the self-questioning of its actual beginning, it is the progressive self-foundation and the ever-renewed self-beginning of its primary data. Man's capacity to think philosophically is *given* "with" the actual beginning of philosophical thinking. Yet both this actual beginning and man's given capacity to think philosophically remain *in question*. Not in the sense of either a sceptical or a methodical doubt, but rather in the sense of a self-questioning capacity and a self-verifying beginning. In philosophical thinking at every step the whole road is at stake. In philosophy every step is "critical!" Every answer re-kindles the whole of our fundamental questioning, every move deepens our need for critical thinking. What philosophical thinking *is* "remains" a philosophical question, and what epistemology *is* "remains" an integral constituent of this question. How the *critical attitude* of the existential thinker implies freedom, a respectful distance and intersubjectivity will be examined in the final chapters of this book.

CHAPTER IX

EXISTENTIAL THINKING AND THE AESTHETIC PHENOMENON

THE NEED FOR TRANSCENDENCY

Let us now try to "illustrate" the transcendency of existential thinking by bringing our example, namely, "the phenomenon of beauty," from the immanency of pre-philosophical phenomenology to the transcendency of phenomenological *philosophy*. In other words, let us now by way of example try to "com-prehend" in the light of the *logos* the phenomenon of beauty which we have already perceived and described in the light of primordial wonder. Our attempt to get to an "original perception" of the aesthetic phenomenon has already resulted in the "self-presentation" of its "original essence." The term "original essence" here should be understood in the light of the pre-philosophical phenomenological reduction. The phenomenon of beauty has presented itself as a unique but complex phenomenon that reveals its structural characteristics and sufficiently differentiates itself from other related phenomena. It may be advisable at this point, despite the length of the quotation, to recall our previous findings concerning the original perception of the phenomenon of beauty.

"Whether I am listening to a beautiful symphony, or a grand vista captivates my eye, whether I am watching the sun sink away blood-red into the wide ocean, or find myself standing before a great cathedral, or breathlessly absorbed in a fascinating novel, my phenomenological analysis always reveals the same unitary phenomenon with the same structural characteristics. I always find that the matter-of-factness of everyday perception loses its obviousness and that a mysterious transparency takes its place. The beautiful object and my intimate self are grasped together in a blissful unity. Space becomes something ethereal and time turns into a reposeful now in which everything is simultaneous. I perceive my beautiful object in its concrete uniqueness as an inexhaustible and translucent fullness of existence to be enjoyed for its own sake. All the dimensions of my ex-sistence are involved in a ravishing harmony when I grasp together the symbolic unity of the individuality of my concrete object and the primordial depth of a cosmic universality. A delightful and awe-inspiring ecstacy makes me transcend the boundaries of my everyday perception, and a new world of wonder remains gravitated around the individual concreteness of my beautiful object."[224]

Although on the pre-philosophical level this brief phenomenological description may suffice, we certainly cannot rest here. The profound mysteriousness, the complexity and authentic sym-bolism of this description is really thought-provoking. Our wonder at beauty has not ceased. On the contrary, this wonder has become intensified to such a degree that the passage from ontic perception to ontological questioning becomes a spontaneous necessity. We feel compelled to ask ourselves a question which up to now has remained unasked: "What is beauty ultimately?" And with this fundamental question we have made the passage from the pre-philosophical phenomenological description to strictly philosophical thinking where phenomenology becomes a constituent of the *logos*. Since we have chosen the phenomenon of beauty merely as an example to demonstrate the unity-in-difference between the pre-philosophical and philosophical structure of phenomenology, we have to restrict our discussion again to some brief but basic observations.[225] We should remember, however, that the *logos* is never "applied" to a phenomenon, but that the *logos* rather invites a phenomenon to participate in its primordial inspiration. We, therefore, do not use the phenomenon of beauty as a mere example or a mere illustration of how a ready-made *logos* is applied to a phenomenon. On the contrary, our "example" enters into a living dialogue with the *logos* and is woven into the very texture of *logos*-thinking.[226]

Now, when we view the phenomenon of beauty in the light of the primordial inspiration of the *logos* its various structural elements converge in a single stroke into a new and fundamental context of meaning. When we put our phenomenological description of the original perception of beauty at the service of the primordial inspiration of the *logos,* then the *logos* in a sudden, spontaneous and inspired convergence of its ontological, phenomenological and dialectical aspects reveals this phenomenon in its onto-logical givenness within the primordial collectedness of Being. For, as we have seen, "phenomena are perceived in their *onto-logical* givenness only when they are com-prehended *in one single stroke* within the irreducible totality emerging from this primordial inspiration."[227] In the light of the primordial inspiration of the *logos* our original perception of beauty manifests itself in one single stroke as *that which brings "the" truth into being.* This sudden revelation, however, brings us also in one single stroke in a "critical" position. For immediately a host of disturbing questions begins to beleaguer us.

A CRITICAL TURNINGPOINT

Is not beauty rather than the truth the proper topic under discussion when we reflect on the aesthetic phenomenon? Is not the primary function of beauty to please, to provide us with relaxation and moral encouragement rather than to inform us about the truth? If "a thing of beauty is a joy for ever," then it certainly cannot be a textbook in philosophy! Does beauty, in fact, have anything at all to do with truth, let alone with *the* truth? Is not beauty a more or less effective emotive utterance, a pseudo-statement rather than a verifiable referential statement?[228]

These and similar questions and objections may spring to our mind at this point. And this is not surprising considering the "critical" nature of this moment. We found the actual beginning of philosophy to be a *decisive* moment in which our de-cision to hold on to the *logos* and to the original data ascertains philosophical authenticity, and prevents this critical "turning point" from going astray. Moreover, every step in philosophy re-begins this critical moment and re-kindles the whole of our fundamental questioning. Now, the encounter between the original immanency of the phenomenon of beauty and the inspirational transcendency of *logos*-thinking is precisely such a critical turning point. It shows that even on the ontological level the need for phenomenological reduction continues to be felt. Phenomenological reduction remains an integral constituent of existential thinking as criteriology. And it is evident that we are also on the ontological level in need of a "pre-view" of that which we are freeing our phenomenological thinking *for* in order to know what we have to free it *from*. On the ontological level phenomenological reduction should free itself for the primordial inspiration of the *logos,* and, therefore, eliminate whatever blocks the transcendency of our *logos*-thinking. Whereas pre-philosophical phenomenology aims at the *original perception* of phenomena in the *ontic* experience of primordial wonder, philosophical phenomenology aims at the *fundamental com-prehension* of original phenomena in the *ontological* thinking of the *logos*.

THE PRINCIPLE OF VERIFICATION

It goes without saying that on the level of philosophical phenomenology we are not trying to "prove" anything in the empirico-logical sense of the term *(beweisen)*. In *logos*-thinking the "critical self-verification" *(aufweisen)* is the proper "verification principle." It is within its dialogue with the *logos* that the original phenomenon of beauty receives its *fundamental* self-givenness, its irreducible and ever-growing self-evidence and the very possibility of its dynamic self-verification. The phenomenon of beauty is ontologically "veri-fied" or "made true" in its inspirational encounter with the *logos*. This, of course, is not to be understood in the conceptual sense of static essences, but rather in the fundamental sense of dynamic presences. The phenomenon of beauty, for instance, is never given once and for all as an "established fact" demonstrated by an external criterion of meaningfulness. On the contrary, the original phenomenon of beauty reveals its self-givenness more and more, becomes more and more self-present, is continually made truer by its dynamic participation in the *logos* as the fundamental universe of discourse. *This ontological "critical self-veri-fication" is precisely the dialectical task of philosophical phenomenology.* In other words, existential thinking is its own veri-fication principle. We know that in modern positivistic and analytic philosophies this verification principle is used in a more restricted sense.[229] Now, it is precisely in the light of this restricted use that the above mentioned questions and objections against "beauty as the birth of truth" have originated. This restricted use of the verification principle is in various ways inspired by the natural scientific methods of verifying scientific data. This verification principle has a legitimate place within the realm of scientific and ob-jectifying thinking. But to extend its use beyond the realm of objectifying thinking and to regard it as the only and ultimate criterion of all meaningfulness entails the arrogation to philosophical ultimacy of merely scientific thinking. This arrogation is the illogical and self-contradictory dogma of "scientism" which we have exposed over and over again in the earlier chapters of this book. There is no need here to repeat our refutations of "scientistic" (not "scientific") thinking.[230] With respect to our phenomenon of beauty, it would be scientifically correct to call this phenomenon "unverifiable," *scientifically* unverifiable, that is. But to deduce from this that the phenomenon of beauty is utterly unrelated to *any* questions concerning the truth, to reduce the phenomenon of beauty to a merely subjective commentary, to a merely emotive utterance or to a pseudo-statement is itself a pseudo-philosophical statement based on an illegitimate and "scientistic" contraction of our experiential world. Once we have eliminated this pseudo-philosophical verification principle, or should we say, once we have broadened and deepened this principle into its ontological dimensions, the above mentioned objections against any relationship between beauty and truth can be discarded.

A DIALOGUE BETWEEN ONTIC AND ONTOLOGICAL PHENOMENOLOGY

We are now prepared to begin our brief re-flection on the phenomenon of beauty on the level of strictly *philosophical* phenomenology as an integral constituent of *logos*-thinking. In the light of the *logos* the whole configuration of the aesthetic phenomenon assumes in a single stroke a *fundamental* meaning through a sudden, spontaneous and overwhelming inspiration. Suddenly the structural characteristics of our original perception of the phenomenon of beauty reveal their fundamental meaning as part of a whole, and the whole phenomenon of beauty falls into place in the totality of all that is. Beauty as we have described it phenomenologically on the pre-philosophical level manifests itself on the philosophical level as *the truth which brings-itself-to-stand in a being.* Beauty is the pure disclosure of Being in the primordial concreteness of an entity. Beauty is the emergence of the extra-ordinary world of primordial inspiration within the ordinary world of our workaday existence. In traditional terminology, beauty is the self-manifestation of spirit in matter. It goes without saying that the terms "spirit" and "matter" here should not be understood in their dualistic sense of respectively "soul substance" and "pure quantity," but rather as the primordial openness to Being and its correlative: primordial concealment.

Beauty is the truth which brings-itself-to-stand in a being.[231] As we have seen, however, this original inspiration will evaporate if it is not "worked out." Philosophy *is* the "working out" of the primordial inspiration of the *logos*. The working out of our *logos*-inspiration concerning beauty will be only brief and sketchy. For it will merely serve as an example of the dialogue between pre-philosophical and philosophical phenomenology in existential thinking. Beauty is the truth which brings-itself-to-stand in a being. In this sudden inspiration the whole phenomenon of beauty falls into place in the totality of all that is. As we have seen, the original perception of the aesthetic phenomenon reveals beauty as the emergence of the primordial World of Wonder in the ordinary world of our workaday existence. In the light of the *logos* we know primordial wonder to be the birthplace of *the truth of Being* as unconcealment or *aletheia*. Now, it is in the sudden inspiration of *logos*-

thinking that beauty manifests its ontological presence and sets itself apart from related fundamental phenomena. In the light of *logos* inspiration beauty manifests itself as the pure disclosure of the truth of Being in the ordinary world of entities, or as the truth which brings-itself-to-stand in a being. And as that which "arrests" Being beauty sets itself apart from philosophy which "thinks" Being and from ethical existence which "lets it become."[232]

THE AESTHETIC PHENOMENON IN THE LIGHT OF THE *Logos*

The Mysterious Transparency of Beauty

Now, it is in the light of the same *logos*-inspiration that the structural characteristics of beauty reveal their fundamental meaning and their original interconnectedness in the totality of the aesthetic phenomenon. *To begin with,* to understand beauty as the emergence of the mystery of Being in our everyday existence makes it ontologically intelligible that in beauty "the matter-of-factness of our everyday existence loses its obviousness." Moreover, during our discussion of the *logos* we found that the mystery of Being revealed itself in the ontological dimension, which is the primordial dimension of depth. Now, it is precisely the understanding of the mystery of Being as primordial depth which makes it fundamentally meaningful that beauty not only transcends our everyday obviousness but also that in beauty "a mysterious transparency takes its place."

Aesthetic Sym-bolism

Secondly, the understanding of beauty as the emergence of the mystery of Being in our everyday existence presents us with a fundamental insight into some other structural characteristics of beauty. For instance, in the aesthetic phenomenon "the beautiful object and our intimate self are grasped together." Now, as we have seen, the mystery of Being is experiential and involves the whole of our ex-sistence. The experiential gift of wonder transcends the subject-object dichotomy. Beauty, therefore is never the merely subjective "experiencing" of an object, nor is it exclusively inherent in merely objective values. We transcend the traditional theories of beauty insofar as they have oscillated between merely subjective experiencing and the beholding of purely objective values. Beauty is rather a "wondering-standing-in-the-world" in which beauty comes neither from "within," nor from "without," but arises as a mode of this Being-in-the-world. And this reminds us of the fact that the aesthetic phenomenon is our "original perception."[233] Our original perception reveals the natural world as it truly *is*, i.e. as it "presents itself" in the primordial world of Being. Our original perception, therefore, is always sym-bolic in the fundamental sense of the term, for in it the world of the usual and the un-usual world of wonder are "thrown together" in their "aesthetic di-stance." Now, the all-encompassing inspiration of wonder reveals itself only in the act in which it is fully received. And this is the very openness of the whole of our human ex-sistence, and not the act of any particular human faculty. In other words, "all the dimensions of our ex-sistence are involved in a ravishing harmony when we grasp together the sym-bolic unity of the individuality of our concrete object and the primordial depth of a cosmic universality."

Aesthetic Joy

Thirdly, in the aesthetic phenomenon the beautiful object and the beholding self are grasped together in a "blissful" unity. This becomes ontologically meaningful in the light of the fact that the mystery of Being is an overwhelming, gratuitous and inspirational experience. "Bliss" is an overwhelming joy, true happiness or heavenly rapture.[234] In beauty we are experientially affected by the transcendent joy and fascination of the overwhelming mystery of Being. This is true "happiness" as the experiential "happening" of the truth of Being.[235] In primordial wonder the truth of Being "happens" experientially as a fundamental "happiness." This "overwhelming" joy of the mystery of Being is the "blissfulness" of beauty which escapes our controlling attitude. "We are," writes Josef Pieper, "whenever happiness comes our way, the recipients of something unforeseen, something unforseeable, and therefore not subject to planning and intention. Happiness is essentially a gift; we are not the forgers of our own felicity."[236] True happiness, however, is never an "unmixed blessing." And this for a twofold reason, due to the twofold concealment of the truth of Being.[237] The mystery of Being, as we have seen, reveals itself only as concealed, as co-original with Nothingness which Heidegger calls "the veil of Being."[238] Authentic happiness, therefore, is permeated with authentic non-happiness. Authentic happiness is co-original with existential (not pathological) anxiety, with the awe-fulness of the mystery of Being.[239] Authentic happiness is not for the weak but for the strong and the courageous. "Courage," says Paul Tillich, "is self-affirmation 'in spite of,' namely in spite of nonbeing."[240] In addition, as we have also seen, Being reveals itself only in a "dia-logue" with beings. In this fundamental "con-flict" or "strife" there is even a certain drifting away from the very mystery of

Being which is nonetheless a constitutive element of its true self-manifestation. True happiness, therefore, is not only in an existential tension with its concealment, with non-happiness, but also with its derivative modes such as sensory pleasure, physical well-being etc. Now, in the *aesthetic joy* this twofold conflict is preserved and arrested, and remains rooted in the twofold strife of the truth of Being. Aesthetic joy, then, is neither purely spiritual happiness nor a mere titillation of the senses, but an essential and arrested "con-flict" of both in the primordial depth of their aesthetic di-stance. This arrested conflict is not a struggle in which the partners try to annihilate one another. On the contrary, this conflict is "ex-sistential," and con-stitutes the very self-affirmation of its respective partners. An intensification of this conflict does not destroy the aesthetic experience, but it rather intensifies its arrested dynamism. Thus aesthetic joy is least of all "sheer pleasure," "comfortable relaxation" or a delicacy for the connoisseur and the aesthete. Aesthetic joy is rather the arrested conflict between happiness and non-happiness on the one hand, and between happiness and its sensory derivatives on the other. In other words, aesthetic joy is "the sensory expression of the intimate gratuitousness of ex-sistence."[241] or the "delightful and awe-inspiring ecstacy which makes man transcend the boundaries of his everyday perception."

Aesthetic Spatiality

Fourthly, spatiality and temporality as perceived in the aesthetic phenomenon differ notably both from our geometrical conception of space and time and from the lived perception of space and time in our everyday existence. We found that in beauty "space becomes something ethereal and time turns into a reposeful now in which everything is simultaneous." The mysteriousness of aesthetic space and time is provocative and invites us to dwell on this point with some greater length. On the one hand, aesthetic space is no longer the mere context of the different places of the "environment" of our everyday concerns, such as a place to eat, a place to sleep, a place to work, etc. On the other hand, aesthetic space has nothing at all to do with the pure abstraction of the absolute space of Newtonian physics.

The spatiality of our "environment" is characterized by the "distance" of the things in our "surrounding" world. This di-stance is determined by the nearness of that which is ready-to-hand to our everyday concern, and not at all in terms of mathematical measurement. When, for instance, a scholar is walking along a street, environmentally his shoes are more "remote" from him than the bookstore across the street, although mathematically speaking the reverse is true. The spatiality of our environment is neither a quality of surrounding things, nor a property of man as a human subject, but rather a structural characteristic of our everyday "being-in-the-world." This everyday "being-in-the-world" is the dynamic context of manifold places "di-stanced" (held apart) by our concernful "ex-sistence" (standing-apart). The spatiality of our environment is not the sum total of all spaces, of all "heres" and all "theres." On the contrary, all spaces, all "heres" and "theres" are only possible as differentiations of the structural totality of our concernful being-in-the-world. "When we let entities within-the-world be encountered in the way which is constitutive for Being-in-the-world, we 'give them space'. This 'giving space', which we also call 'making room' for them, consists in freeing the ready-to-hand for its spatiality."[242] This "making room" is a structural characteristic of everyday ex-sistence. This everyday ex-sistence occupies space in the sense of spatializing what it occupies. Now, in aesthetic space we transcend the space of the everyday world in wonder. The all-encompassing presence of primordial Being reveals a fundamental omnipresence which transcends any sort of "space-for." We will soon return to this.

As contrasted with the space of our everyday existence, the "abstract" conception of the three-dimensional *absolute space* of classical physics is not really perceived. It is not really a "surrounding" world, or, for that matter, a "world" at all. For absolute space is the *absolute objectification*[243] of phenomenal or "lived" space which is the dynamic context of places distanced by our concernful ex-sistence. Absolute space, therefore, would be the absolute "op-posite" of the unitary structure of lived space as ec-static being-in-the-world. Consequently, absolute space would be the absolute lack of unity, of structure, of dynamism, of world and of Being. Absolute space would be the absolute multiplicity of discrete "world-points," absolute homogeneity, absolute passivity, absolute isotropy and absolute self-alienation. In other words, absolute space would be the absolute absence of world and Being, it would be *absolute nothingness*.[244] The absolute objectification of space turns the ob-jects into mathematical "world-points." Absolute ob-jects are no longer related to a sub-ject, they are absolutely standing-over-against-the perceiving sub-ject, they are the absolute opposite of the perceiving ex-sistence and escape all possible perception. Absolute ob-servation is "holding-the-ob-ject" at an infinite di-stance. An absolute ob-ject, therefore, ceases to be an ob-ject at all, and absolute observation is no longer a "perceiving" ob-servation. The ob-ject no longer manifests itself, becomes the vanishing point of being and is reduced to the mere abstraction of a "world-point." Implicit in these points, according to Ulrich Sonnemann, "is the abstraction of facticity itself, the unreality of nothing-but-objects inasmuch as de-phenomenalization has reduced them to mere occupants of such points."[245] Absolute space is neither "the container of all objects," nor "our 'real' space par excellence." The absolute space of classical science cannot be perceived at all, it results from an abstractive contruction of the mind. The perception of absolute space would be a blind gazing into the eternal silence of the night of nothingness. The observer of absolute space would be absolutely de-tached and dis-interested since he would completely have lost his concernful involvement. For him there would be no environment, no di-stance, no per-spective, no depth and no world. It goes without saying that the wondrous phenomenon of aesthetic spatiality has nothing to do with the classical conception of absolute space.

Aesthetic Distance and Primordial Depth

The question of space is a question of di-stance, of per-spective and depth. Distance has been viewed most often as a negative phenomenon. This is a mistake. Di-stance as existential unity-in-opposition implies by necessity both ontological nearness and ontological farness. Insofar as "di-*stance*" is an actual "standing" in the presence of the structural "unity" of ex-sistence, there is ontological "nearness." Insofar as "*di*-stance" is the ex-sistential "standing-*apart*" of the unitary structure of ex-sistence, there is ontological "*remoteness.*" Di-stance as the unity-in-opposition of the near and the remote is *a structural characteristic of the ec-static nature of ex-sistence.* And the *mode* of ex-sistence determines the *mode* of di-stance, the *mode* of per-spective and space of a given situation. Absolute space as the infinite multiplicity of absolute discrete world-points has no unity-in-opposition whatsoever. Absolute space lacks per-spective, lacks all di-stance, any sort of farness and nearness. Mathematical points are neither close nor remote. But, then, it is characteristic of absolute space that it docs not exist.[246] The mode of di-stance in the space of our "surrounding" world is obviously characterized by its "closeness." This closeness, however, is not determined by geometrical measurements, but rather by our familiar tasks and positions, the use of our tools, our particular concerns which articulate our everyday world according to our "particular" needs and interests. We are always involved in "places for something."

In contrast, in the mysterious spatiality of the aesthetic phenomenon a new dimension opens up which is the di-stance of the primordial depth of wonder. Wonder is not differentiated in "places for some-thing," nor does it have its parts "outside one another" as the tradi-tional definition of quantitative space reads. On the contrary, we have encountered wonder as the "oceanic experience." Here the totality of all that is is given, and the totality of all that is remains in suspense. Everything becomes at the same time *infinitely remote* and *infinitely close*. And one's being is reduced to a drop in the infinite ocean while at the same time the ocean is contained by the drop. Things can no longer be localized in our familiar space and time, but they seem to be freely floating while they are drawn into the whirlpool of a mysterious omnipresence.[247] The spatiality which opens up in beauty is not the di-stance of the horizontal depth of our everyday existence, but rather the vertical depth of primordial Being, the interiorizing self-transcendency of wonder in which the intimate nearness and the profound remoteness of all that is fuse into one. A "cosmic sympathy" is born. The space which opens up in the aesthetic phenomenon is the very "open-ness" of the comprehensive universality of primordial wonder. It is this all-encompassing universality of Being which reveals everything within its "omni-presence" and in which everything is everywhere. And this is why the *logos* as the dialectical self-manifestation of Being *in-gathers* all that is in its primordial *to-gether-ness*. Moreover, in the spatiality of beauty the "solidity" of our environmental space is transcended. Origi-nal spatiality as the "dis-closure" of primordial Being "dis-locates" our ordinary perception of the common patterns of everyday spatiality. Original spatiality as the "mysterious transparency" of the primordial depth of wonder manifests itself in beauty as a strange, wondrous and "ethereal" sort of space. "One small part of the world," we quoted Maslow as saying, "is perceived as if it were for the moment all the world."[248] Or, as Thoreau once remarked, "I have traveled a good deal in Concord." All this has a deep ontological significance. For beauty "con-tains" space in the sense that it "holds-together" the original "con-flict" between the segmental space of our environment and the cosmic openness of original spatiality. In this con-flict the "aesthetic di-stance" comes to a stand. The revelation of original space makes us aware of the fact that we are not spatialized on the basis of our *body* alone, but rather on the basis of our "Being-in-the-world."[249] We are not "spatial-ized" in the passive sense of an "established fact," but rather "spatial-izing" in the active sense of "opening up a world." Bullough in his discussion of "aesthetic distance" was right when he spoke of "the *action* of distance."[250] It is, therefore, neither in the absolute space of classical science, nor in the lived space of everyday existence that origi-

nal space manifests itself, but in the mysterious openness of the aesthetic phenomenon. In beauty original spatiality manifests itself as "the
opening up" of the primordial depth of Being in a unity-in-opposition
with the ordinary space of our everyday existence. Fundamentally
speaking, therefore, it would be incorrect to say that we "have" space
or are "in" space. It would be better to say that we "are" spatiality, or,
that we are "spatializing." Or, better still, in our reflection on the
spatiality of beauty we have discovered that original spatiality *has us.*

Primordial Temporality

Fifthly, the strange and fascinating phenomenon of aesthetic temporality will lead us to an analogous discussion. On the one hand, aesthetic temporality is no longer our "having time for" the various
activities and involvements of our everyday existence, such as "a time
for work," "a time for eating," "a time for relaxation," etc. On the
other hand, aesthetic temporality has nothing to do with the traditional
abstractive thinking of time as an infinite sequence of instantaneous
"nows" that successively come along and pass away. Just as in aesthetic
spatiality we transcend any derivative form of space and first encounter
primordial spatiality, so also in aesthetic temporality we transcend any
derivative form of time and witness the birth of primordial temporality.
It is in the light of *primordial temporality* that the derivative forms of
time become fundamentally intelligible and that aesthetic temporality
reveals its ontological significance.

In fact, primordial time was already tacitly assumed in our elucidation of primordial spatiality as "the 'opening up' of the primordial
depth of Being." For, as we have seen,[251] the primordial depth of Being
is our primordial di-stance. This di-stance is our authentic ex-sistence as
original emergence, as original "going beyond." And this "going beyond" is not a "going outside" in a quantitative sense, but rather a
"being one's own beyond," in which the "here" and the "there", the
"now" and the "then," the "close" and the "far" merge. Now, this
"going beyond" of primordial depth, is, as we have also seen,[252] the
coming towards *(future)* one's primary data *(past)* as dis-closure of the
fundamental situation *(present)* of authentic ex-sistence. In other
words, primordial temporality is authentic ex-sistence which "presents
itself" *(present)* as being continually "ahead-of-itself" *(future)* into its
own "original potentiality" *(past).* Also existential thinking as the
thinking of authentic ex-sistence is temporal. It "presents itself" by its
continual "coming towards" its "having been." Primordial temporality
is the "circular ec-stacy," the "interiorizing self-transcendency" or the

"primordial *dis*-closure" of Being. Or, as Heidegger puts it, *"Temporality is the primordial 'outside-of-itself' in and for itself.* We therefore call the phenomena of the future, the character of having been, and the Present, the *'ecstases'* of temporality."[253] This "outside-of-itself" of primordial temporality is, of course, neither the absolute outside of one another of an infinite succession of separate "now-points," nor the outside of one another of our intra-temporal "time-for's" of the daily concerns in our "surrounding" world. The "outside-of-itself" of primordial temporality is the "outside-of-itself" of primordial depth in which the past, the present and the future merge, in which these ecstases are *co-original,* simultaneous and gathered into their original to-gether-ness. To quote Heidegger again, "Temporalizing does not signify that ecstases come in a 'succession'. The future is *not later* than having been, and having been is *not earlier* than the Present. Temporality temporalizes itself as a future which makes present in the process of having been."[254] And by now it should be evident that also primordial spatiality and temporality are co-original, and that we never encounter the one without the other. Primordial spatiality is the "opening up" of the primordial depth of Being as temporalizing. The *logos* is the dwelling-place (spatiality) of temporalizing Being (temporality). What the space-time continuum is for the natural sciences, is the spatio-temporal nature of the *logos* for existential thinking.

Primordial Temporality and Ordinary Time

According to our ordinary conception of time we say that a present event will soon be "a thing of the past," implying thereby that "in the course of time" it will become more and more ab-sent, more and more distant. And "out of sight, out of mind." In the "dis-course" of primordial temporality, however, the *logos* "holds on" to the past as its future possibility. Also here the past becomes more and more past. But this no longer implies becoming more and more distant and absent. On the contrary, the "past" as the "having been" of primordial temporality becomes more and more "present," more and more Being. The authentic past as primary origin becomes more and more "origin-al." Primordial temporality is no longer a fleeting succession of past, present and future "nows," but rather the dynamic and circular ec-stacy of the differentiated self-disclosure of primordial wonder. It is only in unity with its past and future potentialities that Being "presents" itself. The authentic "present," therefore, is never a mere "moment-point," or an absolute "now," but rather the *out-standing movement of primordial dis-closure,* or, as Heidegger calls it, "the moment of vision."[255] The authentic present as the "moment of vision" does not pass away in the course of time as one "now" in an endless sequence of nows that continually arise and pass away without leaving a trace. On the contrary, the authentic present as the "moment of vision" is an integral constituent of the self-temporalizing dis-closure of primordial Being. And, as such, it does not pass away, but becomes more and more "present," it becomes a more and more *out-standing movement* which "pro-motes" the very dis-closure of Being.

As contrasted with primordial temporality, the ordinary time of our "everyday" existence remains unconcerned with the primordial depth of Being. In our "everyday environment"[256] we understand ourselves in terms of our daily work and of the tools required for its fulfillment. Here we have to "use" time effectively, to "take" time for important occupations, and to make sure that we don't "lose" time. In our workaday world, therefore, we have to "reckon with time." Also our ordinary time is experienced in terms of the concernful involvements of our daily occupations and the respective tools to be employed, and not in terms of either primordial Being or mathematical measurements. We may have two hours of "clock-time" without "having time for" a particular visitor because we have a previous engagement elsewhere. Moreover, each of our everyday involvements has its own time. "Now" it is time for working, "earlier" it was time for sleeping, and "later" it will be time for relaxation, etc.

The ordinary time of our workaday world is "lived" and "used," but it is hardly known *as such*. We are only dimly aware that the "present now" is always a "now it is time for," and that this "present now" is our privileged time, our "real" time par excellence. We are also only dimly aware that this "present now" does not stand apart, but that it opens up the horizon of the "earlier" (past "now") and the "later" (future "now"). Both past and future are understood in terms of the "present now" which is not an absolute "time-point," but rather a letting things "present" themselves in the perspective of our daily involvements. In the light of the spatio-temporal nature of the *logos,* however, these vaguely perceived structures of our ordinary time become ontologically significant. Whereas our everyday world conceals the primordial World of Being, it remains nevertheless a derivative form of authentic ex-sistence. Its basic structure is retained, albeit in an unauthentic way. Thus our ordinary time conceals primordial temporality, but it never dissolves into an "endless sequence of 'nows'." Whereas the primordial ecstases of temporality arise from the *interiorizing* self-transcendency or the vertical depth of Being, the time-dimensions of the fragmentized world of our daily existence result from the *exteriorizing* self-transcendency or the horizontal distance of our concernful involvements. This does not dissolve time, but it exteriorizes it. The "present now" is never an "absolute" now in the sense that it is unrelated to any other time or space dimensions. On the contrary, the "present now" is always relational, it is always given in connection with a "no-longer-now" (past) which it retains, and a "not-yet-now" (future) which it awaits. Moreover, the "present now" is never isolated from space either, since it is encountered in the objects of our "environmental" involvements. It precisely consists in making these objects present, or better, in letting them "present" themselves to our daily concerns. As we will see shortly, an "absolute now" could never be perceived, neither in itself nor in succession. Heidegger sums it all up in the following statement: "Saying 'now' . . . is the discursive articulation of a *making-present* which temporalizes itself in a unity with a retentive awaiting."[257] Both primordial temporality and the time of our workaday world dis-close the "being-ahead-of-itself" of ex-sistence. Both relate to spatiality, both reveal an ec-static unity of past, present and future, both are structural characteristics of our entire being-in-the-world. Nevertheless they temporalize themselves in essentially different ways. Primordial temporality by dis-closing the primordial depth of the World of Being in an interiorizing self-transcendency. Our ordinary time by concealing primordial temporality and thus forgetting its own roots in an exteriorizing self-transcendency. Yet, our ordinary time is not the absolute opposite of primordial temporality. On the contrary, our ordinary time retains the structure of primordial temporality in an unauthentic way. It is ontologically understood as a *derivative* form of temporality which temporalizes the fragmentized world of our everyday ex-sistence.

Primordial Temporality and Absolute Time

What is really the absolute opposite of primordial temporality is the *absolute time* of Newtonian physics. Absolute time is an endless succession of absolute "now-points," in which the "present now" is nowhere and arises out of the "not-yet-now" (future) which is nowhere and immediately passes away into the "no-longer-now" (past) which is nowhere. In absolute time the ec-static unity of past, present and future, and the spatio-temporal structure of primordial temporality gets completely lost in a "pure" succession of insignificant "now-points." Ontologically this means that absolute time is the absolute op-posite, or *absolute objectification* of primordial temporality. What we said concerning absolute space also applies, *mutatis mutandis,* to absolute time. Absolute time would be the absolute op-posite of the unitary structure of experiential temporality as dynamic and ec-static being-in-the-world. Consequently, absolute time would be absolute lack of unity, of structure, of dynamism, of world and of Being. In other words, absolute time would be the absolute multiplicity of discrete moments, the absolute "outside-of-one-another" of an infinite number of meaningless "time-points." Absolute time would be characterized by its absolute homogeneity, its absolute passivity and isotropy, its absolute absence of structure and of Being. Absolute time would be the absolute "outside-of-itself" of temporality, it would be "absolute nothingness." The absolute objectification of temporality deprives actual "moments" (L. *momentum*—movement) of their movement, and turns them into static, discrete and absolutely abstract "now-points," or into a blind sequence of "punctiform" instants. Speaking of such instants, Henri Bergson says: "You could never create time out of such instants any more than you could make a line out of mathematical points."[258]

As absolute ob-jects these mathematical "now-points" of absolute time are absolutely standing-over-against the perceiving sub-ject and escape all possible perception. Such an "absolute now" becomes the vanishing point of "real" time which is dissolved into the mere abstraction of a pure succession of "time-points," which symbolize the negative infinity of absolute nothingness. Consequently, as contrasted with the experiential nature of temporality, the "absolute now" cannot be perceived at all. And if this holds true of an "absolute now," then it must be *a fortiori* true of a "pure succession" of such "nows." Such a pure succession, moreover, would be self-contradictory. For an "absolute now" is precisely a "now" that would be considered as unrelated to either the past or the future. It would be by definition a "now-without-succession." The passing away of an "absolute now" would become a pure annegation of itself, a total destruction of "presence," or a schizophrenic loss of orientation to reality. The implication is that our "actual present" is never an "absolute now," but that it is only "present" when it is experienced within the horizon of a past and a future.[259]

Absolute Time and Clock-time

Absolute time and ordinary time are worlds apart. Nevertheless, our customary *conception* of ordinary time tends towards an objectification of it. And this for at least three interrelated reasons. In the first place, ordinary time is perceived through the objects that present themselves to our everyday concerns. Thus our ordinary time itself is easily mistaken for something like an object or a thing. In our everyday existence we are inclined to model our conception of time upon beings-within-the-world rather than upon Being-in-the-world. Secondly, one important "use" of time is to employ it as a "means" to regulate "public life." "Public time" is no longer one's own time, or the "lived" time of one's everyday existence, but it is a time which applies to "everybody, no matter whom." Public time, therefore, has to be "exact" time, it has to conform to the accuracy of mathematical measurement. And this entails the *objectification* of the time of our everyday existence. The concrete time of the "lived" presence in our workaday world turns into the abstract time of the "countable nows" of mechanical "clock-time." Due to the universality of its usage "clock-time" is normally mistaken for *the* time. Thirdly, the fact that scientism or the absolutism of objectifying thinking has become part and parcel of our "natural world" reinforces the danger of confusing time with "clock-time." Nevertheless, it should be noted that although public time approximates absolute time, it is not identical with it. Henri Bergson was right in warning us against mistaking the measurement of time for the reality of time. On the other hand we should also be warned against the opposite mistake of altogether divorcing measurement from reality. Absolute measurement measures absolutely nothing. For measurement also is a measuring-being-in-the-world.[260]

From all this it follows that "clock-time" is still a minimal being-in-the-world, and, therefore, as public time still a minimum of time. This fact is reflected in the characteristics of "clock-time" that would remain unintelligible in terms of absolute time. For example, in clock-time there are on the one hand the "continuity," the "irreversibility" and the "activity" of the hands as "*traveling* pointers," and on the other hand the "presence" of the hands as "traveling *pointers*." These characteristics are only intelligible when public time is regarded as a derivative form of temporality. They would be completely unintelligible, however, in the light of the absolute multiplicity, isotropy, passivity and total lack of spatiality of absolute time.[261]

It was Leibniz who first criticized Newton's conception of absolute space and time. Time, for Leibniz, is not the absolute container of all possible events any more than space is the absolute container of all possible objects. Newton was wrong in treating them as subsisting entities. For Leibniz they are *"phenomena bene fundata,"* well-founded phenomena. Indeed, space and time rather than being absolute entities are *relative* phenomena in several interdependent ways. First, they are not independent, absolute containers, but structural characteristics of the dis-closure of ex-sistence. And as such they are *related* to and firmly rooted in this ex-sistence ("well-founded phenomena"). Secondly, as structural characteristics of the dis-closure of ex-sistence both space and time are modes of being-in-the-world. Consequently, space and time are *interrelated*. They are not only related to ex-sistence, but also to one another. Thirdly, space and time are not exclusively characteristics of the "external" world or of the world of "objects." For the world of "objects" always relates to a world of "subjects." This relationship is an encounter which is only possible on the basis of a spatio-temporal situation which comes neither from "within" nor from "without" but arises as a mode of "being-in-the-world."

Primordial Temporality and Aesthetic Temporality

We are now prepared for a brief elucidation of the wondrous phenomenon of *aesthetic temporality*. It goes without saying that this experiential phenomenon has nothing to do with the objectifications of time, that it has nothing to do with either clock-time or absolute time. In the aesthetic temporality, however, we also transcend the mere "reckoning with" time of our everyday existence. The "time-for's" of our daily concerns are transcended by the "out-standing moment of primordial dis-closure."

In the aesthetic temporality a new dimension opens up which is the "circular ec-stacy," the "interiorizing self-transcendency" or the "original dis-closure" or primordial wonder. In the aesthetic temporality we witness the birth of primordial temporality. It is in the primordial depth of this temporality that the past, the present and the future merge, that these ecstacies are co-original, simultaneous and gathered in their original to-gether-ness. In primordial wonder itself, however, the ecstacies of temporality are not yet differentiated. In this all-encompassing but undifferentiated phenomenon the past, the present and the future fuse into the unique "moment of wonder" implicitly presenting the interiorizing simultaneity of original "movement."

The ontological significance of aesthetic temporality is that it "contains" or "holds-together" the original "con-flict" between environmental time and primordial temporality. In this con-flict the action of "aesthetic di-stance" comes to a stand, and the "moment" (*momentum—* movement) becomes an "ar-rested movement." Aesthetic temporality is no longer cut up in fleeting moments, but it has become an "ar-rested movement" or a "repose-ful now in which everything is simultaneous." An ar-rested movement is no more a dead movement than an arrested man is a dead man. An ar-rested movement is not a mere motionless moment, but rather a "resting movement." A resting movement is a "resting-in-itself," a "gathering-in-peace" which is the highest form of movement precisely in the absence of all "locomotion." A moment of beauty dis-closes the inexhaustible movement of primordial depth.

A Useless "Waste of Time"?

In beauty this unique and inexhaustible fullness of primordial depth is something "to be enjoyed for its own sake." To many of us, however, such an experience would seem to be a "useless waste of time." And at this point we might be tempted to try to demonstrate the usefulness of the aesthetic phenomenon, or, for that matter, of existential thinking which is a fundamental reflection on original perception. Such an attempt, however, would be both futile and unphilosophical. It would be futile because beauty and philosophy *are* useless. It would be unphilosophical because it would rest on the pseudo-philosophical dogma of our functionalized world which states that usefulness is the ultimate end and criterion of all action and meaning.

What has to be shown is not the usefulness of beauty and philosophy, but rather the pre-eminence of non-utilitarian Being. Since utilitarianism is a characteristic of the absolutism of the controlling frame of mind, we have already exposed its pseudo-philosophical dogmatism. Here we could add that questions such as "what can you do with it?" or "what is it good for?" have no answer when they are asked about beauty and philosophy. Questions such as these are also typical of beginning "liberal arts" students, and betray their still calculative and subjectivistic frame of mind. The attempt on the part of the professor to enumerate some possible useful purposes of philosophy and beauty might reinforce the student's utilitarian way of thinking. On the other hand, to declare that beauty and philosophy "serve no purpose" and "are good for nothing" will drive the student into despair. For statements such as these mean to him that he is taking the course "for nothing," and that he is "wasting his time." One might be able to avoid either horn of the dilemma by simply stating that one has to delay one's answer because it would require a much deeper philosophical background on the part of the student. In due time the student will discover the answer to his utilitarian question from his very own response to the primordial inspiration of Being. This "due time" will be "primordial temporality" as the "inspirational dis-closure of wonder." This primordial temporality first opens up in the aesthetic phenomenon, and becomes explicated and differentiated in the course of existential thinking. It is here that the student discovers that the primordial inspiration of temporality *tran-*

scends the time we *have,* and that this "out-standing moment of primor-dial dis-closure" cannot be understood in terms of "time . . . . . for," or in terms of time that can be "used" or "wasted." It is here that the student will understand that it is more correct to say that primordial temporality *has us,* and that he will gain an experiential awareness of the profound remark made by Martin Heidegger: "granted that *we* can-not do anything with philosophy, might not philosophy, if we concern ourselves with it, do something *with us?*"[262]

What really results in "wasted time" is not the temporality of beauty and philosophy, but rather the dogmatic belief in the ultimate useful-ness of time. For it gets us involved in a nihilistic conception of "prog-ress" that actually gets us "nowhere." Long ago Aristotle wrote, that if we "did not desire something for its own sake," instead of choosing everything for the sake of something else, "the process would go on to infinity, so that our desire would be empty and vain."[263] The *activity neurosis* attending our modern activism results from such an exclusive belief in infinite progress which leaves us fundamentally empty. It is not so much a "clinical neurosis," but rather a *nooneurosis,* or "an existen-tial despair over the meaning of life."[264] The "dis-ease" of activism cannot be cured unless we are willing to accept the non-utilitarian inspiration of primordial wonder, and to transcend the workaday world.

Now it is precisely in the aesthetic phenomenon that primordial won-der frees us from our total submergence in the world of work and keeps us "wondering in the face of the world." It is in the aesthetic phenome-non that this fragmentized world is transcended, and that a new world of wonder remains gravitated around the individual concreteness of the beautiful object. Our rootedness in this all-encompassing inspiration is not useless or time wasted. For it keeps our ex-sistence "hale," our philosophy "healthy," our love "wholesome" and our religion "holy."[265]

This brief onto-logical re-flection on the aesthetic phenomenon should suffice to give us an example of the dia-logue between pre-philosophical and philosophical phenomenology. It has also demon-strated that the primordial inspiration of the *logos* sets all things at one single stroke in their primordial to-gether-ness, and that at the same time this inspiration has continually to be worked out in our existential thinking. It has also shown the mysterious fusion in existential thinking of immanency and transcendency, of hard work and primordial inspira-tion, of the ordinary and the extraordinary. In fact, our example has shown that a philosophical example is never merely an example in the sense of an "illustration." A philosophical example is essentially an integral constituent of the actual way of access to Being in which we are involved with the whole of our ex-sistence.

BEAUTY OF ART AND BEAUTY OF NATURE

We could not terminate our example, however, without raising one more issue concerning beauty from the phase of pre-philosophical phenomenology to the level of *logos*-thinking. As was pointed out in the previous chapter, a "radical" distinction between *beauty of art* and *beauty of nature* would violate the original givenness of these phenomena.[266] At first blush beauty of art and beauty of nature seem to be radically different, since the former is man-made and the latter is not. A superficial and prejudiced phenomenology would describe beauty of art as a product manu-factured by man, containing representational symbolism, and beauty of nature as a non-symbolic, self-contained natural thing untouched by the human hand. Existential thinking, however, which is a thinking "in depth" and never a mere fascination with the surface, cuts across this radical dichotomy between both forms of beauty.

Although the words "nature" and "art" are the distinctive marks of these forms of beauty, if they are taken in the restricted sense of their possible "dependency on human activity," they do not define the "beauty" of these respective forms. And, consequently, these marks do not create a radical dichotomy between beauty of art and beauty of nature. This we have to examine more carefully.

VARIOUS MEANINGS OF THE TERM "NATURE"

In the first place, it is a well-known fact that the word "nature" has undergone many historical shifts of meaning causing a great variety of meanings in our present-day usage.[267] A full account of all these meanings would require a whole book, and will, of course, not be attempted here. But a few points must be made. It should be noted that the term "nature" in the sense of "that which is independent of human activity" does not exhaust the usage of the term. We can, for instance, meaningfully ask questions such as: "What is the nature of art?" or "What is the nature of human activity?" or, for that matter, "What is the nature of nature?" Here it is evident that "nature" as "that which is independent of human activity" is taken in a derivative and restricted sense, which is neither historically nor experientially the original meaning of the term.

The Original Sense

For, when we ask ourselves the question "What is the *nature* of that which is independent of human activity?," we ask ourselves a *fundamental* question, i.e. a self-questioning question in the primordial light of wonder or the totality of all that is. In other words, nature in its *original* sense is *the emergence of primordial Being* in which all things pre-sent themselves in their true essence ("be-ing") and original to-gether-ness.[268] Nature in this original sense, therefore, is given in the aesthetic distance of our "original perception," of our "wondering-Being-in-the-world."

Nature as Physis

Now, this original sense of nature is *physis* as it was understood by the pre-Socratic philosophers at the origin of the history of Western thought. C. S. Lewis in his *Studies in Words* mentions two branches of meaning in the words *physis*. The one meaning is "to inhabit," "to dwell," "to remain," or "to be." The other is "to grow," or "to become."[269] Thus, according to Martin Heidegger, the word *physis* "denotes self-blossoming emergence . . . . . , opening up, unfolding, that which manifests itself in such unfolding and perseveres and endures in it; in short, the realm of things that emerge and linger on."[270] *Physis* is the emergence of Being as primordial phenomenon. It is interesting to note that there is even an etymological relationship between the words *physis* and phenomenon. "The radicals *phy* and *pha* name the same thing," says Heidegger. "*Phyein,* self-sufficient emergence, is *phainesthai,* to flare up, to show itself, to appear."[271]

Nature as Natura

The English word "nature" is derived from the Latin *natura* (*nasci*— to be born) which means "birth" or "nature" and is at best only a partial translation of the powerful Greek word, *physis*. With the word "nature" the original Greek inspiration is left behind. For *physis* is not only coming forth, but also enduring. It is not merely the essential character of a thing, but precisely that which enables "everything" to manifest its original presence. *Physis* is not so much that which is defined "in opposition to" something else, but rather that which sets all things apart in their limits within their primordial to-gether-ness of Being. *Physis* is not something that can be defined, but rather that which con-stitutes our "natural world" (in the original sense) by letting things *be* as they *are* in the awe-inspiring and fascinating light of our "original perception." *Physis* is not the physical universe, but the primordial world of wonder.

C. S. Lewis is right, therefore, in stating that "nature" taken in its original sense of *physis* "has no opposite."[272] As soon as one finds that "there is something else besides *physis,*" "nature" is no longer taken in its original sense, but in a derivative, a restricted, or as Lewis calls it, a "demoted" sense.[273] Whenever we conceive "nature" in contradistinction to something else, we understand "nature" in its "restricted" sense, no matter whether that "something else" is man, or spirit, or art, or science, or law, or supernature. It goes without saying that nature in the restricted sense is never to be identified with *the* World (Being). This holds true of any and all "restricted" meanings of "nature" such as: the sum-total of elementary cosmic forces, the raw material for manufacture, the object of natural sciences, the romantic landscape, our earthly existence, the entire physical universe, etc. These "restricted" forms of nature are always encountered "within" *the* World of *physis,* "within" nature in its original sense. Moreover, they are only encountered in their "true nature" in the light of our "original perception," in the light of *physis* as "wonder in the face of the world." And they are only ontologically com-prehended in the primordial inspiration of the *logos* as the dialectical self-manifestation of *physis.*

Beauty of Nature

All this has some important implications for our reflection on beauty of nature and beauty of art. Beauty of nature is not beautiful because of some mystifying property inherent in nature in the restricted sense, but precisely because of the self-revelation of *physis,* or nature in the original sense within nature in the restricted sense. But, then, the same holds true of beauty of art. An artwork is beautiful because it opens up the world of *physis,* because it reveals nature in its original sense. Moreover, beauty of nature is not merely located in that which is "independent of human activity." To be sure, in this beauty of nature "nature" in the restricted sense remains untouched by the human hand, it remains independent of the *controlling* attitude of man. But the revelation of nature in the original sense requires man's fundamental activity, namely his existential openness to allow Being to reveal itself. And this, as we have pointed out in an earlier chapter, involves man's ex-sistence in its entirety.

The Role of Physis in Beauty of Art

On the other hand, the beauty of an artwork is not merely man-made. For the technique of the artist, as we have also seen, is not the mere "manu-facture" of a product, but an inspired technique, or a technique put at the service of the primordial inspiration of *physis*. Beauty of art, therefore, results from an activity which is *not* merely the *controlling* activity of man as a human subject, but which is more basically the *inspired* activity of man as the participant in *physis* as the primordial emergence of Being. The artwork is not merely a handiwork, but more fundamentally the work of nature in its original sense *(physis)* which is neither touched nor touchable by the controlling hand of man. The artist expresses himself *beyond* himself. He is always more than a skillful technician. He always transcends the mere manufacturing of man-made products containing the truth of referential symbols. He would not even be an artist if he were not primarily attuned to the world of *physis* as the unveiler of the primordial truth of Being in the fundamental sym-bolism of his artwork.

In short, beauty of *nature* involves *man* in his fundamental activity, and beauty of *art* involves *nature* in its fundamental sense. Nature is not beautiful because it has a perfectly pleasing property, nor is art beautiful because it is a perfectly made handiwork. Both art and nature are beautiful for the same reason. They are beautiful because they reveal the truth of *physis*. Of course, we do not deny the respective differences of beauty of nature and beauty of art, but we deny that these differences are fundamental.[274] Neither nature in the restricted sense nor art in its restricted or technological sense can ever be beautiful in themselves. They are beautiful only to the extent to which they reveal the truth of *physis,* to the extent in which they are put at the service of the primordial inspiration of Being.

FUNCTIONAL AND FUNDAMENTAL ART

And this brings us to a final point. Just as nature, as we have seen, can be taken in a restricted and in a fundamental sense, so also *technique* (art) can be understood in a restricted and in a fundamental sense. It is precisely because our present-day means-centered culture fails to grasp the fundamental sense of technique that modern man tends to become a slave of technocracy. Technique in the restricted sense is the production and use of tools, instruments and machines for the satisfaction of the needs of our everyday existence. When technique is placed under the guidance of the natural sciences we speak of *technology*. Technology is the "logic" of technique, it is calculative thinking and action aiming at the control of nature. Technology is concerned with the problems of man as *homo faber,* but it does not raise or answer *fundamental* questions. Technology, for instance, does not ask the question what technique ultimately *is*. This question is a self-questioning question, it is a philosophical question, a question concerning the *logos* of *techne,* or a question of *techno-logy.*

"Techno-logy" reveals that the essence of technique is not to be sought in the full uniformity and stifling routine of the mere mechanical mass-production of tools and instruments. The essence of technique is not the mechanical production of instruments, but rather the "producing" of instruments in the original sense of "bringing to light" their respective potentialities. This is also the etymological sense of the verb "to produce" (*pro*—forward, and *ducere*—to lead) as to bring to view, to offer for inspection.[275] Technique in the restricted sense unfolds and unveils the potentialities of nature in the restricted sense. Technique (art) in the fundamental sense, however, puts technique in the restricted sense at the service of nature in the fundamental sense *(physis).* But technique in the restricted sense put at the service of *physis* or the primordial inspiration of wonder is precisely what we have called aesthetic art. Moreover, as we have seen, we grasp the essence of a phenomenon in our original perception of that phenomenon, which is the perception in the light of the primordial phenomenon of wonder. In other words, the essence of technique is aesthetic art. Aesthetic art is not a special kind of art (technique), but any art (technique) is truly art only to the extent to which it approximates aesthetic art, to the extent to which it helps to "pro-duce" the truth of *physis.*[276]

TECHNOCRATIC FUNCTIONALISM

Now, whereas technology simply ignores these fundamental insights of techno-logy, it is *technocracy* which rejects them. Technocracy is the scientistic absolutism of technology. It is the pseudo-philosophical attitude which reduces all beings, and even man himself, to raw material for man's domination over the earth. It is technology which rejects "techno-logy." And by reason of this rejection technocracy reduces all beings to controllable ob-jects standing over against the human subject. It reduces the mystery of Being to a host of solvable pro-blems, it degrades the "sacredness" of the ontological dimension of existential thinking to the mere functionality of calculative thinking, and it dissolves our will to Being into the will to power. Technocracy does violence to the Being of phenomena by regarding them as mere ob-jects, and by decomposing the World into antagonizing "op-posites" thus becoming a factor in the making of war.[277] Technocracy as the scientistic absolutism of the logic of technique makes man forget the essence or fundamental meaning of technique. Technique becomes divorced from the World of human ex-sistence, and is no longer understood as a potential factor in the un-folding of this ex-sistence. On the contrary, technique becomes a thing-in-itself, and man is degraded to an instrument for the promotion of technique. This perverts the natural order of things, and turns the means into an ultimate aim.

This absolute functionalism, this belief in the absolute supremacy of usefulness results in the nihilism of an infinite technical progress without any fundamental meaning whatsoever. Within this scheme of things man himself is reduced to a mere instrument or to a controllable thing in a controllable world. As Marcel says, "Man's mastery of nature is a mastery which has less and less control over itself."[278] Thus man becomes a phase in the nihilistic dialectics of "pantechnicism" (Marcel). Man falls victim to technocracy and becomes the slave of his own creations. He defines himself within the subjectivistic framework of the subject—object polarity. He interprets the Aristotelian definition of man *zoion logon echon (animal rationale)* as "logical animal." And today this often connotes "technological animal." Gabriel Marcel recalls the fact that "in an absurd or chaotic world technical achievements tend to seem more and more the chief, if not the only, mark of man's superiority to the animals."[279]

THE ESSENCE OF MAN

Now, to define man in relation to animals, even when the specific difference of "rationality" differentiates him from them, is at best only a "partial" definition of man. For it is a definition from the viewpoint of calculative and functional thinking which fails to reach the essence of man. Man is never merely a member of the "human species." This makes him an ob-ject of classifying and controlling thinking, and leaves his essential relation to Being unthought. Being transcends all species and genera. The same holds true of the interpretation of rationality as mere "logical" or "technological" thinking. This specific difference differentiates man from other animals as a "machine-making" animal. His calculative thinking, however, may some day be replaced by electronic brains. Be this as it may, the interpretation of rational as "logical" or "technological" fails to disclose man's essence as the unveiler and thinker of Being.

Logos-thinking as the dialectical self-manifestation of Being in man infinitely transcends the qualification of "specific difference." Man can disclose his essence only by escaping from merely logical definitions and from the nihilistic bounds of technocracy. And he can escape only by transcending the merely controlling frame of mind. And he can transcend this frame of mind only by transcending the thinking which we have "at our disposal," by placing it *at the disposal of the logos*. Only in the light of the *logos* can we understand that the "logically" correct definition of man as a *zoion logon echon,* as a "logical animal," has to be transcended into the fundamental truth of the Heideggerian formula: *logos anthropon echon,* "the *logos* which possesses man."[280] Logical thinking is a thinking that we possess, existential thinking is a thinking that possesses us. Existential thinking is "the thinking of Being." And the genitive indicated by the preposition "of" is more fundamentally a "subjective" than an "objective" genitive. It is more the self-thinking of Being in man, than man's thinking about Being. For, fundamentally speaking, man is a being which is at the disposal of the primordial inspiration of the *logos*.

CHAPTER X

EXISTENTIAL THINKING AND ETHICAL EXISTENCE

Man is a being which is at the disposal of the primordial inspiration of the *logos*. This is where the previous chapter ended. Now, as we know from earlier chapters, it is precisely through his original de-cision to listen to this primordial inspiration of the *logos* that man achieves his authentic ex-sistence. And this is why existential thinking is authentic thinking. But this is not the whole story. Existential thinking is not the only way of achieving authenticity. And this is where a new chapter begins.

At this point the reader may question the advisability of adding another chapter, since "existential thinking" and not "authenticity" is the proper topic of our study. The answer is, that as this chapter will demonstrate, "the other way" of achieving authenticity not only runs parallel to but also interlocks with existential thinking. The other way of achieving authenticity is *the ethical way*. Man's ascendency towards authenticity oscillates between a "thinking" and an "ethical" way of placing himself at the disposal of the primordial inspiration of the *logos*. These ways run parallel to one another, not in the sense of remaining independent or side by side, but in the sense of corresponding in their structural characteristics, and of being complementary to each other. There is a duality between these two ways, but not a dualism. This is why it is wrong, strictly speaking, to employ the word "two" in its ordinary mathematical and additive sense, and to speak of "two" ways of achieving authenticity. The "du-ality" between "existential thinking" and "ethical existence" is rather an expression for the essential and necessary failure of man to achieve perfect self-identity in his being at the disposal of the *logos*. Yet it is their "interwovenness" which is most fundamental, and which makes them interdependent and complementary in their respective ways of achieving authenticity. Now, it is precisely insofar as ethical existence sheds light on existential thinking that we want to discuss it in the present chapter. A discussion of ethical existence for its own sake would require another book and would exceed the limits of this study.

The present chapter is merely an *epilogue* (*epi*—upon, in addition; *legein*—to say), an additional statement providing the discussion of this book with a summarizing and final conclusion. In philosophy, however, a summary of final results and definite statements is impossible. Philosophical thinking promotes what it describes and is always caught in the act. A recapitulation of philosophical insights remains meaningless without the inspiration of *logos*-thinking within which they are actually thought. A philosophical epilogue is an *"epi-logos."* A philosophical *"epi-logos"* con-cludes *(con—claudere)* a philosophical discussion by once more involving or enclosing the whole, and bringing it to a close by shedding "added" *(epi)* light upon this fundamental discussion *(logos)*. This light is not added to the whole from without or from beyond, but from within. It is not a "mere addition" in the quantitative sense, but a further differentiation of the *logos* itself. The present chapter is an *"epi-logos"* in which we will re-view existential thinking by shedding added light upon it, by viewing it in the light of the *logos* of *ethos*. This chapter will further differentiate our understanding of existential thinking by viewing it as *a mode of ethical existence*.

The Dual Way of Achieving Authenticity

As we have seen in earlier chapters, there will always be a fundamental distinction or immanent polarity between the phenomenon of primordial Being and the Being of this primordial phenomenon. It is this polar tension which underlies the classical distinction between "essence" (what-ness) and "existence" (that-ness). And it is only in the light of this polar tension that this distinction is fundamentally meaningful. And since man's authentic ex-sistence is a response to the dialectical self-manifestation of Being, his achievement of authenticity will preserve this polar tension. In other words, man's achievement of authenticity takes place in an oscillating du-ality between his responses to the *logos* as the *"self-revelation"* of Being on the one hand, and his responses to the *logos* as the *"self-actualization"* of Being on the other.

To be sure, both the "self-revelation" and the "self-actualization" of Being involve the whole of the *logos* and the whole of our authentic human ex-sistence. Both the "self-revelation" and the "self-actualization" of Being are essential modes of the progressive "self-presentation" of Being in man. The word "presentation" connotes both "bringing to light" and "making present." The unity of these modes of "self-presentation" of Being in man is more fundamental than their respective distinction. This distinction is never to be understood as a separation, but rather as an oscillating *emphasis* of man's responses to the *logos*. The essence of man as the authentic response to the self-presentation of the *logos* oscillates between existential thinking with the *emphasis* on the "self-revelation," and ethical existence with the *emphasis* on the "self-actualization" of Being. Our fundamental reflection on human authenticity, therefore, also moves between two poles that are mutually elucidative, interdependent and complementary, but never completely interchangeable. The one pole is the reflection on existential thinking which been the topic of our entire study, and which has prepared us for an understanding of the other pole. This other pole is the reflection on ethical existence which constitutes the content of the present chapter.

In the present chapter we will ask ourselves some fundamental questions concerning our ethical existence with a view to shedding further light on existential thinking. How do we know the fundamental meaning of ethical existence? How can we arrive at a basic understanding of the nature and structure of our ethical Being? How does this basic understanding of ethicality further differentiate our understanding of existential thinking? Since all these questions are basically interdependent, the answers to these questions will be interdependent too.

THE ESSENCE OF "ETHICALITY"

When we examine what in general and at all times has been understood by "the ethical," then it is found to be the answer to the question: how do I have to act in order to give my life the meaning that it fundamentally has and ought to have? To put it differently, throughout the ages the ethical life of man has been regarded as the self-realization of man *as* man, as the realization of the highest and specifically human values, as the striving of man towards his highest good and the fulfillment of his specific perfection.[281] Although there has been much discussion and disagreement concerning the *content* of this highest good, this general principle has never been debated. As Paul Häberlin puts it: "However much man in his objectifying thinking may be mistaken as to the 'representation' of this ultimate good, as to the 'general principle' he is never mistaken."[282] It is not surprising that our objectifying thinking "mis-represents" the fundamental meaning of our ex-sistence, and reduces ethical life to the fulfillment of limited perspectives such as duty, pleasure, law, self-control etc. For objectifying thinking, as we have seen, deals with particular beings and phenomena from particular standpoints. Objectifying thinking is never concerned with authentic existence, it never raises fundamental issues, it never views things in the primordial light of the *logos*.

The basic question, therefore, that confronts us here is to determine in the light of the *logos* what human action gives our human life its fundamental meaning, what basically is meant by the self-realization of man *as* man or by the fulfillment of his highest perfection. It is the answer to this question which will reveal to us the essence of ethicality. And this answer is not far to seek. The action which establishes the fundamental meaning of human life, and actualizes the existence of man *as* man is the progressive *actualization of man's essence as authentic ex-sistence,* or as the participant in the self-actualization of primordial Being. In other words, ethical existence is the progressive achievement of authentic ex-sistence at the service of the primordial inspiration of the *logos*. In short, ethicality is human action *kata ton logon,* human action in accordance with the *logos*. Ethical ex-sistence is "*logos*-living" just as existential thinking is "*logos*-thinking."

Ethos as Man's Abode with Being

The word "ethical" is derived from the Greek word *ethos*. The original meaning of the Greek word, *ethos,* is dwelling place, abode, man's characteristic place or dis-position in which he "holds his own" in the world (*ethos*—IE. base *swedh,* akin to Goth. *swes*—"one's own"). *Ethos* means the primordial situation or existential place of a person or people.[283] *Ethos* is the way we fundamentally "hold our own" by holding ourselves in Being, by "behaving" in accordance with the *logos*. *Ethos* is the behavior we *are,* the behavior in response to the call of our own authentic Being. To "be-have" (ME *be*—thoroughly, and *have*— to hold oneself, to act) means to have oneself in hand, to hold one's own, to achieve one's own authenticity. Authentic behavior, therefore, is behavior *kata ton logon,* behavior in response to the *logos*. Authentic behavior is essentially ethical and existential. It is ethical as the achievement of authentic ex-sistence at the service of the *logos*. And it is existential since it transcends the subject-object dichotomy, and involves man's entire Being-in-the-World. *Ethos* is "authentic be-havior." In *ethos* man holds his own as the response to the ontological self-presentation of Being *(physis).* And as such *ethos* is a "mode" of *physis.*

As a secondary meaning of *ethos* is often listed: custom, usage and folkways. It should be emphasized, however that this meaning is secondary and derivative. The existential disposition of a people or a community *(ethos)* can be expressed in their folkways (customs). Customs and conventions may also be developmental stages on the road to a people's own authenticity, they may be *ethos* in a nascent state. But, whatever the case may be, the permanency or abode of the *ethos* does not result from one's being "accustomed to Being." This would obviously be self-contradictory. It would mean that one takes primordial wonder for granted, that one is perfectly adjusted to the mystery of Being. The "lasting dis-position" of the *ethos* does not result from "repeated action" (habit), but from its rootedness in Being *(physis)*. For, as we have seen, *physis* "abides" (AS. *a-bidan*—to remain).[284] The word *physis* not only denotes the unfolding and emergence of primordial Being, but also its essential dwelling, enduring or abiding. We will have to say more about this later on.

EXISTENTIAL ETHICS AS THE *Logos* OF *Ethos*

Since *ethos* is the abode of man with Being, there is only one appropriate way of re-flecting on this phenomenon. And this is the way of thinking which thinks Being, this is the way of existential thinking. The philosophy which re-flects on our ethical existence is the *logos* of *ethos,* or "etho-logy."[285] Unfortunately, scientism or rationalism is the dominant persuasion today. And even the study of man's ethical existence has not escaped from its dogmatic despotism. Most of our Western "ethics" or "moral philosophy" is dominated by this persuasion, and is really a "logic of *ethos*" rather than an *ontology* of *ethos* ("etho-logy"). As we have seen, however, the abstractive, calculative and objectifying nature of logical thinking is unable to probe into the very depth of primordial Being. Consequently, many of our rationalistic treatises on ethics or moral philosophy fail to comprehend our ethical life since they have to leave our abode with Being *(ethos)* unthought. They reduce the creative dynamism of *ethos* to the mechanical conformity to an abstract and static set of isolated rules. These rules are the so called "objective" ethical norms. In fact, they are merely external codes that are defined apart from *ethos,* and that live an hypostatized existence apart from their ontological birthplace: Being. And since logic conceals *ethos* rather than revealing it, these uprooted norms do not possess their ethical validity in their own right. They are either surreptitiously borrowed from theory, or else they are attained by absolutizing regional customs *(mores),* usage or folkways. Such a conception of ethical life lacks the creative and open dynamism of *ethos,* and comes close to what Henri Bergson has called "closed morality."

THE RATIONALISTIC ARGUMENT

The argument underlying rationalistic ethics runs something like this. In general, man's acts are ethical to the extent to which they are specifically human, to the extent to which they actualize man's highest potentialities. (In the general principle man is never mistaken.) Now, human acts are specifically human when they are in conformity with human *nature.* Human nature is expressed in the definition *zoon logon echon,* i.e. an animal endowed with reason, or "a logical animal." The "logical reason" constitutes the specific difference which differentiates man from other animals. Acts that are specifically human are acts in accordance with human nature, i.e. acts in conformity with the logical reason. This "right reason" constitutes the basic norm of morality. However, at the end of the previous chapter we have seen that the definition of man as "logical animal" fails to disclose the essence of man since it leaves man's relation of Being unthought. It leaves, therefore, also *ethos* as the abode of man with Being unthought. In other words, the "right reason" of rationalistic ethics is the *wrong* "right reason"! Its abstractive nature contracts the creative richness of *ethos* to the legalistic conformity with a static set of rules. Its ob-jectifying nature pulverizes our respect for life into a hairsplitting casuistry, and its calculative nature reduces life itself to a machine-like existence.

Small wonder that a student who has worked his way through the rigorism, the conformism and the legalism of a rationalistic textbook on ethics gets the sad impression that life is no longer worth living. Small wonder also that in recent times the "rationality" of objectivistic ethics has been challenged by the "ir-rationality" of subjectivistic ethics. But the subjectivistic revolt of psychologism, relativism and "situation ethics" *(Situationsethik)* against the inadequacies of objectivistic ethics does not remedy the situation either. For also the irrationalism of subjectivistic ethics *fails to disclose the essence of man* by defining him in terms of the "human subject" rather than in terms of the *logos.* Both rationalistic and irrationalistic ethics are fundamentally two sides of a single coin. Both belong to the same level of thinking, because both define man within the subject-object dichotomy rather than in the light of the *logos.* Both fail to disclose the essence of man by leaving his relation to Being unthought. Both fail to reveal the essence of *ethos* for their inability to understand it as the abode of man with Being. The argument between subjectivistic and objectivistic ethics is a fight between an elephant and a whale. The argument could go on forever for lack of common ground. A common ground could be found in the *logos* by transcending the subject-object dichotomy, and by transcending both rationalism and irrationalism. Only the *logos* discloses the authentic nature and structure of our ethical existence. And this is what we now want to sketch in broad outline.

PRIMORDIAL WONDER AS THE BEGINNING OF ETHICAL EXISTENCE

It will, of course, come as a surprise to both rationalistic and irrationalistic ethics that we regard *primordial wonder* as the beginning not only of philosophy, but also of our *ethical life*. For the rationalist cannot understand how primordial wonder could have anything to do with perfect, mechanical and problemless conformity to a static set of moral rules. On the other hand, the irrationalist cannot understand how moral life could be anchored in anything other than the human subject. Nevertheless, our ethical life, as the authentic response to the *logos,* also has its birthplace in primordial Being. Since primordial wonder, however, is an implicit and undifferentiated phenomenon, it does not yet disclose the explicit differentiation between the self-revelation and the self-actualization of Being. In other words, the entire content of our chapter on "The Primordial Phenomenon of Wonder" could serve as an introduction to a philosophical reflection on our ethical existence, just as it has served as an introduction to existential thinking. For both ways of achieving authenticity find their implicit beginning and their original undifferentiated unity in this primordial phenomenon. Only the explicit and actual beginning of existential thinking and ethical existence reveals their respective difference of emphasis.

This is why not only the question, "How should we begin philosophy?" but also the question, "How should we begin ethical life?" leads to unsolvable antinomies. For these questions are asked *outside* their actual beginning in Being. And since the all-encompassing universality of Being overwhelms us, we cannot, strictly speaking, control or begin the self-presentation of this phenomenon. Primordial Being is not of our own making, but it posits itself as a primordial question and makes us. *It is Being and not man that has the initiative.* Man does not begin to ex-sist authentically until he opens up "in response to" the *logos*. It is primordial wonder which frees us "from" the bonds of our everyday existence, and makes us free "for" the self-presentation of Being. Man cannot evoke this primordial inspiration at will. Only the reverent and humble abandonment of man's total existence permits him to respond authentically to the authoritative voice of Being. It is only in the total openness and the creative receptivity of man's whole personality that the primordial "gift" of Being is received, and that the phenomenon of wonder becomes a primordial act of "gratitude." The undescribable, undefinable and undemonstrable phenomenon of primordial wonder reveals itself only to our unconditional acceptance of its self-manifestation, or it does not reveal itself at all. It is interesting to note that on the one hand we hear ethical undertones in our very description of wonder, and that on the other hand ethicality as such remains inplicit in this undifferentiated phenomenon.

THE PRIMITIVE ETHICAL INTENTION

It is only in *the actual beginning* of ethical life that the distinction between existential thinking and ethical existence becomes explicit. Just as in philosophy, the most *decisive* moment in ethical life is its actual beginning. And just as in philosophy this actual beginning of ethical life consists in a "turning back upon" primordial Being. But it is also at the very beginning that they part company with respect to their respective *ways* of turning back upon Being. The actual beginning of philosophy is the "primitive cognitive intention," the first re-flection on primordial Being which "reveals" the primary data (first principles) of philosophy as a unitary structure. This unitary structure, as we know, is the *self-revelation* of our Being-together-with-others-in-the-world. It is our authentic ex-sistence as multi-dimensional *self-revelation* focalized by our essential *openness* to Being.

Now, the actual beginning of *ethical life* is the "primitive ethical intention," the first turning back into Being which "presents" the primary data (first principles) of ethical life as a unitary structure. This unitary structure is the *self-actualization* of our Being-together-with-others-in-the-world. It is our authentic ex-sistence as multi-dimensional *be-havior* focalized by our essential *dynamism* towards Being. It is this actual beginning, this "primitive ethical intention" (the "good intention") which ethicizes our very ex-sistence, and which makes our human life *virtuous* in the sense of "endowed with ethical excellence" (*virtus*—excellence; *vir*—man). The virtuousness of the actual beginning of our ethical life is neither one single virtue, nor many unconnected virtues, but a unitary structure. Just as the actual beginning of philosophy is neither the one nor the many, so also the actual beginning of our ethical life is neither the one nor the many. The actual beginning of virtuous ex-sistence is neither one first principle nor many first principles, but a polar tension between the one and the many. It is a response to the dialectical self-actualization of Being, a human action *kata ton logon,* in accordance with the *logos.* Virtue is in the whole!

CREATIVE ETHICS

Moreover, just as the actual beginning of philosophy is *creative,* so also the beginning of our ethical life is creative. As a response to the dialectical self-actualization of Being the beginning of ethical existence does not lead us away from this all-encompassing phenomenon, but it rather *brings us back into it.* Ethical existence actually begins as a self-actualizing spontaneity, as an immanent dialectics or as a circular movement. What the medieval thinkers called *synderesis* is precisely this self-actualizing spontaneity or this spontaneous self-beginning of ethical life.

Now, this actual beginning of ethical life remains the *pro-ject* of all ethical self-actualization. Ethicality is the differentiated returning upon itself of the fundamental self-actualization of the integral totality of all that is *(logos).* Ethicality *is* the progressive self-actualization of its primitive ethical intention, or of its own actual beginning. Ethical life is the progressive self-foundation, the deeper and deeper self-actualization of its primary data. And this ever renewed and enriched self-beginning is the essential *creativity* of our ethical existence.

Whereas the very thought of a "creative ethics" is a nail in the coffin of the formalist and the legalist, a thinker like Gabriel Marcel expresses the *need* for such a creative ethics. Marcel is correct in his claim that only creative ethics can save us from the narrowness of monadic individualism, and from the glum repetition and killing routine of ethical formalism. Only creative ethics can safeguard man's experiential uniqueness and personal dignity, and recover the universal openness of his primordial situation.[286] What we said in an earlier chapter concerning the creativity of existential thinking applies *mutatis mutandis* to the creativity of our ethical existence. Ethical life actually begins, becomes "present," or "presents itself" (present) by presenting its primary data (past) as possibilities for something "to come" (future). Ethical life presents its primary data as "re-search pro-ject," it "re-news" the old by "re-peating" its original data as immanent finality, or by the self-enriching ad-venture of going back into its own original foundations. As a self-enriching ad-venture ethical life both continues and advances what it has begun. And in this sense ethical life is truly *self-creative.*[287] It is this self-creative re-petition (*re*—again; *petere*—to seek), and not the mechanical repetition of "habits" that constitutes virtuousness. We will revert to this shortly.

THE PRIMORDIAL "DE-CISION" AS THE EXISTENTIAL "WILL-TO-BEING"

But before turning to a comparison between virtues and habits, we must once again focus our attention on the actual beginning of ethical ex-sistence as its most *decisive* moment. Again, the word "decisive" here is taken in both its etymological sense and with all its possible connotations.[288] The word "de-cision," as we have seen, is etymologically derived from the Latin *decidere* which means: to cut off, to separate, to decide (*de*—off, from; *caedere*—to cut). Now, the actual beginning of ethical life as the response to the dialectical self-actualization of Being is the *primordial de-cision* (setting apart) to respond to this differentiated call of the *logos*.[289] This primordial de-cision (setting apart) is an ex-sistential de-cision. It is the "ec-static pro-jection" into primordial Being which con-stitutes (sets together) our human essence as authentic "ex-sistence." Being, as we know, gives itself only in the act in which it is fully and unconditionally received, namely in the total openness of our authentic ex-sistence. In other words, it is *one and the same primitive ethical intention* which gives birth to the dialectical self-actualization of Being *(logos),* and to our primordial de-cision to ex-sist authentically. Consequently, this primordial de-cision is not so much a de-cision *we make,* but rather a de-cision *we are.* Or, better still, it is a de-cision which *makes us.* It is not until we have made this de-cision that we can regard ourselves as qualified to make it.

It goes without saying that the primordial de-cision is not any particular decision, not any particular act of the will to choose, to act or to judge.[290] On the contrary, the primordial de-cision constitutes man's *fundamental* will, which is the "will-to-Being," the will in accordance with the *logos*.[291] This fundamental will, therefore, ethicizes our authentic ex-sistence in its entirety, and could be called the "ethical" or the "existential" will. Ethical life is the life of the existential will. The existential will as the response to the all-encompassing phenomenon of Being, transcends the subject-object dichotomy. In other words, the existential will cannot be an "ob-ject" or a thing to be controlled, nor can it be an "instrument" for the control of the world to be employed by a human subject.

The existential will transcends any such categories. The primordial de-cision of the existential will to respond to Being involves *the whole of our ex-sistence.* In fact, it *constitutes* this authentic ex-sistence and gives rise to our Being-in-the-world. And as a fundamental mode of Being-in-the-world the existential will cannot possibly be a separate human faculty in the restricted and traditional sense of the term. The existential will is the will we *are,* rather than the will we *use.* The existential will as primordial de-cision constitutes the very openness of our authentic ex-sistence. This is why Martin Heidegger is right in saying that "To will is to be resolved" (*Erschlossenheit*—openness, decisiveness).[292] And just as the primordial question of Being is not a mere question among other questions, but the critical beginning of philosophy that anticipates and permeates all other questions, so also "Resolve is not a mere decision to act, but the crucial beginning of action that anticipates and reaches through all action."[293]

THE DECISIVE MOMENT OF ETHICAL EXISTENCE

The actual beginning of ethical existence is also its most *decisive* moment in the sense of crucial, critical or risky. The birth of ethical life as the "separation" from the womb of primordial Being, and the explicitly turning back into it is a critical "turning point." At this very moment our ethical life is in danger of mistaking some particular or subordinate ethical phenomenon, such as pleasure, duty or law for the primitive ethical intention, or of substituting a part for the whole.

Furthermore, the actual beginning of our ethical life is its most *decisive* moment in the sense that it *decides upon* its authenticity at any stage of its development. Human action is strictly ethical to the extent in which its ethical intention is focalized by the dialectical self-actualization of Being. In other words, the actual beginning of ethical ex-sistence as "human action in accordance with the *logos*" is the *criterion* which ascertains ethical authenticity.

And, finally, the actual beginning of our ethical life is its most *decisive* moment in the sense that it provides our ethical existence with its fundamental *certainty.* This, of course, was already implied in the just mentioned fact that human action in accordance with the *logos* is the criterion which *ascertains* our ethical authenticity. The primordial "decision" provides ethical existence with its "terra firma," its "solid ground" to "hold on to," to "stand on" or to "trust." In other words, the actual beginning gives ethical life its "stability," its "trustworthiness" or its "reliability." It is important to note, however, that existential certainty is rooted in the dialectical self-presentation of *primordial Being,* and that this phenomenon transcends the subject-object dichotomy. This entails that existential certainty is neither a merely "objective" nor a merely "subjective" certainty. Existential certainty is neither logical, nor psychological but ontological. Existential certainty arises out of our Being-in-the-world, and involves our authentic ex-sistence in its entirety. The existential "certainty" of our authentic existence is a state of "having parted ways" (*cerno*—to separate, to decide) with the unauthentic which enables us to "discern" (*dis* and *cerno*) between good and evil.[294] Only the fullness of primordial Being can fulfill the primitive ethical intention. The fulfillment of authentic "ex-sistence" is what constitutes existential certainty. It is the experiential reliability of Being rather than the conformity to abstract rules or *mores* which defines the ethicality of the good.

The existential certainty of our ethical life is rooted in the primordial phenomenon of Being. This entails that it is rooted in both the dynamism and the mystery of this primordial phenomenon. Rationalistic and legalistic ethicists, however, will reject the very idea of existential certainty. For it contradicts the unchanging solidity *(terra firma)* and Cartesian clarity of their own conception of certainty. "Before the spectacle of this universal mobility," says Henri Bergson, "there may be some who will be seized with dizziness. They are accustomed to terra firma; they cannot get used to the rolling and pitching. They must have "fixed" points to which they can attach thought and existence."[295]

Nevertheless, existential certainty constantly demands to be certified still further. For ethical life, as we have seen, comes into its "own," "presents itself" as "authentic" and "certain" by turning back into its "past" as the *ground* of its "future" possibilities. Now, this dynamic self-grounding ground is the most fundamental and, therefore, the most solid possible ground. To quote Bergson again: "Its solidity is infinitely superior to that of a fixity which is only an ephemeral arrangement between mobilities."[296] The existential certainty of ethical life rests creatively *in* the dynamic, self-grounding ground of the *logos*, rather than immutably *on* the *terra firma* of the fixity of unchanging principles. As rooted in the dialectical self-actualization of primordial wonder, the existential certainty of our ethical life remains our most "wonder-ful" and most "suspense-ful" ad-venture. This, of course, is a far cry from the dehydrated procedures of our legalistic cookbook morality.

ETHICAL CONSCIENCE

Inadequate Interpretations

Now, the creative certainty of authentic ex-sistence as "having to be a response to the dialectical self-actualization of Being" reveals itself in our *conscience*. Or, as Luijpen puts it, conscience is the "understanding of Being as the unveiling of existence-as-norm."[297] Nevertheless, to many ethicists, psychologists and sociologists conscience is nothing but the interiorization of some external authority. And no matter whether this authority is God, a parent, a social group, a tradition, or one's past history, what this conscience reveals is a far cry from what we called a most wonder-ful and suspense-ful adventure. What it reveals is rather the fixity of an inhibiting force which reduces one's life to a soul-killing routine which is laid down in a forbidding list of prohibitions and taboos. Conscience, in this case, is always the uncritical and more or less mechanical echo of a voice coming from without. According to this opinion a healthy, critical and mature personality is one who has freed himself from the bonds of his conscience.

On the other hand, there are those who claim that conscience cannot be affected by its biological, psychological or sociological substructures. For, in their opinion, conscience presents us with the norms, the laws and the rules of human behavior which are general, timeless and abso-lute. The "dis-position" or involvement of the acting person is irrele-vant. The only criterion that decides upon the morality of an action is its more or less mechanical conformity with the laws (legalism). A moral personality is one whose conscience has freed itself from both all moral substructures and all existential involvement.

Fundamentally speaking, however, these opposite interpretations of conscience are only two sides of a single coin. Both have in common that they interpret the "voice" of conscience as something coming "from without." Both reduce conscience to something authoritarian, mechanical and non-creative. Both "detotalize" the original structure of conscience due to their common failure to face the human situation.

In Accordance with the Logos

As we have seen, the ethical way of achieving authenticity is given to man in his response to the *logos* as the dialectical self-actualization of Being. Now, the self-actualization of Being, as we have also seen, is one pole of the oscillating self-"presentation" of Being in man. In other words, the ethical self-presentation of Being is at the same time a self-*revelation,* but with the emphasis on self-*actualization.* The ethical self-actualization of Being is an *ethical way of self-revelation.* Now, *con-science* is the self-revelation of the self-presentation of Being *as self-actualization.* To put it differently, conscience is the consciousness of man as ethical ex-sistence, or the consciousness of the entire ethical personality. It is only in the light of this basic insight into the Being of conscience that we can understand the fundamental meaning and coher-ency of the structural characteristics of mature conscience. The authen-tic "voice" of conscience is all-encompassing rather than the voice of a special human faculty. This authentic voice of conscience is creative rather than mechanical, free and responsible rather than culturally determined, and authoritative rather than authoritarian.

No Special Faculty

As the conscious response to the dialectical self-actualization of Being conscience involves the *all-encompassing* phenomenon of Being. It is experiential and concerns our ex-sistence in its entirety. Authentic conscience, therefore, is always more than a "special faculty," a "moral sense," an "interiorization of external authority," a "conformity to a set of rules," a "sense of duty," an "inner voice," etc. In fact, an accurate phenomenological description of the "voice of conscience" reveals that it is neither a little "inner voice," nor a voice that comes merely "from without." Conscience is the voice of self-actualizing Being in man, and arises from our entire Being-in-the-world. Authentic conscience, therefore, not only calls us *beyond* our ethical substructures and our everyday existence, but it also fully *includes* them. Just as existential thinking is a mysterious synthesis between immanency and transcendency or a thinking with the mind, the heart and the hands, so also ethical existence is a synthesis between immanency and transcendency or a conscientious living with the heart, the mind and the entire body.

Creative Conscience

Moreover, as the conscious response to the dialectical self-actualization of Being conscience reveals our *creative* and *multi-dimensional ethical responsibility*. Conscience is *creative*. For, as we know, ethical life presents its primary data as "re-search pro-ject," it "repeats" its original data as immanent finality. Conscience is the self-enriching or creative consciousness of our ethical ad-venture which "holds its own" by "holding on" to its actual beginning with "creative fidelity."

Multi-dimensionality of Conscience

But this is also why conscience is *multi-dimensional*. For ethical "ex-sistence" is only faithful to its actual beginning by responding to the *differentiated* voice of Being. It is only faithful to its actual beginning by becoming the ethical will-to-Being as the free and creative "ability to respond" (responsibility) to the dialectical self-actualization of Being, or to engage in the ethical "dia-logue." Ethical responsibility, therefore, is never rectilinear and one-dimensional, but always *circular* and multi-dimensional. Every ethical act turns back into the all-encompassing phenomenon of Being in its multi-dimensional self-actualization. In every ethical act the whole of our ethical ex-sistence is at stake. Every ethical act re-begins our primitive ethical intention.

Authoritative Conscience

And this brings us to a final point concerning conscience, and on this point we will dwell in greater length. Authentic conscience is *authoritative rather than authoritarian*. Unfortunately, in our functionalized world the fundamental distinction between these terms is hardly noticed. Don't we mean by "authoritative" conscience a conscience which presents itself as an "authority?" And is not authority something we have to outgrow, something needed to control the immature, the weak and the helpless, but also something that suppresses the freedom, the initiative and creativity of the strong and the mature? Is not authoritative conscience precisely the internalized external authority which we have rejected as unauthentic? The answer is that it is not. But in order to understand this we have to transcend the current legalistic and functional meaning of authority, and to probe deeper in the fundamental meaning of authority. In other words, we should free ourselves from our present-day unauthentic understanding of authority by making an ontological distinction between functional, existential and autocratic authority.

VARIOUS MEANINGS OF THE TERM "AUTHORITY"

When we ask ourselves the question what the word "authority" means, then a glance at the dictionary will tell us that it means: "the power to command obedience." This seems to be the common denominator and the basic meaning of the definitions of authority. As more or less derivative and weaker meanings are also listed: "personal influence resulting from prestige, respect and confidence," and "expert authority." Now, it is important to note that the common definition of authority as "the power to command obedience" permits at least three basically different interpretations. Firstly, it can be taken in the *juridical* sense of the legal right to prescribe laws, to give orders and to command obedience. Since this authority is characteristic of the functional level of our existence, we call this authority *functional* authority. Secondly, the definition can also be understood in the sense of a *de facto physical power* to boss people around by force, fear and suppression. This perverted and fixated authority is autocratic authority or *autocracy*. And, finally, "the power to command obedience" may also be interpreted in a more *existential* or *fundamental* sense as "a personal influence or ethical power which commands one's respect and invites one to *listen (obedire)* to the voice of Being in authentic 'ex-sistence.' " The obvious name for this authority is *existential* authority.

EXISTENTIAL AUTHORITY AS ETHICAL AUTHORITY

Etymologically, an authority is one who is an "author," one who originates something. The word "author" is derived from the Latin word *augere* which means *to give increase,* to author something, rather than to command. Now, it goes without saying that the most fundamental and authentic meaning of authority is our most fundamental way of originating something. And our most fundamental way of originating something is the very creativity of our response to the dialectical self-actualization of Being. In other words, existential authority is the very dynamism of our authentic ex-sistence as "emergence," as "going beyond" or as "primary initiative." Authentic authority is existential authority. Existential authority *is* our authentic exsistence as primary initiative. And conscience as the revealer of existential authority is authoritative conscience. Existential authority is ethical authority.

Existential authority as ethical authority is not something which originates in our controlling or objectifying attitude of life. It springs from our abode with Being. Existential authority, therefore, is not something we possess, but rather something which *possesses us*. Existential authority as the creativity of our abode with Being is inspirational and wonder-ful. Instead of suppressing freedom and stifling initiative, the fascinating and awe-inspiring phenomenon of existential authority creates openness and respect, and is the very source of authentic freedom and initiative. Existential authority as the creativity of our abode with Being is never an accomplished fact or an unchanging state of being. On the contrary, it only manifests itself as an ideal, an adventure and an inexhaustible task.

CO-AUTHORITY AND CO-OBEDIENCE

Moreover, existential authority is *never unilateral authority*. It does not come from within or from without, but it originates in our multidimensional *dia-logue* with Being. Existential authority arises as the creativity of the "mutual response-ability" of our Being-together-with-others-in-the-world. Or, to put it differently, since man's Being is co-Being and his authentic ex-sistence and co-existence, existential authority is essentially *co-authority*.

Fundamentally speaking, the world is not, or should we say, should not be divided into two segments: those in authority and those who obey. For those who obey do so as "listeners" *(ob—audire)* to the differentiated voice of the *logos*. And this constitutes them as authorities. An existential authority should not say "I have authority," but rather "We are in authority." Within the world of existential authority nobody has *absolute* authority over the community or over any of its members. But every member *is* in authority, every member "gives increase" to the whole of the community. Instead of suppressing personal or group initiative, existential authority is their lasting source and inspiration. Even he who is in supreme authority is not merely "ruling" his people in the functional and legalistic sense. He is rather the "inspirer in chief" of his co-authorities, the "supreme listener" who orientates his co-listeners towards their common good, towards their *ethos* or their very own abode with the primordial inspiration of Being.[298]

Not only existential authority, but also *existential obedience* is never unilateral. For those who obey are also in authority, and those who are in authority also obey. We have already seen that those who obey or listen are in authority, since authority is co-authority, and listening to the creativity of the *logos* constitutes existential authority. But the reverse is equally true. Those in authority have to obey or to "listen" to existential authority. Here obedience (*ob* and *audire*—to listen to that which transcends or is superior) is taken in the fundamental sense of listening to the *logos* as the differentiated self-actualization of the primordial initiative of Being. This onto-logical understanding of ethical obedience reveals that this obedience is a mutual listening to the voice of authentic authority in each other and in ourselves. It is a co-listening to the authoritative voice of the *logos*. He who is in existential authority does not only have to obey the authority of those who obey him, but he also has to obey his own existential authority. In other words, he who is in existential authority has to obey the nature, the personality, the uniqueness, the initiative and the developmental stage of the one who obeys; but he has also to obey his own unique authority, his own limits and his own place in the community and the world.

EXISTENTIAL AUTHORITY AND FUNDAMENTAL FREEDOM

From all this it follows that existential authority is *not arbitrary*. Genuine authority does not have the freedom to suppress the freedom of others by merely unilateral decisions. It does not have the freedom to reduce the obedience of others to a merely mechanical, uncritical and unquestioning kind of listening. The freedom of existential authority is not the freedom of arbitrariness, the freedom of indifference or the freedom to deal with other freedoms at will. On the contrary, the freedom of existential authority is *fundamental* freedom, the freedom to be oneself and the freedom to allow beings to manifest themselves as being what they "are." "Freedom unveils itself here," says Heidegger, "as the letting-be of beings."[299]

This fundamental freedom is the freedom of the ethical will. This ethical will, therefore, is not so much the freedom of "choice" or indifference, but more fundamentally the freedom of "engagement" (Gabriel Marcel). On the fundamental level existential authority and freedom are not opposites, but mutually inclusive components of authenticity. Existential authority does not suppress freedom but rather appeals to it, constitutes it and makes it grow. Existential authority is "obedient authority" which increases the *co-listening* of the personality and the community. Existential authority is "authoritative obedience" which increases the *co-authority* of the personality and the community. Also ethical obedience as the existential listening of our abode with Being is mutual, creative, wonder-ful, critical, respect-ful, free, self-questioning, responsible and inspired.[300]

THE ROLE OF FUNCTIONAL AUTHORITY

Existential authority, it goes without saying, is not a free floating entity hovering over the workshop of our everyday existence. As an authentic mode of Being-in-the-world it not only transcends this everyday world, but it is also fully immanent in it. Existential authority is incarnated in the world of our unauthentic existence of functional relationships where *functional authority* is "in force." Functional authority is the legal power to prescribe laws and rules, and to command obedience by "enforcing law and order." This functional authority is immersed in the "environment" *(Umwelt)* and its utilitarian values, its social functions and organizations.

In this world of human labor, of supply and demand, of human needs and drives and their satisfactions functional authority is subjected to the more or less mechanical interactions and stimulus-response situations which characterize this world.[301] This functional authority, however, is no more unworthy of existential authority and human freedom than the rules of a language are unworthy of creative writing and free expression. "A language," says Dorothy Lee, "is full of regulations—yet it is freeing. Through learning the rules I am enabled to communicate with others, I am free to express myself. I am not hampered by the rigid taboo against using a singular verb for a plural subject; I am not outraged when I am commanded to add *ed* to *wash* when I refer to yesterday."[302]

Functional authority is the canvas into which the tapestry of authenticity or the freedom of existential authority has to be woven. Functional authority is "instrumental" in preserving "law and order." Existential authority, on the other hand, *never* functions as an instrument. The "order" created by existential authority is the order of the *logos* which, as we have seen, sets all beings in their original limits by setting them apart in their primordial unity of Being *(sapientis est ordinare)*. Functional authority maintains order by placing things at a "controllable" distance. Existential authority creates order by allowing things to "be" within a "respectful" distance. Without "order" human life would fall into a state of chaos. But with only functional authority human life would fall into a state of stupor. Functional authority is essential to, but never the essence of genuine authority. Functional authority is not meaningful and human *unless it is placed at the service of the primordial inspiration of existential authority*. Functional authority can be formalized and abstracted from the person in authority, existential authority never. For existential authority is experiential; it always involves the personality in its entirety.

Accordingly, we conclude that existential authority is not something that originates in our needs or deficiencies. Existential authority is not something that suppresses freedom and initiative and has to be outgrown and eliminated. On the contrary, existential authority originates in the plenitude and richness of Being and is a structural characteristic of our authentic ex-sistence. To suppress existential authority is to suppress freedom and initiative. To suppress existential authority is to suppress our "common good" of the comprehensive universality of Being. Functional authority, on the other hand, is concerned with our "common need." And as such it is essential to existential authority as its necessary substructure. Put at the service of existential authority also functional authority promotes freedom and increases the initiative and creativity of the community and its members. What really suppresses freedom and initiative in man is neither existential authority nor the proper "use" of functional authority, but rather its destructive "ab-use."

THE DESTRUCTIVENESS OF AUTOCRACY

Now, this "ab-use" of functional authority is called *autocracy*. Autocracy is the divorce of the legal motive from the ethical motive. It is the dogma of the absolute ultimacy of functional authority. What scientism is to existential thinking autocracy is to ethical existence. The absolute supremacy of the functional level blocks any possible union between immanency and transcendency. The autocrat *(auto-krates—*

self-ruling) wants *absolute* authority over others. For to the extent to which his power over others is limited, he is not a complete self-ruler, he is not in absolute control over the situation, and his autocracy remains imperfect. The autocrat can arrive at absolute authority only by perverting the very nature of authentic *ex-sistence* as standing out, as emergence, as multi-dimensional openness. He can only become an absolute ruler by setting himself up as the absolute center of the universe, and by restricting his existential authority or the "will-to-be" to the mere functional authority or the "will-to-power." He assumes as his fundamental attitude the "controlling" attitude, thereby reducing the others to mere "ob-jects" standing over against him or to things to be subjected to the unrestricted force of his power. He demands absolute submission or unquestioning obedience. His unilateral authority not only takes the joy out of obedience, it even takes the "listening" (obedience) out of obedience. For objects or things are, in fact, unable to listen. Moreover, the autocrat does not ex-sist "authentically." And the narrow ego of his shrunken self offers no authoritative voice to "listen to," or to be "inter-ested" in (*interesse*—to participate).[303]

The autocrat reduces obedience to mechanical conformity which interdicts free action, and thereby the very possibility of truly ethical obedience. Even if on the surface the behavior obtained by the dictates of an autocrat may resemble genuine ethical behavior, when we penetrate to the core we discover its lack of freedom and creative responsibility. The responsibility of such an unquestioning obedience is not the ethical responsibility of our authoritative conscience, but rather the automatism of a stimulus-response situation which characterizes the authoritarian conscience. This automatism which progressively substitutes habit for virtue deprives our behavior of precisely that which constitutes its ethical dimension, namely, its free and creative response to the *logos*.

VIRTUES AND HABITS

But are we here not contradicting a respectable tradition in philosophy that equates virtue with a "good habit?" Is it not true that virtue is acquired by repeated acts, and that a repetition of acts results in a habit (L. *habitus*—habit)? The answer is that virtue is not a habit, and that the tradition was only respectable as long as the Greek *hexis* or its Latin equivalent *habitus* meant something like "authentic be-havior," and were not yet rendered by the modern word "habit." For the translation of the word *habitus* by "habit" deprives this Latin word of its original meaning and ontological flavor, and amounts to an inflation of the word *habitus*. In order to restore the word virtue to the full ontological significance it formerly possessed we have to abandon the term "habit."

Virtue, as we have seen, is the excellence of authentic human action. It is "authentic human be-havior" which is be-havior in accordance with the *logos*. Authentic be-havior is the be-havior we *are*, the be-havior which constitutes the very *authenticity* of our ex-sistence. Now, it is "authentic be-havior" rather than "habit" which renders the original meaning of the Greek *hexis*, the Latin *habitus* and the English "be-havior." These words are not merely derived from the respective verbs *echein, habere* and "to have" that all mean "to possess," but from *houtoos echein, sese habere* and to "be-have," expressions that signify "to be" rather than "to have." Their common meaning is: to have oneself, to have oneself in hand, to hold one's own, to achieve one's own ex-sistence.

Apparent Similarities

At first blush it may seem that the notion of "habit" corresponds very well to the meaning of *"habitus"* as authentic and virtuous behavior. Their structural characteristics are seemingly identical. Both habit and *habitus* are acquired by a *repetition* of the same acts which makes these acts more and more *effortless*, more and more rooted in a *permanent disposition*. Yet a careful phenomenological description reveals a fundamental difference in *the way in which* "virtuous be-havior" and "routine habits" manifest these structural characteristics.

Phenomenological Differences

A "routine habit" is acquired by the repetition of a series of identical acts which makes the acts less and less voluntary, less and less conscious and more and more mechanical. These acts become progressively effortless to the extent in which they become rooted in the permanent disposition of a bodily automatism. "Virtuous be-havior," on the other hand, shows quite a different picture.

"Virtuous be-havior" *begins* in a turning back into primordial Being as the self-creative, self-actualizing *re-petition* of this primordial phenomenon (*re*—again; *petere*—to search). The progressive achievement of "virtuous be-havior" proceeds through a "re-newal" of the primary data, through advancing the self-actualization of Being it has begun, through "presenting" its "past" data as "future" possibilities. And in the process the primitive ethical intention, the freedom of the ethical will and the awareness of the ethical conscience become more and more intensified, more and more conscious, more and more creative. In addition, the acts of "virtuous be-havior" become progressively effortless to the extent in which they become rooted in the permanent dis-position of authentic ex-sistence. It goes without saying that the seemingly identical characteristics of virtuous be-havior and of routine habits realize themselves, phenomenologically speaking, in diametrically opposite ways.

The Ontological Meaning of the Phenomenological Differences

Now, it is of the greatest importance to understand the ontological meaning of these phenomenological differences. "Virtuous be-havior," as we have seen, is "authentic be-havior." And authentic be-havior is man's response to the dialectical self-actualization of Being. And this involves man's ex-sistence in its entirety. Virtue is in the whole. Now, the re-petition of action required for the acquisition of virtue is *essentially* different from the repetition of a series of identical exterior acts. It is the self-enriching "going back into" the self-actualization of Being *(re—petere)*. Every virtuous action is creative, every virtuous action involves the whole of our ex-sistence, in every virtuous action our entire ethical life is at stake. Moreover, as the creativity of our authentic be-havior virtue "holds its own" by holding on to our primordial dis-position. This primordial dis-position is our "differentiated" response to the self-actualization of Being as *physis*. And *physis,* as we know, denotes both the "emergence" and the "abiding" of primordial Being. In other words, virtue is characterized by effortlessness and permanency to the extent to which it is deeper and deeper rooted in *physis*. Far from engendering a "settled" disposition to act in a stereotyped or automatic manner, virtue is a "permanent" dis-position to act in a creative way. Virtue is the excellence *(virtus)* of the ever growing self-perfection of our authentic ex-sistence as the creative response to the primordial inspiration of *physis*.

Poles apart is the structure of the routine habit which indeed is a "settled" disposition to act in a stereotyped or automatic fashion. Here the habit is acquired by frequent repetition of a series of identical acts until the performance becomes quite involuntary and mechanical. Such an automatic activity becomes more and more ingrained in our psychosomatic substructures and their mechanical stimulus-response situations. Such an automatic activity *withdraws from authentic ex-sistence*. Consequently, it implies a diminution and gradual extinction of its structural characteristics such as freedom, self-consciousness, originality, creativity, universal openness and experiential involvement.

Rather than constituting virtuous be-havior the automatic behavior of the routine habits deprives our human action of its ethical dimension.

No wonder that a human life based on such habits diminishes its ethical excellence, and turns it into the glum repetition and killing routine of conformism. In such a life the permanency of disposition and the facility of action do not result from being rooted in the enduring emergence of *physis,* but rather from being ingrained in the *physical* determinisms of our psychosomatic substructures. Only a continual *vigilance* on our part can prevent our ethical ex-sistence from dwindling into the external night of blind repetition, from vanishing into the meaninglessness of negative infinity or primary matter.[304]

The Function of Routine Habits in Ethical Life

This is not to say that routine habits, customs or conformity with rules and laws have no place in our ethical life. On the contrary, they are as necessary in ethical life as the rules of grammar are in literature or the beating of time in music. And just as in literature and music these rules and mechanical procedures become meaningful only when put at the service of our primordial inspiration. However, were we to *substitute* habits for virtuous be-havior a community of ethical personalities would resemble a collection of perfectly identical automatons for whom the following of "correct procedures" constitutes the ultimate of ethical excellence.

ETHICAL FORMALISM AND HYPOCRISY

This is ethical "formalism" which observes the "correct form" of ethical behavior but neglects its "spirit." Ethical formalism obeys the law to the letter, but it ignores its primordial inspiration (spirit). The ethical formalist brings the whole ethical situation down to the controlling and ob-jectifying level of his existence. On this level he can get things "under perfect control." He reduces his ethical existence to an automatic and problemless conformity to a static set of rules, and falsely calls it "self-control." And since the freedom, the ethical intention and the originality of his authentic ex-sistence have vanished, the fundamental dis-position of the acting person becomes entirely irrelevant. His impersonal conformism assumes the nature of a universal norm in matters of morality which applies univocally to no matter whom.

The formalist, therefore, automatically presents his own behavior as a norm for others, and he calls it "giving a good example." This good example, however, is merely the external manifestation of static correctness devoid of genuine ethical intention. Such an example, therefore, is strictly an "ob-ject" that the formalist holds in-front-of others for "ob-servation" and unquestioning imitation. No wonder that the autocratic "good example" that the formalist *gives* has the opposite effect of the good example that the authoritative ethical personality *is*. Instead of inspiring to participation, this moral exhibitionism is literally *repulsive*. No wonder, also, that the rigidity of the conformist results in a self-righteous attitude of intolerance, condemnation and aggression whenever he is confronted with the creativity of authentic, virtuous behavior.

It goes without saying that both formalism and legalism are *hypocrisies (hypokrinesthai*—to pretend to be what one is not). Both formalism and legalism pretend to be ethical excellence which they certainly are not. They present their ethical degradation as ethical excellence.[305] Formalism is a degradation of ethical life just as scientism is a degradation of philosophy. In fact, ethical formalism is to ethical existence what scientism is to existential thinking. For, both formalism and scientism impair our fundamental ways of achieving authenticity by insisting on inappropriate methods. Both formalism and scientism are unfaithful to their original data by substituting ob-jectifying methods for creative fidelity.

ETHICAL EX-SISTENCE AS METHOD

And this brings us to a brief comparison between ethical life and existential thinking as fundamental methods of achieving authenticity. Ways of dealing with authenticity are never merely "correct procedures to be followed" as in baking a cake. They involve our entire Being-in-the-world. The philosophical *way* of thinking *is* the dialectical self-manifestation of Being, just as the ethical *way* of living *is* the dialectical self-actualization of this primordial phenomenon. Consequently, what we said concerning philosophy as *method* applies *mutatis mutandis* to our ethical way of life.

Our ethical ex-sistence as "method" cannot be formalized just as existential thinking as "method" cannot be formalized. For formalization, as we have seen in connection with existential thinking, presupposes the possibility of abstraction, of ob-jectification, of dichotomization between subject and object. But since ethical life is action in accordance with the *logos,* it always involves the all-encompassing phenomenon of Being and transcends the subject-object dichotomy. Every ethical action involves the self-actualization of Being, and, therefore, our entire Being-in-the-world. The ethical *way* of life is never given "apart from" this experiential world. It always involves the entire ethical personality, and cannot be formalized or defined in terms of "correct rules to be followed." This is what the ethical formalist does not understand.

The ethical *way* of life begins as an original and creative moment in the lived spontaneity of our fundamental dis-position. And it develops in a "strictly ethical way" *not* by its "exact conformity to correct procedures," but by its creative fidelity to the actual ethical beginning. This actual beginning is the circular movement of the self-actualization of the concrete and all-encompassing phenomenon of Being. Virtuous behavior as our authentic be-havior does not *have* a method; it *is* a method. It is the very movement of the self-actualization of the *logos*. Hence virtuous be-havior as an ethical *way* of life is inseparable from its ethical content. Ethical life does not follow a set of directions that guide the process automatically to its desired result. Virtuous action does not follow a "beaten path" but it creatively projects its own road in response to the call of the *logos*. Virtuous be-havior is not instrumental action; it is not the procuring of the means for the attainment of a ready-made result. Virtuous be-havior does away with the separation between the result and the process of arriving at it. In virtuous be-havior there is a fusion of means and aim, of method and content, of beginning and end.

ETHICAL EX-SISTENCE AS SYS-TEM

But if the truly ethical method does not consist in "conformity with correct procedures," then we may have to follow the lead of other thinkers who regard *consistency* as the criterion of ethicality. Is not, indeed, consistency a typical characteristic of maturity, of greatness, of ethical excellence? But, then, there are consistent liars. There are consistent murderers. And . . . . there are consistent formalists.[306] We immediately recognize here the parallel between the ethical theories of conformity and consistency on the one hand, and the philosophical theories of correspondence and of coherency on the other. Our discussion of these philosophical theories[307] together with our elucidation of virtuous be-havior provides us with an answer to the question concerning ethical consistency.

Ethical "con-sistency" is ethical "ex-sistence" as a sys-tem, as an organized whole, as a "standing-together" *(con-sistere)* of ethical attitudes, virtues and actions in their original ethical unity. Virtuous behavior *is* con-sistent as ex-sistent. It is con-sistent as the dialectical self-actualization of primordial wonder or as be-havior in accordance with the *logos*. It is the *logos* that assigns the ethical phenomena their proper limits by setting them to-gether (con-sistency!) in their primordial collectedness of Being. Consequently, virtuous be-havior is not ethical be-cause it is consistent, but it is con-sistent because it is ethical, because it differentiates our abode with Being. Ethical con-sistency, therefore, is creative, open, free and growth-provoking. It has nothing to do with the rigidity of a closed morality, with the merely logical consistency of a static system or with the rigorous schematism of the formalist's classi-fying frame of mind. Neither virtue as "conformity" nor virtue as "con-sistency" are sufficiently fundamental to ethicize our human behavior. The con-sistency of human be-havior is ethical only when it creatively conforms to the dynamism of the *logos*.

ETHICAL ASCETICISM

Let us illustrate this with an example. As our example we have chosen the conception of ethical life as *asceticism*. We want to demon-strate that asceticism is not ethical unless it is con-sistent with the *logos,* and that asceticism as the consistency of rigid "self-control" is strictly unethical. Moreover, this example will further elucidate our comparison between existential thinking and ethical existence by revealing the im-portant parallel between phenomenological reduction on the one hand, and asceticism on the other. Asceticism is to ethical living what phe-nomenological reduction is to existential thinking. Generally speaking, asceticism is the practice of self-discipline for the attainment of some ideal or goal (*askeoo*—to exercise). It is the nature of the goal which determines the nature and scope of the respective form of asceticism. And the variety of human goals, such as military, bodily, education, philosophical, artistic, ethical or religious excellence, entails a corre-sponding variety of ascetical practices. A common characteristic, how-ever, of all ascetical practices is the differentiation into a positive and a negative aspect. We are namely freeing ourselves *from* something (neg-ative or carthartic aspect) in order to free ourselves *for* the attainment of a certain goal (positive or revelatory aspect). True asceticism in whatever form is never merely a "running away," but first and foremost a "running for." Let us restrict our discussion to a comparison between ethical asceticism and philosophical reduction which Paul Ricoeur has aptly called a "special asceticism."

Ethical Asceticism and Phenomenological Reduction

Just as existential thinking has to reflect on the natural world, or the world as it really *is,* unspoiled by preconceived ideas, and uncorrupted by prejudices or uncritically accepted "self-evidences," so also our ethi-cal existence has to return to the original world in which subjectivistic attitudes have been cleared out, and from which the screens that filter our authentic encounter with Being have been removed. In either case this "return to the original world" requires laborious techniques, great effort, painful self-discipline and a lifetime of hard work on our part. Yet, neither phenomenological reduction nor ethical asceticism know what to free our experiential world *from* unless at the same time they know what to *free* this experience *for*. Their cathartic and revelatory elements are dialectically related. Both reduction and asceticism, therefore, are authentic only to the extent to which they prepare human existence for an encounter with Being, to the extent to which they are put at the service of the primordial inspiration of the *logos*. Just as phenomenological reduction, so also ethical asceticism is a mysterious union between painful work and primordial "in-spiration" (spirit). Ethical asceticism, therefore, also involves man's ex-sistence in its entirety. Consequently, a disembodying soul cult is just as unethical as a soul-killing body cult. Ethical asceticism is the art of achieving ethical authenticity, the art of acting in accordance with the *logos,* and not the art of killing our bodily existence.

Asceticism as Anti-body Self-control

This anti-body asceticism has flourished whenever a dualistic conception of human existence was prevalent, such as, for instance, in the post-Platonic and the post-Cartesian eras. The aim of this anti-body asceticism is to bring the body "under perfect control." "Self-control" has become the paragon of ethical excellence. Such a perfect self-control, however, can only be achieved by suppressing the spontaneous drives, feelings and emotions of the human body, by reducing this body to a physical ob-ject and by treating it as a material thing standing over against us. This anti-body asceticism mistakes "self-control" for the ethical will. It reduces the ascetical practice to the level of our "controlling" attitude. This asceticism impairs rather than promotes our access to the *logos,* and it reduces the authoritative will to Being to the autocratic will to power. Anti-body asceticism does to our ethical life what rationalistic abstractionism does to our existential thinking. Both coagulate the creative openness of our primordial initiative into the fixity of a closed system.

Anti-body "self-control" is out of tune with our abode with Being, and stifles rather than promotes our authoritative will to Being. This authoritative will transcends the controlling level of our existence. This authoritative will-to-Being is tuned in to the all-encompassing totality of all that is, and therefore, is overwhelming and inspirational rather than controlling. The authentic will does not, strictly speaking, "possess" or "control" itself, but it rather allows itself to "be possessed" and to "be governed" by the primordial inspiration of the *logos*. Moreover, we would also fail to grasp the ethical meaning of asceticism if we should interpret "self-control" in terms of the control of the "lower" self by the "higher" self. For, again, we would reduce the authoritative will-to-Being to the controlling level of the will-to-power and thus place the unauthentic self *outside* our authentic ex-sistence as an ob-ject. We would relapse into the Cartesian dualism, and substitute the selfish, autocratic and disembodied will of the autistic ego for the creative openness of the ethical will.

Authentic and Unauthentic Self-discipline

The ethical way to deal with one's passions, feelings and emotions is not to squelch them or to put them in a strait-jacket, but to let them "be," i.e. to let them "respond" to the will-to-Being, to make them *disciples* (listeners) of the authoritative voice of the *logos*. Asceticism is not ethical as "self-control," but rather as "self-discipline" in the just mentioned fundamental sense of the term. One becomes, so to speak, one's own "superior," who orientates his subjects, i.e., his feelings, desires, drives etc. towards their common *ethos,* who inspires them to fulfill themselves by becoming co-listeners to the primordial inspiration of the *logos*. The obedient authority of the ethical will does not diminish our "lower" self, but it rather allows for the emergence of its true Being.

Although "self-discipline" can be a painful "self-denial" at times, it is not ethical to the extent to which it is painful, but to the extent to which it "denies" everything in our ex-sistence that impairs action in accordance with the *logos*. Self-denial as self-control suppresses both the "lower" and the "higher" self, and it looks very much like "self-torture" for its own sake. It takes the joy out of self-discipline, because it takes the inspired "listening" out of self-discipline and is no longer practiced at the service of the primordial enthusiasm of the *logos*. This negativistic reduction to insensitivity is the dominant conception of asceticism in a scientistic age. "It is," says Erich Fromm, "one of the unfortunate aspects of our Western concept of discipline (as of every virtue) that its practice is supposed to be somewhat painful and only if it is painful can it be good."[308] No small wonder that the interest in such a self-discipline is waning, and that even the word has become taboo. How can we truly love an asceticism that frees us "from" precisely that which it is supposed to free us "for," namely: *existential love.*[309]

CHAPTER XI

EXISTENTIAL THINKING AND EXISTENTIAL LOVING

Apparent Irreconcilability of Human Love and Ethical Life

This chapter brings our epilogue to its climax. The parallel between existential thinking and ethical existence is ultimately *a parallel between existential thinking and existential loving*. In other words, ethical existence is existential love, and love is existential and authentic to the extent to which it is ethical. But is not this identification of ethical life with authentic love somewhat presumptuous and hasty? Don't the phenomenological descriptions of ethical existence and of love reveal different and often even mutually exclusive characteristics? How, for instance, can we reconcile the stern sense of moral duty with the blissful feelings of human love? How can we conciliate the objectivity of ethical codes with the subjectivity of emotional attractions? Moreover, there are various kinds of love, such as self-love, motherly love, romantic love, etc. that seem to have little or nothing to do with our ethical existence. And, finally, granted that such a thing as ethical love exists, shouldn't this be regarded as one virtue among other virtues? How to account for an identification of the virtue of love with our ethical life in its entirety, if in addition to love we encounter other distinct virtues, such as humility, temperance, justice, etc.?

Rationalistic Prejudices

The observant reader will have noticed that questions such as these have arisen within the framework of our representational thinking which is manipulative rather than responsive, constructive rather than perceptive. This abstractive mentality, as we have seen, reduces the life-world to an atomic dust of unrelated entities, to a mere collection of separate beings, or to a mere juxtaposition of things. This calculative thinking fails to perceive the original phenomena in their primordial unity and ontological depth. It fails to think in accordance with the *logos* which gathers all things in their primordial collectedness of Being.

As for our ethical existence, we have already demonstrated that the understanding of ethical excellence as a stern sense of duty, as a mere conformity with moral codes or as the cultivation of a list of isolated virtues rests on rationalistic prejudices. It remains to be shown that also the conception of love as a merely subjective emotional feeling is inadequate and based on the same prejudices. Once we begin to view human love in the light of the *logos* its cosmic structure becomes manifest. It will no longer be possible to maintain that authentic love is a merely emotional attraction or simply one virtue among others. The reasons that prevented us from seeing the interrelatedness of human love and ethical existence will evaporate. The problem of the irreconcilability of human love and ethical life will appear to be a pseudo-problem created by the prejudiced world-view of rationalistic thinking.

"Phenomeno-logy" of Existential Love

Now, the phenomenon of human love manifests itself in a variety of authentic forms that represent a variety of embodiments of this authentic love, and constitute an *ordo amoris,* or a hierarchical order of its morpho-logy. Authentic love, for instance, appears in the form of love of one's neighbor (brotherly love), love of friendship, parental love, heterosexual love, religious love, etc. Yet, in spite of their morphological differences these authentic forms of human love have basic structural characteristics in common. We give the unitary phenomenon which reveals these structural characteristics of human love the name of *existential love*. Existential love, therefore, is not one form of human love among others, but rather that which constitutes the very *authenticity* of any form of human love. The structural characteristics of existential love reveal themselves at one stroke in their ontological meaning and original togetherness in the light of the primordial inspiration of the *logos*. In a complete philosophy of love this inspiration would have to be "worked out." But a complete philosophy of love is, of course, beyond the scope of this study. We merely attempt in the light of the *logos* to give a brief but accurate description of the structural phenomena of existential love in order to reveal their ontological meaning and primordial togetherness.

Existential Love as Co-Being-in-the-World

Existential love establishes a profound, experiential and personal bond between the partners. The achievement of such an interpersonal union is among the things in life that human beings seem to be craving for in the core of their existence. Now, in the light of the *logos* it becomes immediately evident that this profound bond is the experiential depth of our very ex-sistence as "co-Being." This is why in love we overcome our self-estrangement, our loneliness, our experience of being isolated from others. For in existential love we are no longer "standing alone." The "standing out" of our "ex-sistence" is fundamentally a "mutual-standing-in-the-world." We are called by Being to become co-participants in its inexhaustible Presence. And by our free co-responding we "present" ourselves to one another as "mutual self-presences." And it is this creative co-responding which constitutes our mutual self-fulfillment.

In the intimacy of true love a new dimension opens up, the original dimension of our existential togetherness, of our original "Being-with" others, of our fundamental union in Being. This new dimension is the mutual presence of the "I—Thou" relationship which invites us to transcend the narrow confines of our everyday existence, of any subject-object dichotomy and of the self-centeredness of our subjectivistic ego. Existential love is World-wide. It never restricts itself to the loving subject or to the beloved object alone; it never originates exclusively within the inner self or in the outer world, but it springs forth as a fundamental mode of our "co-Being-in-the-world." Existential love is experienced as something that transfigures and enlivens our ordinary world, as something that enriches our entire ex-sistence and that makes us return to our original integrity with all that is.

Existential love calls man out of the narrow confines of his self-centered ego by making him move towards the other and merge into an existential union of mutual self-discovery and mutual self-actualization. In the light of the *logos* this characteristic can readily be understood as the oscillating co-achievement of authentic ex-sistence as co-Being. In other words, existential love is not the self-actualization of a previously constituted self that enters into some relationship with another fully constituted self. On the contrary, it is the I—Thou dimension of existential love that constitutes the authentic self of the respective partners as authentic ex-sistence, as multi-dimensional co-Being-in-the-world. Existential love, therefore, is not "caused" in terms of mechanical and unilateral causation. It begins as a mutual response to a mutual appeal, it begins dialectically. And just as existential thinking begins as the dialectical self-manifestation of Being in man, so also existential loving begins as the dialectical self-actualization of Being in man. Both ways of achieving authenticity are characterized by their dialectical, phenomenological and ontological aspects.

EXISTENTIAL LOVE AS TRANSCENDENCY

The ontological characteristic of existential loving should not be over-looked. The existential union of the loving relationship does not isolate the partners from the rest of the world. On the contrary, it is precisely existential love that opens up the primordial context of our experiential oneness with all Being, and makes us return to our original integrity with all that is. Existential love is authentic when it creatively mediates the all-encompassing self-presentation of primordial wonder. An accurate phenomenological description reveals that existential love is never exclusively a union between two persons, but that it always *transcends* such a union, that it always includes our relatedness to all Being.

Within existential love we are all one, because we participate in the same source of transcendency, in the same primordial depth of Being. Erich Fromm refers to this transcendency in a more psychological terminology. "Love," he says, "is not primarily a relationship to a specific person; it is an *attitude,* an *orientation* of *character* which determines the relatedness of a person to the world as a whole, not toward one 'object' of love."[310] Or, as Ignace Lepp puts it: "According to the celebrated postulate of Karl Jaspers, there can be no authentic individual existence without an intrinsic reference to the Transcendent. In the same way, a love which cements the existence of a couple has equally to be integrated into a Love which transcends the couple."[311] And elsewhere, speaking of friendship, he says: "If it is a genuine friendship, it presupposes the sharing together of friends in one and the same transcendent reality, in something which surpasses themselves and their friendship."[312] In short, existential love is always "to-getherness" within the context of the primordial "all-togetherness" of the *logos.* Both existential thinking and existential loving are essentially a mysterious union between immanency and transcendency.

EXISTENTIAL LOVE AND PRIMORDIAL WONDER

Involving the all-encompassing phenomenon of primordial Being existential love is an overwhelming and inspirational experience. This experience is not given to those who are possessed by the will to power, but rather to those who have the freedom to allow love to "be," to those who are able to let it "happen." Only then does the profound "happiness" of love make itself felt in its mysterious union of primordial enthusiasm and reverential awe. This is why the relationship of authentic lovers is characterized by a respectful distance, rather than by a possessive closeness. The attitude of authentic lovers is that of mutual ad-miration rather than of mutual control. Existential love is authentic be-havior as co-Being. *Ad-miration* (*ad*—at; *mirari*—to wonder) *is primordial wonder as co-wonder*. It is the distance of admiration, the infinite farness and infinite nearness of the mystery of Being, which places true lovers at the *optimal* distance from one another and which at the same time creates their profound intimacy in Being. In the presence of one another within *the original depth of primordial Being* existential lovers attain the unexpected depth and inexhaustible originality of their own intimate self. Existential love is *deep* love, and the depth dimension is an essential criterion for the authenticity of human love. Erich Fromm has stated that "There is only one proof for the presence of love: the depth of the relationship, and the aliveness and strength in each person concerned."[313]

EXISTENTIAL LOVE ETHICIZES HUMAN EX-SISTENCE

By now our elucidation of existential loving has sufficiently advanced to understand its *ethicality*. As we have just seen, existential love manifests itself as the original depth of our existential togetherness, as our primordial "Being-with" others, as our fundamental union in Being. Existential love appears to be our mutual self-creation and mutual self-discovery which opens up the original context of our experiential oneness with all that is. In the light of the *logos* this means that existential love is the co-achievement of authentic ex-sistence as co-Being. In other words, existential love is *the self-actualization of our Being-together-with-others-in-the-world*. Now, it is precisely this unitary but structured phenomenon that we have found to be the primary datum of our ethical ex-sistence.[314] Consequently, *it is existential love that ethicizes our ex-sistence,* that constitutes the virtuousness of our authentic be-havior, that makes us be-have in accordance with the *logos*. In short, existential love is the very life of our ethical will-to-Being.

Now, it is in turn our understanding of existential love as the ethical will-to-Being which helps us further elucidate the nature and unity of the structural characteristics of existential love. In the first place, we have seen that our ethical will-to-Being ethicizes our authentic ex-sistence in its entirety.[315] Virtue is in the whole![316] In other words, existential love as the ethical will-to-Being is not one virtue among others, but rather our primitive ethical intention which ethicizes our ex-sistence in its entirety, and constitutes the ultimate virtuousness of any particular virtue. It is this that St. Thomas Aquinas meant when he said "Love is the form of all virtues."[317] Existential love is not one virtue among other virtues, but rather "a principle of life,"[318] or "the *style of life* that is willed in and through each of the virtues."[319] In each virtue the whole of existential love is at stake. Each particular virtue is a special expression of existential love.[320]

EXISTENTIAL LOVE AS THE ETHICAL WILL-TO-BEING

Furthermore, we have also seen, that the ethical will-to-Being originates in our primordial de-cision to be open or to *ex-sist* authentically. And this is why Martin Heidegger is right in stating that "To will is to be resolved" (*Entschlossenheit*—openness; decisiveness, courage).[321] It is evident, therefore, that existential love as the ethical will-to-Being cannot possibly be a merely emotional attraction, a purely passive affection or a sentimental "falling for." On the contrary, existential love is the courageous de-cision of our ethical will to be "open," to "stand-out," to accept our responsibility to the beloved one within the multi-dimensional response-ability towards all Being. And this insight presents us with the ontological foundation of Erich Fromm's definition of authentic human love. "Genuine love," he says, "is an expression of productiveness and implies care, respect, responsibility, and knowledge. It is not an 'affect' in the sense of being affected by somebody, but an active striving for the growth and happiness of the loved person, rooted in one's own capacity to love."[322]

As the courageous will to be *open,* to be affected by reality in its entirety, and to let beings "be," existential love is precisely that which gives rise to our authentic Being-in-the-world. Consequently, an existential analysis of the "openness," the "standing-out," or the "Being-in" of our Being-in-the-world will further differentiate our fundamental elucidation of existential love. This brief analysis, finally, will focus our attention on three more structural elements that are co-original and constitutive of existential love, namely: 1) its primordial enthusiasm; 2) its creative understanding; and 3) its dialogical structure.[323]

EXISTENTIAL LOVE AND PRIMORDIAL ENTHUSIASM

Although existential love is not a merely emotional attraction, it is not a neutral attitude that leaves our existence colorless and unaffected either. On the contrary, existential love "moves" us to the core of our ex-sistence. For existential love as the co-achievement of authentic ex-sistence involves the all-encompassing phenomenon of primordial Being. In existential love, therefore, man is "tuned in" *(gestimmt)* to Being or the totality of all that is. In existential love man's ex-sistence in its entirety is *affected* by his Being-in-the-world. Now, it is in this primordial affectedness, this being-tuned-in to that which transcends in its totality that we have called with Heidegger "primordial mood" *(Befind-lichkeit)* or with Eugen Fink "primordial enthusiasm" (being-in-transcendent-Being). This primordial enthusiasm is a structural characteristic of existential love. It is through the ecstasy of primordial enthusiasm that existential lovers overstep their narrow ego towards their harmony with the *logos* and that they establish their personal bond in Being.

Motivation and Spontaneity

From this it follows that in existential love we are profoundly "moved" by primordial enthusiasm rather than by any particular or visible "motive" *(movere*—to move). Existential love is not so much determined by a particular content as by the fundamental "how" of an existential attitude. As that which gives rise to our "Being-in-the-world" existential love reveals the original "spontaneity" of our ex-sistence or "the *unmotivated* upsurge of the world."[324] In existential love we do not break away from our feelings, passions and emotions, but we break with our acceptance of them as the only and ultimate "motives" of authentic human love. Our particular feelings and emotions play an important role in existential love, but only to the extent to which they remain gravitated around primordial enthusiasm as their permanent source and inspiration.

These particular feelings and emotions are not the "internal" reactions of a basically "mood-less" self to "external" events, but rather *dialectical* modifications of our primordial affectedness. No particular "reason" or "motive" is great enough an incentive to induce a person to enter into an existential love relationship. We are neither "pushed" nor "pulled" into existential love; it is not caused by either "internal" or "external" motives; there are no particular reasons for this authentic love; there is no separation of meaning from the act of existential loving.[325] Existential love originates as a spontaneous and unmotivated upsurge of our co-Being-in-the-world. Existential love is not "motivated" by anything other than itself. St. Bernard expressed this beautifully: "Love seeks no cause beyond itself and no limit; it is its own fruit, its own enjoyment. I love because I love; I love in order that I may love . . ."[326]

In existential love as the unmotivated upsurge of our co-Being-in-the-world man reaches the very height of *spontaneity*. According to Maslow "Spontaneity at the self-actualizing level—being healthy, natural—is unmotivated; indeed it is the contradiction of motivation."[327] Negatively speaking, spontaneity is the absence of control, inhibition, repression, fixation, role-playing, defenses, artificiality. Positively speaking, spontaneity is any uncontrolled or self-acting action or behavior (*sponte*—of free will). Control and spontaneity are by definition antithetical. But, then, there is authentic and unauthentic self-acting behavior. This distinction gives rise to two different meanings of the word spontaneity. In the first place there is the *authentic* spontaneity of our will-to-Being which transcends our controlling will-to-power. This authentic spontaneity is voluntary, it is the very freedom of our authentic be-havior. This authentic spontaneity is the ethical will to let beings "be," and to let Being "happen." And, secondly, there is the *unauthentic* spontaneity of involuntary action which can be impulsive, instinctive or automatic. Thus the words "voluntary" and "involuntary," which are really antonyms of each other, are both at the same time partial synonyms of the word "spontaneous."

Existential love as the will-to-Being is authentic spontaneity. All serious writers on the subject of human love have stressed spontaneity as a structural characteristic of authentic love.[328] Existential love as the will-to-co-Being is spontaneity in the sense of freedom-to-be. Existential love lets beings "be" by letting the "event" of Being "happen" (*ex* and *venire*—to come out; *happ*—occurrence without prevision). The freedom thereby gained is not a withdrawal from feelings and emotions, but a withdrawal from fixated and repressed emotions that block the spontaneous emergence of primordial enthusiasm.

Asceticism as the Interplay of Authentic and Unauthentic Spontaneity

It is here that the genuine conception of asceticism comes in. For the spontaneous enthusiasm of existential love is not an acosmic or absolute freedom, but rather an incarnated or "situated freedom." To be sure, the authentic spontaneity of existential love *transcends* the unauthentic spontaneity of the more or less deterministic processes and causal reactions of our emotional and instinctive life. Yet, *without this embodiment* in the unauthentic spontaneity of our emotional life the transcendency of authentic spontaneity, the spontaneity of primordial enthusiasm, could not emerge either. As Luijpen puts it, "The meaning of asceticism in human life can never consist in 'killing' man's facticity, for without this facticity the person is not capable of anything."[329] In other words, in existential love we are primarily but not exclusively "moved" by the authentic spontaneity of primordial enthusiasm. For the unauthentic spontaneity of our passions and emotions also plays an essential role. Not "by themselves," however, but as participants in authentic spontaneity are they able to contribute to the emergence of existential love. Existential love lets these feelings and emotions "be," i.e. it lets them respond to the will-to-Being, and thus it makes them *disciples* of the authoritative spontaneity of the *logos*.

Genuine asceticism does not kill, control or suppress our feelings, emotions or drives, but it "orientates" them towards their common *ethos*. This common *ethos* is existential love which is so "superior" and "authoritative" that it is able to transcend the forces of our facticity without suppressing or eliminating them. The obedient authority of existential love is, in accordance with the *logos,* capable of setting all the conflicting forces of our embodiment apart in their primordial togetherness of authentic spontaneity. The obedient authority of existential love does not induce emotional paralysis, it does not suppress our freedom to feel, it does not petrify the original spontaneity of our life-world. On the contrary, the authoritative spontaneity of existential love inspires our feelings and emotions to fulfill themselves, and to emerge in their true Being as co-listeners to the primordial inspiration of the *logos*. Existential love enables man to live his emotional resources in a healthy and spontaneous way by accepting them as "co-sources" or "co-motives" of his authentic spontaneity. Only in the unity of their reciprocal implication do authentic and unauthentic spontaneity contribute to the emergence of authentic love.

The Viewpoint of the Rationalistic Moralist

From all that has been said it follows that the authentic spontaneity of existential love should never be confused with *irresponsibility*. And this is exactly what the rationalistic moralist is prone to do. For just as the rationalistic philosopher regards everything that transcends his controlling thinking as irrational, so also the rationalistic moralist (the formalist or the legalist) regards everything that transcends his controlling attitude as irresponsible. For his only responsibility is to the deterministic conformity with an abstract set of static rules that control his life. He is afraid of a spontaneous way of life which entails unpredictable changes that upset the reliable and predictable center of his moral activities. He has never experienced the full spontaneity of ethical existence. His conception of asceticism as self-control results in emotional paralysis, ethical insensitivity and the extinction of genuine love. He has never permitted himself to be affected by reality in its entirety. He knows little or nothing of the integrating, cathartic and revelatory meaning of genuine asceticism. He mistakes the "second naïveté" (Santayana) of authentic spontaneity for childish maladjustment, and frowns upon any manifestation of spontaneity as immature or immoral irresponsibility.

Yet, what is really "irresponsible" is the unwillingness on the part of the rationalistic moralist to "respond" to the authentic spontaneity of existential love. This unwillingness entails the refusal to act in accordance with the primordial spontaneity of the *logos* or the refusal to accept this basic criterion of all ethical action. The authentic spontaneity of existential love, instead of being irresponsible, guarantees ethical authenticity. For, in the first place, existential love does not permit the licentious spontaneity of our emotions to take its own course, but it orientates these conflicting forces towards the authentic spontaneity of primordial enthusiasm. And, secondly, this authentic spontaneity of primordial enthusiasm is not the irresponsible freedom of arbitrariness either. On the contrary, this authentic spontaneity is freedom in accordance with the *logos,* or spontaneity that "responds" to the binding criterion of all truly ethical action. Genuine asceticism does not suppress the spontaneity of our ethical ex-sistence. True asceticism frees our emotional spontaneity *from* its suppressions, inhibitions and artificiality (the cathartic aspect) in order to free it *for* its integration in the authentic spontaneity of existential love (the revelatory aspect).

The Spontaneity of Existential Love

Existential love as the authentic spontaneity of primordial enthusiasm is not of our own making and it escapes our control. Existential love does not occur by command, but it comes to us as an "overwhelming" experience, as an original inspiration, as a primordial gift. Genuine love is graced. Existential love is not a gift that we "possess," but rather a gift that "possesses us." It is a gift that constitutes the very authenticity (self) of our human ex-sistence. Existential love is the gift we *are*.[330] This gift is never an "accomplished fact," or an unchanging "state of being." For this would reduce existential love to the fixity and rigidity of a "thing," which as a fundamental mode of co-Being-in-the-world it could not possibly be. Existential love is an original gift renewed in time, a gift which never ceases to give its originative giving. "The original," says Heidegger, "remains original only if it never loses the possibility of being what it is: origin as emergence."[331]

The "Happiness" of Existential Love

Now, the "happiness" of existential love consists precisely in this, that its authentic spontaneity permits this "event" (coming out) of original inspiration (breathing into) to "happen" (occur without prevision). As we have seen before, this "happiness" as the experiential "happening" of the "event" of Being is born in *spontaneity;* it is not subject to control or calculation. According to Josef Pieper "Happiness is essentially a gift; we are not the forgers of our own felicity."[332] Or, as Alan Watts puts it: "Enjoyment is always gratuitous and can come no other way than of itself, spontaneously."[333] The happiness of existential love is always experienced as a *gift*.

We have also seen, however, that the happiness of authentic spontaneity is never an "unmixed blessing."[334] For the "fascination" with the "event" of Being is a fascination with the *mystery* of Being. This fascination, therefore, is always blended with existential anxiety which discloses authentic Nothingness and the radical finitude of our ex-sistence. This experience of radical finitude is further emphasized by the facticity of our situation, by the awareness that we are not the origin of our own originality, and that we cannot ex-sist without an essential dependency on other beings. In other words, existential love discloses both the fascinating inexhaustibility of Being and the awesome finitude of human ex-sistence. Existential love reveals both the fullness and the emptiness of the universe of man. In addition to all this, the inspiration of love's happiness has to be "worked out" through a lifetime of asceticism, laborious efforts and often painful struggles. Small wonder, therefore, that the happy spontaneity of existential love is not for the weak but for the strong and the courageous.

EXISTENTIAL LOVE AND CREATIVE UNDERSTANDING

Up to now we have drawn our parallel between existential thinking and existential loving from the viewpoint of primordial enthusiasm. And the observant reader will undoubtedly have recognized inspirational characteristics such as gratuitousness, spontaneity, transcendency, ecstasy and enthusiasm. We now want to continue our comparison by discussing the second structural element of the "openness" of existential love: *creative understanding*. This creative understanding of existential love is the counter-phenomenon of its primordial enthusiasm. By creative understanding we do not mean intellectual or mere theoretical understanding, but rather *the creative "standing" of authentic ex-sistence "under" the originative openness of Being*. In the following pages we want to discuss the creative acceptance of existential love of the translucent self-actualization of Being in man. And this will reveal more inspirational characteristics of love, such as its creativity, its suddenness and unexpectedness, its dream-like consciousness and its capacity to penetrate to the essence of a thing in one single stroke.

Creative Receptivity

As we have seen earlier, the primordial gift of wonder is received in a way which is neither absolutely creative, nor purely passive.[335] On the level of authentic perception the ordinary categories of activity and passivity should be abandoned, and replaced by the fundamental conception of "creative receptivity." (Gabriel Marcel) For the reception of our primordial inspiration is our highest creativity. This "creative receptivity" is the fundamental willingness to surrender to the "oceanic feeling" of primordial wonder. In our elucidation of authentic inspiration we found that this creative receptivity is the dream-like consciousness which is characteristic of the mystic, the seer and the existential thinker.[336] And, here, we could add "of the existential lover as well."

For the willingness to surrender to the "oceanic feeling" of primordial Being is the very will-to-Being which defines existential love. The original integrity with reality in its entirety, "the feeling of fusion, of oneness ('oceanic feeling')," says Erich Fromm, "is the essence of mystical experience and the root of the most intense sense of union with one other person or with one's fellow men."[337] Existential love as creative receptivity is never a merely passive "being loved." Nor is it ever a mere "being driven," or a purely passive form of union (masochism). On the other hand, it is equally impossible that existential love is a mere activistic giving of love without receiving, or a purely active form of fusion (sadism). Existential love as creative receptivity is a reciprocity of giving and receiving through which both partners achieve their ever growing personal integrity. Existential love is the mutual self-creativity through the reception of the gift of Being as co-Being. And it is the mutuality of this creative receptivity which constitutes the "creative fidelity" of existential lovers (Gabriel Marcel).

Divination of Dormant Potentialities

Existential love as the creative receptivity of the "natural light" or the ontological translucency of the self-actualization of Being in man "stands" creatively "under" the originative openness of Being. Existential love has a "creative under-standing" of its own, which is not identical with philosophical under-standing, although, of course, their structural characteristics are analogous. The creative understanding of existential love enables the lover to penetrate to the core of the beloved one's personality in one single perception. Moreover, the creative understanding of existential love invests the lovers with the power to divine and actualize dormant potentialities in one another, and to lend a continued freshness of appreciation to their mutual admiration. Although these cognitive and divining characteristics of genuine love have often been recognized, they have seldom been understood in their ontological meaning and depth. To arrive at such an understanding is the task we set ourselves in the following pages.

Just as existential thinking begins as a turning back into the all-encompassing gift of Being, so also existential loving begins as a turning back into primordial Being. This turning back into primordial Being is the dialectical self-creative and self-actualizing re-petition *(Wiederholung)* of this primordial phenomenon. The progressive achievement of existential love, therefore, proceeds through a renewal of the primary data, through advancing the self-actualization of Being it had begun, through "presenting" its "past" data as "future" possibilities. In other words, existential love is creatively receiving its data. To employ the terminology of Heidegger, existential love is "under-standing" *(Verstehen),* i.e. its *standing* under the inspiration of Being *(stehen)* is a creative going *beyond* itself *(ver).*

Existential love as creative self-transcendency *is* shedding light, *is* illuminating Being, *is* an existential project, *is* actualization of potentialities, *is* progressive disclosure of the meaning of the self-actualization of our co-Being-in-the-world. It should never be overlooked, however, that every man's creativity is a gift from Being rather than a merely human activity. For, as Heidegger puts it, "All projection—and, consequently, even man's 'creative' activity—is *thrown.*"[338] Existential love is a "thrown project," a "creative receptivity," a "dia-logue."

The I—Thou Relationship

This creative understanding of existential love, since it is a standing under the inspiration of the *logos,* is a *fundamental* understanding. This is why the existential lover has the capacity to discover the *central value* of the beloved one in a single stroke. For, in the light of the *logos,* as we have seen, essences present themselves in a single stroke as fundamental "presences."[339] The inspiration of the *logos* enables existential lovers to penetrate into the very depth of one another's personality which remains hidden from the uninspired. The lover's gaze is never fixed on merely "visible qualities," but it sees right through them down to the "original data" ("gift of Being") of the beloved one's ex-sistence.[340] The mutual understanding of existential lovers never limits itself to observable qualities, characteristics or traits of character. For their mutual understanding is a co-standing under Being. In fact, existential lovers set only little value on "visible" characteristics, but they attach fundamental importance to the very Being of one another's personality.[341]

The true encounter of existential lovers, therefore, takes place in their transcendency rather than in their peripheral facticity. Their *I—Thou* relationship transcends the subject-object dichotomy, and is an immediate and reciprocal self-presence in Being. This is why existential lovers transcend the matter-of-factness, the density and ponderousness of the workaday world. They find themselves and one another transfigured within the "wonder-ful" depth of Being. The existential lover cannot objectify his relationship without destroying it.

An attempt to objectify the *I—Thou* relationship would reduce it to an *I—he* relationship, in which the *he* stands for a human ob-ject, and the *I* for a human sub-ject. An objectified *Thou* would no longer be encountered in the transcendency of their mutual presence in Being, but rather as a *thing* that stands over against an observer, as a thing that can be "seen" and know in terms of predicates or "particulars" listed on an "official dossier." (Gabriel Marcel) Or, to put it differently, the *I—Thou* can be degraded into the *I—it* relationship. From the monologue of this *I—it* relationship the dialogue of the mutual presence of the "essential we" has vanished. The "essential we" has degenerated into a subject-object relationship, in which the object, the "it" is known as the sum total of its "observable characteristics." (Martin Buber)

Existential lovers, therefore, do not love one another because of any particular characteristics. Gabriel Marcel says it very aptly: "It is vain for the lover to enumerate the characteristics and the merits of the beloved. He is certain *a priori* that any such inventory will not give him his love, which is transparent in itself. Even if he managed to pick out a special characteristic, this special characteristic would still be unexplainable to him: it is inasmuch as this characteristic is not treated as such [but in their mutual presence in Being] that it is active."[342] The existential lover would not say: "I love you because of *this* or *that* special characteristic," but rather: "I love you because you are you," Or, more accurately yet: "I love you!"[343]

The Suddenness of its Beginning

Another inspirational characteristic of existential love is its *suddenness* and unexpectedness. The creative understanding of existential love is inspired understanding. For it is the creative receptivity of primordial enthusiasm. And inspiration, as we have seen, manifests itself "at one stroke" in an undivided and indivisible act of creation. Inspiration does not arrive in a succession of "separate" parts of "discrete" moments.[344]

The authentic spontaneity of existential love, therèfore, arrives suddenly and unexpectedly. The sudden beginning of authentic inspiration, however, is usually some germinal insight that has to "grow" and to be "worked out." This holds true for existential love just as much as we found it to be true for existential thinking and artistic creativity. Erich Fromm has recognized the fact that love has to be "worked out," and rightly emphasized that love is an "art." But he has strangely overlooked the other fact, namely, that love is a sudden inspiration.[345] Oswald Schwarz, among others, has been more predominantly concerned with these inspirational characteristics of authentic love. "Love, he says, "always begins suddenly. It need not always be the *coup de foudre,* the dramatic 'love at first sight', but even if a love seems to grow gradually from inconspicuous beginnings, even if one seems to start loving a person one has known for some time—even then, the beginning is sudden."[346]

"Love at First Sight"

Existential love always begins suddenly and unexpectedly. But does not this imply that existential love is always such a dramatic "love at first sight?" From our foregoing elucidations it should be immediately clear that the meaning of this much debated issue of "love at first sight" hinges on the interpretation of the word "sight." If by "sight" is meant the sensory act of "seeing" or a surface fascination with "visible" qualities, then this love has nothing to do with existential love. Existential love never limits itself to external qualities or visible characteristics. "Love at first sight" in the sense of *seeing* is at best a mere emotional attraction, a sensual fascination with surface characteristics, or some sort of sticky sentimentality. If, on the other hand, the word "sight" is understood in the sense of fundamental "insight," then we may be confronted with existential love. For existential love grasps the central value or the Being of the beloved one's personality in an "original perception" which is a veritable "insight." Existential love is "love at first sight" in the sense that it "creatively under-stands" the very depth of the beloved one's "presence" in one single stroke, or in one original, sudden and unexpected perception.

Consequently, that which decides on the authenticity of our "love at first sight" is again the criterion of depth.[347] This criterion, as we have seen, is inherent in the original perception itself.[348] Original perception precisely differs from mere sense-perception in this that it opens up the primordial depth of the all-encompassing phenomenon of wonder. Just as in existential thinking the assurance of the truth is found in the *beginning,* and is veri-fied or made truer or more trustworthy by nothing other than itself, so also existential loving has the fundamental assurance in its very *beginning,* and validates *itself* rather than by any outside criterion. The understanding of existential love is self-justifying and self-validating in the never-ending ad-venture of its creative receptivity. In existential thinking it is the phenomenological reduction which prevents us from lapsing into the simple and fortuitous "seeing" of a naive and uncritical intuitionism.[349] In existential loving it is the respectful and courageous reception of inspired "insight," and the laborious "working out" of this inspiration that safeguard us against the easy intuitionism of "love at first 'sight'."

It is against this naive and uncritical intuitionism of "love at first 'sight'," against this easy and effortless "falling in love" that Erich Fromm has written his excellent book *The Art of Loving.*[350] He correctly warns us in his own words, against "the confusion between the initial experience of *'falling'* in love, and the permanent state of *being* in love, or as we might better say, of 'standing' in love."[351] Indeed, this "out-standing" phenomenon of "ex-sistential" love should not be confused with *erotic love* which is its beautiful beginning or initial stage of fascination. But, on the other hand, erotic love should not be confused with the easy intuitionism of "love at first 'sight'" either.

The Ontological Meaning of Erotic Love

Theories of *erotic love* have oscillated between two opposite extremes. On the one hand, erotic love has been interpreted as morbid excitement, dark and irrational passion, unholy and earthy sensualism, silly sentimentalism or beautiful illusion. On the other hand, many have regarded erotic love as the paragon of human love, as the enjoyment of sheer supernatural beauty or as sublime enthusiasm which reaches the summit in its union with the divine. In actual fact, the former set of interpretations underestimates the ontological significance of erotic love, whereas the latter conceptions overrate it.

Erotic love is *the original perception of existential love.* As we have seen earlier, the original perception is the aesthetic perception, it is the experiential and sym-bolic encounter of the world of the usual and the un-usual world of wonder. In the original perception of a phenomenon this phenomenon "presents itself" in its "original givenness."[352] The *ontological significance* of erotic love, therefore, is that it presents the phenomenon of existential love in its *original givenness.* Erotic love is *beautiful love,* it is the experiential, wonder-ful and undifferentiated beginning of existential love. In the beauty of erotic love the lovers encounter one another in the sym-bolic union between the wonder-ful Being and its visible embodiment. In erotic love the lovers love one another's body not as an object of lust, of dark passion or unholy sensuality, but rather as the "holy" incarnation of the spirituality of their personal Being. In erotic love the lovers love one another with their *whole body* and *whole soul* in an *undifferentiated unity*.[353] Erotic love, therefore, is "love at first sight" in the unique sense of a sym-bolic encounter between "first sight" and "originative insight."[354] The ordinary expressions we use for erotic love, at least if we understand them authentically, are: "falling in love," or "being in love." "Being in love" is the undifferentiated incipience of the existential love of Being. And just as in terms of existential thinking the aesthetic perception is that which brings the truth into ex-sistence, so also in terms of existential loving erotic love is that which brings authentic love into ex-sistence.

The Ethical Relevancy of Erotic Love

It may come as a shock to the rationalistic moralist that we think of erotic love as being invested with ethical relevancy. Yet, this insight is a necessary implication of our foregoing elucidations of erotic love. In short, if erotic love is that which brings authentic love into ex-sistence, and if authentic love is ethical love, then erotic love is that which brings ethical love into ex-sistence. This inescapable conclusion is utterly unacceptable to the rationalistic moralist, and a far cry from the conception of erotic love as unbridled sensuality. If, indeed, erotic love is reduced to unbridled sensuality, and if morality is a mere conformity to a set of rules kept under control by "hardening" mortification, then ethical life and erotic love are irreconcilable phenomena. Small wonder that nowadays the aesthetic phenomenon, or for that matter the phenomenon of love are regarded as mere irrelevancies in matters of morality. It is *a fortiori erotic love* as the beautiful love that is considered to be amoral, if not outright immoral.

But if ethical existence is existential love as the will-to-Being, then erotic love as the original perception of authentic love "presents" us with the undifferentiated, beautiful and *pre-ethical* source of ethical life.[355] We say "presents" us in its fundamental, ontological sense of creative emergence, of giving birth to. Once again, our original perception does not merely perceive what is there already, but it is also creative and constitutive of our authentic ex-sistence. Erotic love as the original perception of existential love does not merely take a snap-shot of this love as if it were an already established fact. On the contrary, the original perception of existential love brings this love into ex-sistence, it constitutes its beautiful and undifferentiated beginning and promotes what it perceives.[356]

"De-finition" of Erotic Love

Erotic love is the original perception of existential love. It is precisely this insight which reveals to us both the ontological significance and the fundamental limits of erotic love. Erotic love is essentially more than a beautiful illusion or an unbridled passion. For erotic love brings existential love into ex-sistence. It opens up the spiritual dimension in the embodiment of the lovers.[357] Erotic love as authentic "falling in love" or "being in love" is a genuine experience of revelation, and not a mere "infatuation." Erotic love discloses a profound intimacy of Being, a real depth of feeling, a genuine experience of beauty and a true potentiality for existential loving. This is why, as Jersild says, those who have fallen in love "seek one another's company as something of supreme value," and are "confronted with an inner wealth which they never knew they had."[358]

Erotic love as the original perception of existential love is the beautiful onset of the self-actualization of one's co-Being-in-the-world. This is the ontological significance of erotic love. On the other hand, this beautiful onset is not the primordial de-cision of the will-to-Being yet. And this is the ontological limitation of erotic love. Erotic love is not the paragon of human love; it has to be transcended. Erotic love is not the *actual* existential love, it is not the *de-cisive* will-to-Being, it is not the *differentiated* or *dia-logical* self-actualization of Being in man. The inspiration of erotic love has not yet been "worked out." Those who underestimate erotic love ignore its spiritual relevancy and reduce it to a sticky sentimentality. Those who overestimate erotic love ignore its need to be transcended and fixate it into a sticky sentimentality also.

Erich Fromm on Erotic Love

Erotic love as the authentic "love at first 'insight' " is beautiful, sudden and spontaneous. In other words, it is truly a "falling in love" which is authentic and has ontological relevancy. It is wrong, therefore, to deprive erotic love of its inspirational characteristics, and to regard it as a particular form of existential love. And it is equally wrong to reduce the meaning of "falling in love" *as such* to the easy intuitionism of "love at first 'sight'." Erotic love as the *authentic* "falling in love" should never be confused with the *unauthentic* "falling in love" of "infatuations." It is here that Eric Fromm makes his basic mistake. By dint of emphasizing the responsibility, the care, the commitment and the decisiveness of existential love, he ascribes features such as beauty, inspiration, suddenness, spontaneity and wonder exclusively to the easy intuitionism of unauthentic "falling in love." He complains that erotic love "is often confused with the explosive experience of 'falling' in love."[359] And "falling in love" he understands as an "infatuation," a "being 'crazy' about each other," which lovers often mistake "for proof of the intensity of their love, while it may only prove the degree of their preceding loneliness."[360] Here he underrates the ontological significance of true erotic love by ignoring the revelatory power of its beauty, its suddenness, its inspiration and its wonder-fulness.

Yet, at the same time he overestimates erotic love by investing it with "will," "decision" and "judgment."[361] "If love were only a feeling," he says, "there would be no basis for the promise to love each other forever."[362] Indeed, when "falling in love" is merely based on feelings and emotions, it is unauthentic, and holds little promise for the future. But erotic love is *not* merely based on feelings and emotions; and the only alternative is *not,* as Fromm thinks, that it is based on "will," "decision" and "judgment." There is a third possibility which Fromm has overlooked, namely that erotic love is based on the *original perception* of existential love. Erotic love is the original perception which constitutes the initial and beautiful disclosure of the will-to-Being. Although erotic love is more than mere feelings and emotions, it is less than the existential will. As the pre-reflective, undifferentiated and beautiful beginning of existential love, erotic love is not the differentiated self-actualization of Being in man. Erotic love is not the de-cisive will of existential love as Fromm suggests.

For Fromm erotic love is one particular form of existential love. And its distinctive mark is "exclusiveness." We agree with Fromm when he regards exclusiveness as a characteristic of erotic love, and also when he asserts that this characteristic does not separate us from the rest of the world. Fromm is right in stating that the erotic lovers love one another in "the essence of their being," and that in one another they love (at least implicitly) "all of mankind, all that is alive."[363] However, we do not agree with Fromm where he regards *exclusiveness* rather than *original perception* as the distinctive mark of erotic love. It is not its exclusiveness that distinguishes erotic love from other forms of existential love, but it is the originality of its perception that distinguishes erotic love from *any* form of existential love, and, for that matter, from any unauthentic form of "falling in love" also.

Erotic love is not one particular form of existential love among others, but rather the initial and pre-reflective stage, and a structural element in the dialectics of *any* form of existential love. In the first place, as the beautiful anticipation of existential love it is the initial stage not only of existential heterosexual love, but also of other forms of existential love, such as authentic friendship, religious love etc. It is just as wrong to exclude beauty, wonderfulness and inspiration from erotic love as it is to include the existential de-cision of the ethical will in its structure. Moreover, just as existential thinking is a turning back into the original perception of wonder which remains its lasting source and guiding light, so also existential loving turns back into the wonder-ful perception of erotic love as the permanent source and lasting inspiration of its dialectical self-actualization. We are now, finally, able to understand a strange omission in the otherwise so profound analyses of existential love in the works of Erich Fromm. In his analyses of human love we look in vain for inspirational characteristics such as beauty, wonder, humor, playfulness, spontaneity, happiness etc. Since Fromm has eliminated these characteristics from the beautiful beginning of existential love, we do not find them as a lasting inspiration in its dialectical structure either. It is not without foundation that Maslow makes his terse remark that Fromm's definition of existential love "sounds a little like a pact or a partnership of some kind rather than a spontaneous sportiveness."[364]

Participation in the Self-project of One Another's Being

So far we have discussed the creative understanding of existential love as fundamental *understanding*. This fundamental understanding enables the lovers to penetrate to the essential value of each other's personality in one single and inspired perception. We now want to elucidate how the *creativity* of this understanding invests the lovers with the power to divine dormant potentialities in one another, and to lend a continued freshness of appreciation to their mutual admiration.

The creative understanding of existential love is, as we have seen, self-transcendency. It is shedding light, it is both the progressive self-actualizing and self-illuminating disclosure of our co-Being-in-the-world. Existential lovers, therefore, always perceive one another *in the act of becoming.* In other words, they encounter each other in what they *are,* which is not the *status quo* of their facticity, but rather the dynamism of their ex-sistence as "emergence." They always understand one another "ahead of themselves," "beyond their facticity," or as "being more than they are." The existential lover understands creatively his beloved one, which means that he divines still dormant potentialities in him, and that at the same time he helps him actualize what he is capable of becoming *(Seinkönnen)*. To understand a person merely in the *status quo* of his facticity means to fixate him into the rigidity of a "thing," and to prevent him from "Being." No one has expressed this more beautifully than the German poet Goethe (we quote from memory): "If we take people as they are, we make them worse. If we treat them as if they were what they ought to be, we help them to become what they are capable of becoming."

Existential love as creative understanding is a co-project in which both partners constitute and increase each other's ex-sistence in a never ending ad-venture of mutual self-discovery and mutual self-creativity. William Luijpen quotes Buitendijk as saying that "to know the essence and orientation of a concrete human being is possible only by participation in the self-project of his being."[365] And then he adds: "Such a participation is called love."[366] Existential love as the creative participation in the self-project of the other's ex-sistence promotes what it understands, and understands what it promotes. Existential love gives the other to himself, it helps him become, and it makes him ex-sist authentically. And all this "happens" in a non-deterministic, non-causal and non-methodical way. Or, rather, existential love *is* the appeal that awakens the other's freedom, it *is* the fundamental *way (methodos)* to beget the freedom-to-be.

"Healing through Meeting"

It should be mentioned in passing that here we are touching on the paramount importance of the *person* in education and in psychotherapy. Educational methods and therapeutic techniques are of little or no avail without the self-actualizing co-Being, without the existential love of the therapist or the educator. Methods and techniques, rooted as they are in the determinisms of man's facticity, become effective only as *co-motives* of the creative understanding of the other's self-project. It comes, therefore, as a surprise to learn that the psychologists are practically silent on the subject of human love.[367] We know of two main reasons for this strange omission. The first one is the misconception of authentic love as a merely emotional attachment, and the justified fear on the part of the psychologist to become entangled in such an emotional involvement. The second reason is the ontological depth of existential love which remains inaccessible to the psychologist who calls himself "empirical." "Psychologists," says D'Arcy, "are strangely silent on the subject of love. Perhaps it is because they feel precluded as empirical investigators from dwelling on a matter which seems to extend beyond their field of study."[368]

The situation could be remedied if the psychologist transcends his merely "experimental" approach by also opening up to the "experiential" data of our authentic ex-sistence. Precisely by doing this Ludwig Binswanger was able to show that what he calls the *objectivity of love* is a fundamental ingredient of our psychological knowledge of man.[369] Once the psychologist is able to grasp existential love as a fundamental mode of co-Being-in-the-world, he will understand that he is involved in primordial Being rather than in subjectivistic emotions. It is *primordial wonder* which keeps the psychologist's existential love at a "respectful" distance from his client. It is the primordial *depth* of this wonder which guarantees the authenticity of his loving attitude. And it is the *comprehensive universality* of wonder which keeps the therapist at a proper distance from both the subjectivism of merely emotional involvements, and the disinterested objectivism of merely manipulatory activities. Whatever methods and techniques may be employed, the client cannot be helped or even found in his personal value without the creative understanding of the self-project of his being, without the personal inspiration of existential love, without "healing through meeting" (Martin Buber). And, it goes without saying, all this applies *mutatis mutandis* to the educator who is true to his vocation. As Buber puts it, "Only in his whole being, in all his spontaneity can the educator truly affect the whole being of his pupil . . . . His aliveness streams out to them and affects them most strongly and purely when he has no thought of affecting them."[370] The non-utilitarian spontaneity of authentic inspiration is the most effective and growth-provoking discipline.

Creative Admiration and the Alleged Blindness of Love

A last structural element of the creative understanding of existential lovers is the *continued freshness of their mutual admiration.* As a creative standing under the never ending emergence of the inspiration of wonder, the mutual self-actualization of existential lovers is never static or final, but always self-enriching, always new and original. Existential love continually enriches the past by receiving it as the possibility of its future self-project. Thus its original data become more and more "origin-al." We have already quoted Heidegger as saying that "The original remains original only if it never loses the possibility of being what it is: origin as emergence."[371] Existential love constantly re-creates the openness of Being by re-peating its origin. This re-peating of existential love is not the mechanical repetition of routine habits which characterizes our merely physical behavior, and which leads to boredom and exhaustion. On the contrary, the re-peating of existential love is the creative re-petition (*re* and *petere*—to seek again; *Wiederholung*) of the original beginning of our authentic be-havior as the most fascinating ad-venture of our ex-sistence. "A purely physical coitus," says Schwarz, "is almost inevitably followed by exhaustion and the indifference or tedium of satiation, whereas lovers awake from their ecstasy refreshed, new-born, looking at each other full of wonderment, as if they had not known each other before. And they have not, really."[372] Indeed, they have not known each other to the extent in which existential lovers understand each other creatively. They always understand each other "ahead of one another," their understanding is always new, enriched and origin-al. Their mutual admiration is never a static gazing that grows old and stale. Existential lovers have the "wonder-ful" capacity to admire one another again and again as an ever-renewed and inexhaustible source of mutual happiness, wonder, awe and fascination. Their mutual understanding is creative understanding; their mutual admiration (co-wonder) is *creative admiration*.[373]

Our elucidations of existential love as creative understanding have a corollary. Nothing is farther from the truth than the commonly accepted saying that "love is blind." For the creative understanding of existential love penetrates into the very essence of a person's Being. To be sure, the understanding of existential love involves us in the mystery of Being. But this is characteristic of *any* fundamental insight. And, as we know, the primordial obscurity of the mystery of Being is by no means tantamount to unknowableness. On the contrary, existential love reveals a depth of insight that far transcends the rational clarity of objectifying thinking. The incommunicability between existential lovers is due to the inexhaustible depth of Being, which sets them apart at a "respectful" di-stance. This incommunicability is not a blind spot or a subjective inaccessibility in existential love, but rather a constitutive characteristic of its very depth.[374] Also erotic lovers, as we have seen, know the essence of one another's Being. Due to the undifferentiated nature of this love, however, they may be somewhat blind to each other's imperfections and limitations. What is really blind is the easy intuitionism of the unauthentic "falling in love" which is based on merely physical or emotional attractions. Such a love fails to penetrate into the being of the loved one's personality, and really remains a being lonesome together, or a blind egotism *à deux*.[375] Authentic love, however, rather than causing blindness presents us with the deepest of insights. Maslow has come to the same conclusion on psychological grounds. "Far from accepting the common platitude that love makes people blind," he says, "I become more and more inclined to think of the *opposite* as true, namely, that non-love makes us blind."[376]

THE DIALOGICAL STRUCTURE OF EXISTENTIAL LOVE

This, finally brings us to the third and last structural element which characterizes the way in which existential love is "in the world." This third characteristic, co-original with primordial enthusiasm and creative understanding is the *dialogical structure* of existential love. Not only existential thinking, but also existential loving has its own dialectics. It is especially this structural element which reveals existential love as "dialogue," as existential "de-cision," and as authentic "response-ability." Since this third structural element has been implied throughout our foregoing elucidations of existential love, we will here restrict ourselves to some basic observations.

Existential Love as Primordial De-cision

As we know, man does not ex-sist authentically until he opens up his entire Being "in response to the self-presentation of the *logos*." Just as existential thinking begins as the dialogue of the dialectical self-manifestation of Being, so also existential loving begins as a dialogue, namely the dialogue of the dialectical self-actualization of Being in man. And just as fundamental meaning in existential thinking results from an encounter between original data and a primary intention, so also the fundamental meaning of existential loving originates in such an encounter, which is the encounter between the primary ethical data and our existential will-to-Being. In other words, existential loving begins as the dialectical self-actualization of our Being-together-with-others-in-the-world. Existential loving begins as a unitary structure, as a unity-in-opposition, as a dia-logue. Existential loving begins as a differentiated response, as a multi-dimensional answer to an appeal, as a polar tension between the one and the many. And this polar tension is the mainspring of its very dynamism.

Existential love, therefore, begins in the primordial de-cision to *respond* to the dialectical self-actualization of Being. Love is not existential unless it manifests itself in the articulated context of *the* world *(logos)* as the horizon of all authentic self-actualization. Love is not existential unless it is world-wide.[377] Moreover, this primordial de-cision, as we have seen, is not so much a de-cision *we make,* but rather a de-cision which *makes us.* Existential love as our primordial de-cision to *be* constitutes the whole of our ex-sistence, and gives rise to our co-

Being in the world. It is only in this context that the "essential we" (Buber) of 'the *I—Thou* relationship presents itself as an original and irreducible phenomenon.

Existential Love and Authentic Asceticism

It is important to remember that the primordial de-cision of existential love is *not* a *particular* decision, and that it is not a decision among other decisions, such as acts of the will to choose, to judge or to control. The de-cision of existential love is the de-cision which underlies and permeates all our particular decisions and acts of the will. It is the primordial de-cision to respond to the call of the *logos*. Consequently, the *decisiveness* of existential love has nothing to do with force, control or coercion. On the contrary, this decisiveness is rather the *authentic spontaneity* which continually *ascertains* the orientation of our entire existence towards the primordial inspiration of the *logos*. In other words, existential love is "decisive spontaneity" which constitutes and continually promotes our freedom to be, our freedom to be with others, our freedom to be in the world, and our freedom to use our emotional resources in a healthy and spontaneous way. And, once again, we come upon asceticism as spontaneity rather than control. Once again we find that the fundamental meaning of asceticism (*askeein*—to excercise) is creative spontaneity rather than self-control, self-denial or self-mortification. Asceticism is the spontaneous "practice" of ethical love to set all things at one stroke in their dialectical orientation towards the *logos*. This insight into the essence of asceticism has been beautifully worded by Martin Buber. "It is a cruelly hazardous enterprise, this becoming a whole . . . Everything in the nature of inclinations, of indolence, of habits, of fondness for possibilities swashbuckling within us, must be overcome, and overcome, not by elimination, by suppression . . . Rather must all these mobile or static forces, seized by the soul's rapture, plunge of their own accord, as it were, into the mightiness of decision and dissolve within it."[378] And it is also in this sense that we should interpret the classical plea for ethical spontaneity: "*Ama et fac quod vis.*" "Love and do what you want" (St. Augustine).

A Personal Dialogue based on Motives of Appeal

The dialectics of existential love, just as the dialectics of existential thinking is, as we have seen, experiential rather than abstractive, creative rather than mechanical, and circular rather than rectilinear.[379] Since existential lovers meet one another in the self-project of their Being, their dialectical *I—Thou* relationship is a personal dialogue rather than a deterministic dialectics, an encounter based on freedom rather than on compulsion. Their encounter takes place within the very freedom of their ex-sistence rather than in the determinisms of their facticity that are to be seized and dissolved within the decisive spontaneity of their soul's rapture. Employing the terminology of Henri Bergson we could say that existential lovers are moved by "motives of appeal" rather than by "motives of force." It is ultimately the call of Being in existential lovers that makes them appeal to one another, and that invites them to transcend their facticity into the freedom of their co-Being. And what the call says is the unspoken invitation: "Be-with-me-in-the-world."

In fact, existential lovers do not primarily *have* an appeal; they *are* an appeal. And the existential answer to which they are invited is the *free* response of their whole ex-sistence. This is why the true lover has to take the risk that his appeal is not accepted, that his invitation is ignored, or that his call remains unanswered. Love based on compulsion, on "motives of force" reduces the beloved to a controllable object, and ceases to be love. There is no love or happiness in compulsion, and love that is not shared freely is no love. Compulsion degrades the free dialogue between the lovers to the mechanical dialectics of a deterministic existence. We cannot force love upon a person any more than we can force freedom, maturity, happiness or authenticity upon him. It is essential to genuine love that it is an overwhelming gift of Being, and that its recipient considers it an undeserved favor which he freely accepts in an act of humility and gratitude. "Humility" is not antithetical to the "greatness" of the gift, but rather a constituent element of its reception.

Existential Love is neither a Quality nor a Function

The existential dialogue of true lovers is first and foremost a dialogue between two persons within the all-encompassing phenomenon of Being. This implies that existential love cannot possibly be used as a "means" to an end, even if that end is the love of another person or the love of God. This would "functionalize" existential love and destroy its authentic dialectics which is always an end in itself. It would reduce the dignity of the beloved to a mere "quality" or to a merely commercial value. According to the famous saying of Immanuel Kant "All things have a price, man alone has dignity." To functionalize an authentic love relationship would violate the categorical imperative as stated by Kant: "So act as to treat humanity, whether in your own person or in that of any other, always at the same time as an end, and never merely as a means."[380]

The Embodiment of Existential Love

Existential love as the self-actualization of our co-Being-in-the-world includes the *world* in the structure of its dialectics. A disembodied or worldless existential love would be a contradiction in terms. Such a love would not "ex-sist," it would not be embodied, it would not be our co-Being-in-the-world. When we ask ourselves the question if it is possible to truly love "objects," or "things," or our "bodily" being, then a distinction should be made. We *cannot* truly love objects, things or human bodies *in their isolation,* apart from our self-actualization as co-Being. For existential love always transcends our facticity. *"Nihil amicum meum sine amico meo,"* "Nothing is lovable without my friend" (St. Augustine). On the other hand, without the "immanency" of our embodiment in the world we could not "transcend" our facticity either. Existential love involves human ex-sistence in its entirety. In other words, the "things" of the world and the "bodily" being of the lovers can only be loved as necessary "co-sources" or "co-motives" of the spontaneous call of existential love. "This call implies," says Luijpen, "that I will his bodily being and that I will his world for him. Otherwise my love would be an illusion. The man who loves his fellow man cares for his body, is concerned with what he needs for his material life, builds hospitals, constructs roads, harnesses rivers and seas, establishes traffic rules, builds schools and prisons—all to make it possible for the other to attain to *self*-realization in the world."[381] Existential lovers, therefore, are actively and essentially concerned with the well-being of each other's bodily being in the world; and it is in and through this embodiment that they meet one another. Their love has no meaning if they don't find it in the world, and their world has no meaning if they don't find it in their love.

Dialectical Conscience

Another dialectical characteristic of existential love is the *articulation* of its consciousness. Just as the existential thinker has a creative "comprehension" (grasping-together) of fundamental phenomena in their permanent togetherness of Being, so also the existential lover has a creative "con-science" (knowing-together) of his basic response-abilities in their primordial collectedness of Being. Con-science, as we have seen, reveals itself as our "having to be a response to the dialectical self-actualization of Being." Con-science is the creative understanding of Being as the "dis-closure" of response-able co-Being as norm. In other words, conscience is the existential disclosure of our being bound by the multi-dimensional responsibility of ethical love. Conscience is the consciousness of ex-sistential love; it reveals the creativity, the mutuality and the multi-dimensionality of its responsibility. "My own conscience," therefore, is never "my own" in the sense of private property, or in the sense of something I possess. On the contrary, conscience as the articulated consciousness of ex-sistential love reveals that my love is dialectical. *My* love is only authentic when it at the same time responds to my own ex-sistence, to the self-project of the other's Being, to the world of my environment, and to the primordial World of Being.

The Dilemma of Selfish or Unselfish Love

And it is here that we come upon an answer to the age-old dilemma between the immorality of *selfish* love and the apparent impossibility of *unselfish* or *disinterested* love. The answer is that the dilemma is a false one. For the articulated consciousness of existential love shows that a person who is exclusively bent on promoting his own interests does not love authentically, but that, on the other hand, a person who neglects his responsibility to self-love cannot truly love either. For in either case the *dia-logical* structure of existential love would be destroyed.

Both existential loving and existential thinking involve, as we know, the primordial phenomenon of Being. This is why they are, strictly speaking, undefinable. But it is their respective acting or thinking in accordance with the *logos* which de-fines all beings by setting them apart in their primordial unity of Being. This unity-in-opposition, this polar tension, this ontological "con-flict" is not destructive, but rather constitutive of the dialectical structure of both existential thinking and loving, and should always be preserved. In other words, the problem whether authentic love should be love for oneself or love for others is a pseudo-problem. It contradicts the dia-logical nature of ex-sistence as co-Being. For self-love *includes* in its very dialectics the participation in the self-project of the other's Being.[382]

The Unselfishness of Self-love

Without this dialogical participation self-love simply is not self-love, but rather *selfish love*. In selfish love the person is *exclusively* bent on promoting his own private interests. The selfish lover reduces his object to a mere instrument for his own private purposes. He reduces the other to a "thing," and degrades the "essential we" of the *I—Thou* dialogue to an impersonal *I—it* monologue. The selfish lover *excludes* any genuine concern for the self-project of the other's Being. And thus he *ex-*

cludes any real concern for his own authentic self. He no longer ex-sists authentically, he becomes an "egoist," one who loves the narrowness of his shrunken self *at the expense* of the other's self-project. One who loves his narrow "ego" at the expense of the other's self-project does this at the expense of the self-project of his *own* Being. Selfish love destroys self-love. *"Selfishness and self-love,"* says Fromm, *"far from being identical, are actually opposites.* The selfish person does not love himself too much but too little; in fact he hates himself."[383]

Now *self-love* is *unselfish* in a twofold sense. Self-love is unselfish in the sense that it has purged away all the traces of selfish love. Self-love is also unselfish in the sense that it does not restrict itself to the boundaries of a "closed" self. For the authentic self is "ex-sistence," it always "transcends" itself, it is always "open" to the other self and to primordial Being. True self-love is existential love. There is a commonly accepted interpretation of unselfishness, however, that tends to purge it of any trace of self-love. Here unselfishness is taken in the sense of loving others at the expense of oneself, of excluding oneself altogether, of giving oneself up. Yet, he who can only love others and not himself destroys the dialogical relationship of existential love, and cannot truly love at all. Unselfish love in this negativistic sense is a giving without receiving, whereas selfish love is receiving without giving. Neither of these alternatives is genuine love. For existential love, as we have seen, is always both giving and receiving; authentic love is "creative receptivity."

The Disinterestedness of Self-love

There is good and bad unselfishness, there is wise and foolish *disinterestedness.* The disinterestedness of authentic love also can be interpreted in a twofold sense. Disinterestedness can be taken in the sense that one has cleared out any tendency to use the loved one for *selfish* interests. Another, related meaning is that one refuses to restrict one's love *exclusively* to self-interest. Taken in either sense disinterestedness is wise and praiseworthy, and results from genuine asceticism. Disinterestedness becomes foolish, however, when it means unselfishness in the pejorative sense of the word. Disinterestedness as a giving without receiving, as we have seen, could not be love at all. It would be a total lack of participation or involvement (*interesse*—to be involved) in the self-project of the other's Being. But this would flatly contradict our phenomenological findings concerning the nature and structure of existential loving.

But the most fundamental reason why neither existential thinking nor existential loving can be disinterested ways of achieving authenticity is their involvement in the all-encompassing phenomenon of Being. The existential thinker and the existential lover are involved with the whole of their ex-sistence in the transcendency of primordial enthusiasm. Their existential *involvement* in that which *transcends* originates their *unselfish interest* in the self-presentation of all that is. And this is why we conclude our discussion on existential loving the same way as we brought our elucidation of existential thinking to an end. Existential love always involves self-love. And self-love is always ex-sistential, it always transcends itself, it always responds to the self-actualization of Being. Existential love is not a love we possess, but rather a love which possesses us. Existential love is "the loving of Being." The genitive indicated by the preposition "of" is more fundamentally a "subjective" than an "objective" genitive. It is more the self-loving of Being in man, than man's loving of Being which constitutes the authenticity of existential love. For, fundamentally speaking, man is more of Being than of himself. Man is himself only by being at the disposal of the primordial inspiration of the *logos*.

THE INEXHAUSTIBILITY OF PHILO-SOPHY

Having arrived at the end of this study we have come to realize one thing: we are not yet at the end of our journey. We started in the all-encompassing question of primordial wonder. We had to answer this question both in thought and in action. For a separation of thought and action would have contradicted the fact that the truth is in the whole, and that primordial wonder is an all-encompassing phenomenon. We found that wonder becomes explicated in the oscillation of two interdependent ways: existential thinking, or the dialectical self-manifestation of Being in man, and existential loving or the dialectical self-actualization of Being in man. Both ways are interdependent and interwoven, and involve the whole of our ex-sistence. We cannot advance fundamental thinking without fundamental action, and vice versa. In other words, existential thinking is also a partial self-actualization, and existential loving a partial self-illumination. Existential thinking is a loving-knowing, and existential loving is a knowing-loving. The well-known saying of St. Thomas: *"nihil volitum nisi praecognitum,"* "nothing is willed before it is known," should always be balanced by the less well-known saying of St. Augustine: *"non intratur in veritatem nisi per caritatem,"* "we cannot enter the truth except through love." Or as D'Arcy puts it: "It remains true that we do associate wisdom with love, because knowledge and love should be inseparably joined."[384]

Yet, one may have the impression that we never left our beginning behind, that our questioning never came off the ground. The answer is that this impression is correct. In fact, every fundamental question we answered put us deeper into the ground, every answer made our beginning more beginning, every answer returned as a more fundamental question. Every answer in existential thinking is but the last step in our fundamental questioning. The concern of the existential thinker is not only to answer philosophical questions, but just as much to keep these questions open. One question that will forever loom at the philosophical horizon, in fact, that *is* the philosophical horizon, is the primordial experience of wonder, the "wonder of wonders that beings are . . ."[385] And since wonder is the permanent source and lasting inspiration of existential thinking, it will always keep us "under way" *(homines viatores)*. We will never arrive at the end of the philosophical way of thinking which would be the full understanding and full possession of its very beginning. The philosophical way of thinking is a road that knows no end.

NOTES

1. Gabriel Marcel, trans., *The Philosophy of Existence,* New York, 1949, p. 3.

2. A philosophy may contain a crippling "lived" contradiction without containing any "systematic" contradiction. Ask, for instance, *for whom* the solipsist is writing his books on solipsism, or *why* the determinist says "thank you," or *how* the philosophical relativist can be absolutely sure of his relativistic philosophy.

3. *Metaphysics,* 1049 b 29–32.

4. Martin Heidegger, trans., *An Introduction to Metaphysics,* New Haven, 1959, p. 19.

5. *Metaphysics,* 982 b 12–13.

6. We write the word *Being* with a capital 'B' to signify the all-encompassing phenomenon of primordial Being, whereas *being* with a small 'b' stands for particular beings.

7. Gabriel Marcel, trans., *Man against Mass Society,* Chicago, 1952, p. 61.

8. *Ibid.,* p. 74.

9. Albert Dondeyne, trans., *Contemporary European Thought and Christian Faith,* Pittsburgh, 1958, p. 18.

10. Cf. Martin Heidegger, trans., *Being and Time,* New York, 1962, p. 80.

11. Dondeyne, *Contemporary European Thought,* p. 10.

12. William Luijpen, *Existential Phenomenology,* Pittsburgh, 1960, p. 15.

13. Cf., Heidegger, *Being and Time,* p. 67. Here we are obviously not taking the term "existence" in its traditional sense in opposition to "essence," but rather in its etymological sense of "standing-out."

14. Luijpen, *Existential Phenomenology,* p. 88.

15. Heidegger, *Being and Time,* p. 263: "Disclosedness . . . . . pertains equi-primordially to the world, to Being-in, and to the Self."

16. The Greek word *aletheia* (lit.: *un-concealment*) was one of the terms used by Aristotle for *truth*. Cf. Heidegger, *Being and Time,* pp. 256ff.

17. Objectivity as an attitude, or the subject pole of objectivity as truth is based on a primordial de-cision of the will which "con-stitutes" our authentic "ex-sistence." More about this later on.

18. Quoted by Rollo May, "The Origins and Significance of the Existential Movement in Psychology," in *Existence: A New Dimension in Psychiatry and Psychology,* eds. Rollo May, Ernest Angel and Henri F. Ellenberger, New York, 1958, p. 26.

19. *Ibid.*, p. 27.
20. Gabriel Marcel, trans., *The Philosophy of Existence,* New York, 1949, p. 3.
21. Dondeyne, *Contemporary European Thought,* p. 23.
22. Josef Pieper, trans., *Leisure the Basis of Culture,* New York, 1952, p. 90.
23. Martin Heidegger, trans., *An Introduction to Metaphysics,* New Haven, 1959, p. 26.
24. Here we are not referring to the Aristotelean meaning of *"sensus communis,"* nor to some sort of "moral prudence." The "sound common sense" is the pseudo-philosophical tendency to regard nothing as real or meaningful which is not given in the world of our everyday existence, or which does not belong to the world of the "common man."
25. Martin Heidegger, *On the Essence of Truth,* trans., in *Existence and Being,* ed. Werner Brock, Chicago, 1949, p. 320.
26. Cf. Karl Jaspers, *Philosophie,* Berlin, 1948, pp. 467ff; 475ff; 483ff; 508ff; 518ff.
27. Martin Heidegger, *What is Metaphysics?,* trans., in *Existence and Being,* ed. Werner Brock, Chicago, 1949, p. 364.
28. Albert Camus, *Le Mythe de Sisyphe,* Paris, 1942, p. 27. Trans. ours.
29. Jaspers, *Philosophie,* p. 539, Trans. ours.
30. Cf. Max Scheler, *Vom Ewigen im Menschen,* Leipzig, 1923, pp. 105-11.
31. *De Docta Ignorantia* (On the Learned Ignorance) is the title of a well-known work by Nicholas of Cusa (1401–1464) dealing with this kind of ignorance. Cf. Jaspers, *Philosophie,* pp. 518–20.
32. Cf. Plato, *Apol.* 21 A.
33. Jacques Maritain, *Existence and the Existent,* New York, 1948, p. 20.
34. Here, of course, the term "givenness" is not used in the *empirical* sense *à la* Francis Bacon, nor in the *experimental* sense of the physical sciences, but in the profound *experiential* sense of the fundamental "data" of our human "existence."
35. *Metaphysics,* 982 b, 28–29.
36. *Quaest. disp. de virtutibus cardinalibus,* 1.
37. Josef Pieper, trans., *Leisure the Basis of Culture,* New York, 1952, p. 123.
38. *Ibid.*
39. *Anal. Post.,* 72 b 5–7.
40. *Anal. Post.,* 72 b 7–8.
41. *Metaphysics,* 1011 a 12–13.
42. *Anal. Post.,* 72 b 18–23. Cf. *Metaphysics,* 994 a 1–34; 994 b 1–30; 1006 a 8–15; 1011 a 8–13; 1063 b 8–12.
43. Pieper, *Leisure,* p. 137.
44. This experience is accepted as a fact by many modern psychologists. In our opinion, the primordial phenomenon of wonder is both the point of contact and the dividing line between phenomenological psychology and fundamental philosophy. More on this later on.
45. *Theaetetus,* 155 D.
46. Jacques Maritain, trans., *The Degrees of Knowledge,* London, 1959, p. 279.
47. Pieper, *Leisure,* p. 135.
48. Some commentators of Heidegger's *Introduction to Metaphysics* think that the question "Why is there anything at all and not rather nothing?" is the most fundamental question for Heidegger. This is wrong. For although this question is

indeed a fundamental question of metaphysics, metaphysics itself is not fundamental philosophy for Heidegger. His *Introduction* is precisely an introduction to the understanding of the *Being* of metaphysics. In the light of Being we understand that the Being of metaphysics, and, consequently of the forementioned question is the partial concealment of the *primordial* question. Consequently, the question "Why is there anything at all and not rather nothing?" *is not our most fundamental question.*

49. Albert Dondeyne, trans., *Contemporary European Thought and Christian Faith,* Pittsburgh, 1958, pp. 9–35.

50. *Theaetetus,* 155 D.

51. Throughout this book we hyphenate the word "ex-sistence" to express etymologically our fundamental human nature 1) as multi-dimensional "standing-out," 2) as ontologically "standing-beyond" the realm of the ontic, and 3) as fundamental "emergence." Although these meanings are co-original, any one of them may be emphasized in a particular context.

52. Here the hyphenation indicates the "articulated unity" or the "unity-in-opposition" of the primitive cognitive intention. Our ample use of hyphenation throughout the entire work should not be misconstrued as some sort of word-mysticism. We merely want to use it as a technical device to indicate 1) the unity-in-opposition of fundamental phenomena, and 2) the un-usual or origin-al meaning of a usual word.

53. G.W.F. Hegel, trans., *The Phenomenology of Mind,"* London, 1949, p. 81.

54. Gabriel Marcel, trans., *The Philosophy of Existence,* New York, 1949, p. 8.

55. Cf. Albert Dondeyne, trans., *Contemporary European Thought and Christian Faith,* Pittsburgh, 1958, p. 93.

56. Martin Heidegger, *Kant und das Problem der Metaphysik,* Frankfurt a. M., 1951, p. 212. Trans. ours.

57. Cf. Marcel, *Philosophy of Existence,* pp. 20–23.

58. Dondeyne, *Contemporary European Thought,* p. 122. Second italics ours.

59. *Ibid.,* p. 149.

60. Our interest in etymology does not imply that we are building philosophy upon etymology. Rather the reverse is true. Of course, etymology as the science of the construction and derivation of "word-objects" is both interesting and legitimate. But etymology as the logical science of words cannot arrive at the *logos* of the experiential fulness of their *etymon* (truth, original meaning). In the present volume we are mainly interested in "etymo-logy" which studies the "truth" appearing as words, or words as the "house of Being" (Heidegger). "Etymology" which studies "word-things" in their more or less deterministic connections and derivations is important, but remains a derivative of "etymo-logy."

61. Martin Heidegger, trans., *An Introduction to Metaphysics,* New Haven, 1959, p. 25.

62. *Ibid.*

63. Martin Heidegger, trans., *What is Metaphysics?* in *Existence and Being,* ed. Werner Brock, Chicago, 1949, p. 387.

64. *Metaphysics,* 995 a 15–20.

65. Pitirim Sorokin, *Fads and Foibles in Modern Sociology and Related Sciences,* Chicago, 1956, p. 82.

66. *Metaphysics,* 995 a 6–10.

67. Cf. André Lalande, *Vocabulaire Technique et Critique de la Philosophie,* Paris, 1951, pp. 623–25.

68. Cf. H. van de Hulst, C. van Peursen, *Phaenomenologie en Natuurwetenschap,* Utrecht, 1953, pp. 126–34.

69. Werner Heisenberg, *Physics and Philosophy: The Revolution in Modern Science,* New York, 1958: "This again emphasizes a subjective element in the description of atomic events, since the measuring device has been constructed by the observer, and we have to remember that what we observe is not nature itself but nature exposed to our method of questioning." (p. 58) "Natural science does not simply describe and explain nature; it is a part of the interplay between nature and ourselves; it describes nature as exposed to our method of questioning." (p. 81).

70. Cf. p. 15, fn. 7.

71. We have borrowed this term from Eugen Fink. Cf. Eugen Fink, *Vom Wesen des Enthusiasmus,* Freiburg i. Br., 1947.

72. Henri Bergson, trans., *Creative Evolution,* New York, 1944, p. 59.

73. J. Rimaud, *Thomisme et Méthode,* Paris, 1925, p. 4.

74. Henri Bergson, trans., *Creative Evolution,* New York, 1944, p. 45.

75. Cf. p. 54.

76. Dietrich von Hildebrand, *Christian Ethics,* New York, 1953, p. 10.

77. Husserl himself was a Doctor of Science.

78. Edmund Husserl, *Ideen* I, Husserliana III, den Haag, 1950, p. 46. Trans. ours.

79. *Ibid.*

80. Dagobert D. Runes, ed., *The Dictionary of Philosophy,* New York, pp. 145–46.

81. Cf. pp. 55–57.

82. We will revert to the nature of "original perception" in the following chapter.

83. Cf. pp. 53–54.

84. Cf. p. 77.

85. Martin Heidegger, trans., *An Introduction to Metaphysics,* New Haven, 1959, p. 62.

86. This juridico-ontological meaning is still preserved in the English expression "The Last Judgement," and in its Dutch equivalent "Het Laatste Oordeel."

87. Cf. Martin Heidegger, *What is Metaphysics?,* trans., in *Existence and Being,* ed. Werner Brock, Chicago, 1949, p. 392.

88. Cf. p. 96.

89. Heidegger, *What is Metaphysics?,* p. 372.

90. *Ibid.,* p. 378.

91. Henri Bergson, trans., *The Creative Mind,* New York, 1946, p. 40.

92. The distinction between "scientific pro-blems" and the "ontological mystery" was first brought into sharp focus by the works of Gabriel Marcel.

93. Cf. Gabriel Marcel, trans., *The Mystery of Being,* Vol. I, London, Chapter IX, especially pp. 192–94.

94. Primordial depth is circular because it is "wonder-ful." We re-peat (*re* and *petere*—to seek again) this experience by going back into its all-encompassing universality. (*Wieder-holung*) We will revert to this later on.

95. Cf. p. 39.

96. Note that the Latin noun *essentia* is derived from *essens*, a participle of *esse* which means: *to be*.

97. The dynamism of philosophical phenomena should *not* be interpreted as a change into "something other" than what they are, but rather as a "becoming of what they are."

98. Cf. Albert Dondeyne, trans., *Contemporary European Thought and Christian Faith*, Pittsburgh, 1958, pp. 119–21.

99. Cf. Bernard Boelen, *Eudaimonie en het Wezen der Ethiek*, Louvain, 1949, pp. 147–55; August Brunner, *Der Stufenbau der Welt*, München, 1950, p. 117; Stephan Strasser, *The Soul in Metaphysical and Empirical Psychology*, Pittsburgh, 1957, pp. 46f., pp. 54ff., pp. 68ff.; De Waelhens, *Phénoménologie et Vérité*, Paris, 1953, pp. 46–60.

100. Rationalistic ontology is "de-ontologized" thinking. It has lost the ontological dimension of the existential "openness" and the dynamic "emergence" of primordial Being. As a result, rationalism reduces the world of the *logos* to an atomic dust of solidified beings ("things") that make up the only content of its pseudo-philosophical abstractionism.

101. Cf. Dondeyne, *Contemporary European Thought*, pp. 112–14.

102. Søren Kierkegaard, trans., *Concluding Unscientific Postscript*, Princeton, 1944, p. 18.

103. *Ibid.*, p. 107.

104. *Ibid.*, p. 99.

105. Cf. Ibid., pp. 99 and 111.

106. *Ibid.*, p. 276.

107. Bergson, *Creative Evolution*, p. 45.

108. Gabriel Marcel, trans., *The Philosophy of Existence*, New York, 1949, p. 88.

109. Maurice Merleau-Ponty, *Sens et Non-sens*, Paris, 1948, p. 189. Trans. ours.

110. Both the truth of correspondence and the truth of coherency *presuppose* an un-hiddenness, a sphere of openness which makes the very encounter between the judgement and the judged or between one truth and another possible. This un-hiddenness, this un-concealment *(a-letheia)*, therefore, is the more fundamental truth. These insights have been masterly developed by Martin Heidegger in his essay *On the Essence of Truth* (in *Existence and Being*, pp. 319–51). Gabriel Marcel develops basically the same insights, and declares himself in fundamental agreement with the views expounded in Heidegger's essay *(The Mystery of Being*, Vol. I, Chap. IV).

111. Cf. p. 77.

112. This attitude is very common today, and it is difficult to change it. For it is *not based upon logic*, but on a *fixated contraction* of our very ex-sistence, which Marcel calls "the spirit of abstraction." Man tends to protect his fixations with a great variety of "defense mechanisms."

113. Gabriel Marcel, trans., *Man against Mass Society*, Chicago, 1952, p. 1. Cf. pp. 114–21.

114. John Wild, *The Challenge of Existentialism*, Bloomington, 1963, p. 97.

115. *Ibid.*, p. 22.

116. *Ibid.*, p. 97.

117. Karl Jaspers, trans., *The Future of Mankind*, Chicago, 1963, p. 168.

118. *Ibid.*, p. 207.

119. *Ibid.,* p. 208.

120. *Ibid.,* p. 209.

121. *Ibid.,* p. 199.

122. Both the word and the meaning of "logic" are derived from *"logos."* It is often said that the word *logos* is a very difficult word. Yet it is not more difficult to "say" *logos* than to "say" logic. What makes *logos*—"thinking" more difficult, however, is its originative nature, and the fact that it corrodes the fixated "spirit of abstraction." Cf. Heidegger, *Introduction,* pp. 120–23; pp. 185–96.

123. *zoion logon echon* is the classical definition of man: "The animal endowed with reason."

124. This is in accordance with Heidegger's famous reversal of the classical definition. Heidegger, *Introduction,* p. 175: *"physis* [Being] is *logos anthropon echon:* being, overpowering appearing, necessitates the gathering which pervades and grounds being-human."

125. Cf. p. 61.

126. The idea of "phenomenological reduction" originated with Edmund Husserl. Although we agree with Husserl's aim, namely, to arrive at the original "self-givenness" of the phenomena, we differ with him in scope and method. Phenomenological reduction is, as we will see, a flexible thing. Husserl himself found it necessary to constantly revise his views on reduction, and the history of phenomenology confirms the diversity and flexibility of its nature. Our discussion of phenomenological reduction will probe into the reasons why this reduction cannot be used as an independent tool, as a ready-made technique or a formalized method.

127. Herbert Spiegelberg, *The Phenomenological Movement,* Vol. II, The Hague, 1960, p. 672.

128. Martin Heidegger, *Being and Time,* trans., New York, 1962, p. 60.

129. James Jarrett, *The Quest for Beauty,* Englewood Cliffs, 1957, p. 27.

130. "Where remains the blossoming tree in the brain-currents that can be scientifically recorded?" asks Martin Heidegger discussing the same example in *Was Heisst Denken?,* Tübingen, 1954, p. 17. Trans. ours.

131. Sometimes the phenomenologist uses the first person in his phenomenological descriptions. This, of course, is not to suggest that his descriptions are "merely subjective," but rather to indicate that they are "experiential" and "first-person experiences" (Heidegger's *"Jemeinigkeit"*—"mine-ness").

132. Under the influence of logical positivism we have a general tendency to invest referential signs with absolute priority.

133. Susanne Langer, *Feeling and Form.* New York, 1953, p. 22.

134. Stephen Strasser calls such an uncritical intuitionism: "Phenomenological Impressionism," *Phenomenology and the Human Sciences,* Pittsburgh, 1963, p. 296.

135. Cf. pp. 14–15.

136. Ernest Nagel in "Symbolism and Science," as quoted in Susanne Langer, *Problems of Art,* New York, 1957, p. 130.

137. Cf. Paul Ricoeur, "The Hermeneutics of Symbols and Philosophical Reflection," *International Philosophical Quarterly,* Vol. II, No. 2 (1962), 194. Cf. also Ricoeur, "The Symbol, Food for Thought," *Philosophy Today,* Vol. IV, No. 3 (1960) pp. 199–210.

138. Cf. Ricoeur, "Hermeneutics of Symbols," pp. 192–93; "Symbol, Food for Thought," pp. 201–207.
139. Mikel Dufrenne, *Phénoménologie de l'Expérience Esthétique*, Vol. I, Paris, 1953, p. 166. Trans. ours.
140. Langer, *Problems of Arts*, pp. 133–34.
141. *Ibid.*, p. 125.
142. Cf. *Ibid.*, pp. 124–39.
143. *Ibid.*, p. 127. Italics ours. Cf. Ulrich Sonneman, *Existence and Therapy*, New York, 1954, p. 337.
144. *Ibid.*, p. 134.
145. Karl Jaspers, *Philosophie*, Berlin, 1948, p. 796, Trans. ours.
146. Paul Tillich, *Systematic Theology*, Vol. I, Chicago, 1951, p. 241.
147. Rudolf Otto, trans., *The Idea of the Holy*, New York, 1958. Cf. especially pp. 136–42.
148. Tillich, *Systematic Theology*, Vol. I, p. 215.
149. *Ibid.*, p. 216.
150. Note the etymological relationship of the words "whole," "holy," "wholesome," "hale," "health," and "healing" that all go back to the AS *hal* (sound, healthy, whole).
151. Such a conception of Being is rightly called *Seinsmystik* (mysticism of being).
152. Josef Pieper, trans., *Leisure the Basis of Culture*, New York, 1960, p. 127.
153. *Ibid.*
154. Gabriel Marcel, trans., *The Mystery of Being*, Vol. I, London, 1950, p. 47. We are not dealing here with a "transcending of experience," but rather with an "experience of transcending." Cf. *Ibid.*, Chap. III.
155. Pieper, *Leisure*, p. 129.
156. We, therefore, cannot agree with John Wild where he accuses Heidegger of *Seinsmystik* because he allegedly "slips into a strange transcendentalism which places being *(Sein)* beyond the world." *(Existence and the World of Freedom*, Englewood Cliffs, 1963, p. 201, note).
157. Edward Bullough, " 'Psychical Distance' as a Factor in Art and an Esthetic Principle," *British Journal of Psychology*, Vol. IV, as quoted in Melvin Rader, *A Modern Book of Esthetics*, 1960, pp. 394–411.
158. *Ibid.*, p. 397.
159. *Ibid.*, p. 396.
160. Maurice Merleau-Ponty, trans., *Phenomenology of Perception*, New York, 1962, p. XIII.
161. We have discussed "original perception" merely to elucidate this phenomenon as the pre-reflective beginning of existential thinking. An exhaustive treatment of this phenomenon, and a comparison with other forms of perception, such as imagination, memory, sensation etc. is beyond the scope of this book.
162. Paris, 1964, p. 243.
163. Merleau-Ponty, *Phenomenology*, p. 3.
164. Cf. p. 17.
165. Marcel, *Mystery of Being*, p. 107.
166. *Ibid.*, p. 67.
167. trans., Berkeley and London, 1954.

168, Immanuel Kant, *Critique of Pure Reason,* trans., Garden City, 1961, in the "Preface to the Second Edition," p. 516, n.

169. Heidegger, *Being and Time,* p. 249, Italics Heidegger's.

170. Cf. H. De Vleeschauwer, *Immanuel Kant,* Antwerpen, 1931, p. 313.

171. John Locke, *Some Thoughts concerning Education,* Cambridge, 1899, p. 152.

172. Søren Kierkegaard, trans., *Either/Or,* Vol. II, Princeton, 1949, p. 194. For Kierkegaard's discussions of aestheticism cf. also: *Either/Or,* Vol. I; *Stages on Life's Way,* Princeton, 1945, pp. 25–93; *Repetition,* Princeton, 1946.

173. An excellent example of *"fundamental* aesthetics" is Martin Heidegger's "Der Ursprung des Kunstwerkes," in *Holzwege,* Frankfurt a. M., 1950, pp. 7–68. Otto Pöggeler rightly states that this essay is not a *"Philosophie der Kunst,"* or a philosophical aesthetics in our sense of the term. (*Der Denkweg Martin Heideggers,* Pfullingen, 1963, p. 207).

174. An excellent example of *philosophical* aesthetics is Mikel Dufrenne's *Phénoménologie de l'Expérience Esthétique,* 2 vols., Paris, 1953. Dufrenne combines a genuine appreciation for the ontological significance of the aesthetic phenomenon as a revelation of Being (fundamental aesthetics) with a great familiarity with the fine arts (experiential aesthetics). His authentic dialogue between the two creates an important *"philosophical* aesthetics." (Cf. also Spiegelberg, *Phenomenological Movement,* pp. 579–85).

175. Cf. pp. 128–129.

176. Maurice Merleau-Ponty, trans., *Phenomenology of Perception,* New York, 1962, p. XIV.

177. *Ibid.*

178. Henri Bergson, trans., *The Creative Mind,* New York, 1946, p. 22.

179. Merleau-Ponty, *Perception,* p. XXI.

180. Gabriel Marcel, trans., *Man against Mass Society,* Chicago, 1952, pp. 28–29.

181. Cf. Gordon Allport, *Pattern and Growth in Personality,* New York, 1961, p. 566; Abraham Maslow, *Toward a Psychology of Being,* Princeton, 1962, p. 10.

182. Gordon Allport, *Becoming,* New Haven, 1960, p. 7.

183. Cf. Abraham Maslow, *Motivation and Personality,* New York, 1954, p. 24.

184. Carl Rogers, *On Becoming a Person,* Boston, 1961, p. 174.

185. Cf. Maslow, *Motivation,* p. 216.

186. Cf. Maslow, *Being,* p. 82.

187. *Ibid.,* p. 83.

188. The phenomenologist who in principle denies the possibility of ontological transcendency runs the risk of falling a victim to some sort of phenomenological positivism.

189. It goes without saying that the characteristics of the creative process and the characteristics of inspiration are interlocking.

190. Edmund Sinnott, "The Creativeness of Life," in *Creativity and its Cultivation,* ed. Harold Anderson, New York, 1959, p. 24.

191. F. Dostoevsky, *Letters to his Family and Friends,* trans., London, 1914, pp. 100–101.

192. Henry Bugbee, Jr., *The Inward Morning,* State College, 1958, pp. 33–34. Italics Bugbee's.

193. Modeste Tchaikovsky, *The Life and Letters of Peter Ilich Tchaikovsky,* as quoted by Rosamond Harding, in *An Anatomy of Inspiration,* Cambridge, 1948, p. 8.

194. Cf. p. 46.

195. Harding, *Anatomy,* p. 15.

196. *Ion,* 534.

197. Cf. p. 42.

198. Bugbee, *Inward Morning,* p. 130.

199. Harding, *Anatomy,* p. 6.

200. The pivotal importance of this dream-like consciousness for education should be evident. The dreaming, wondering, musing etc. of the adolescent between 15 and 25 years of age is too often regarded as laziness, waste of time or mere loafing, whereas, in fact, it is the gateway to self-discovery, to creative thinking and to authentic ex-sistence.

201. It is here that the classical doctrine of the "active" and the "passive" intellect has its ontological roots. This doctrine is meaningless, however, if it is interpreted in the physicalistic sense of separate "functions" or "faculties."

202. Gabriel Marcel, trans., *The Mystery of Being,* Vol. I, London, 1950, p. 67.

203. Martin Heidegger, trans., *Kant and the Problem of Metaphysics,* Bloomington, 1962, p. 244.

204. Cf. p. 17.

205. Martin Heidegger, trans., *Being and Time,* New York, 1962, p. 172.

206. Cf. Eugen Fink, *Vom Wesen des Enthusiasmus,* Freiburg i. Br., 1947.

207. Cf. fn. 45.

208. Heidegger, *Being and Time,* p. 176.

209. Cf. p. 111.

210. Cf. 155.

211. Cf. fn. 60.

212. This goes to show that in the genuine teaching of philosophy the so called "historical approach" and the "thematic approach" are utterly inseparable.

213. Eugen Fink, "L'Analyse Intentionelle et le Problème de la Pensée Spéculative," in *Problèmes Actuels de la Phénoménologie,* ed. H. Van Breda, 1951, p. 54. Trans. ours.

214. Cf. p. 63. In this and the following seven points we are summarizing the findings of our whole book from the viewpoint of ontology *as* "epistemology."

215. Cf. p. 63.

216. Cf. pp. 87–88.

217. Cf. pp. 93–95.

218. Cf. p. 93.

219. Here, just as in aesthetics, we can distinguish between 1) *fundamental* epistemology (an integral part of existential thinking), 2) empirical or *experiential* epistemology (a non-philosophical study of the data of human knowledge), and 3) *philosophical* epistemology (a dialogue between 1 and 2).

220. It should be noted that experiential epistemology can be genuinely *scientific,* whereas the *denial* of the possibility or value of philosophical epistemology is neither scientific nor philosophical. It would be another manifestation of the pseudo-philosophical *scientism.*

221. Cf. pp. 139–140.

222. p. 105.

223. Cf. pp. 57–58.

224. p. 118.

225. Once again, philosophical aesthetics is beyond the scope of this book.

226. Just as an "ethical" example, as we will see, is woven into the very texture of *logos*-living. Cf. pp. 228–29.

227. p. 166.

228. Questions such as these are typical in the camp of neo-positivism and linquistic analysis. Cf. among others: A. J. Ayer, *Language, Truth and Logic,* London, 1948; Max Eastman, *The Literary Mind,* New York, 1931; C. K. Ogden and I. A. Richards, *The Meaning of Meaning,* London, 1927; I. A. Richards, *Science and Poetry,* London, 1935.

229. Generally speaking, a sentence, a proposition or a statement is meaningful (true or false) if it is verifiable (in principle), i.e., if any empirical observation would be relevant to the establishing of its truth or falsity.

230. Cf. p. 175. Here we found that in philosophy no verification is possible "before" or "independent of" its actual beginning. Cf. also Maxwell Charlesworth, *Philosophy and Linguistic Analysis,* Pittsburgh, 1959, pp. 126–49.

231. *"zustande bringen"* (Heidegger).

232. Cf. Chap. X.

233. Cf. pp. 134–137.

234. "bliss" (from OE *blithe*—joyful) means: great joy, spiritual joy, heavenly rapture. A Dutch child is *blij* when an unexpected joy fills his whole ex-sistence (existential joy).

235. "happiness" from ME *happe(n)*—to occur without prevision.

236. Josef Pieper, trans., *Happiness and Contemplation,* New York, 1958, p. 25.

237. This twofold concealment is 1) the concealment of Being *as mystery;* 2) the concealment of the concealment of Being as mystery in the theatre of beings as the dwelling place of Being (the "ontological difference"). Cf. Martin Heidegger, *On the Essence of Truth,* trans., ed. Werner Brock, Chicago, 1949, pp. 340–47.

238. Martin Heidegger, *What is Metaphysics?,* trans., in *Existence and Being,* p. 392.

239. Cf. Bernard Boelen, *Eudaimonie en het Wezen der Ethiek,* Louvain, 1949, pp. 185–86; Pieper, *Happiness,* pp. 107–109.

240. Paul Tillich, *The Courage to Be,* New Haven, 1959, p. 66.

241. Emmanuel Mounier, *Le Personalisme,* Paris, 1951, p. 96. Trans. ours.

242. Martin Heidegger, trans., *Being and Time,* New York, 1962, p. 146.

243. The objectification of the natural sciences, as we have seen, is not absolute. For the scientist, to a degree, encounters himself in the results of his science. For a brief phenomenological analysis of the birth of scientific objectification cf. Heidegger, *Being and Time,* pp. 408–15.

244. It would be the *"prōte hyle"* (primary matter) of Aristotle, or the*"schlichte Unendlichkeit"* (negative infinity) of Hegel.

245. Ulrich Sonneman, *Existence and Therapy,* New York, 1954, p. 201.

246. Its existence is denied not only by the existential thinkers, such as Heidegger, Merleau-Ponty, Jaspers etc., but also by the modern mathematico-empirical scientists.

247. Cf. p. 46.

248. fn. 187.

249. Or, speaking in the terminology of M. Merleau-Ponty, we are not "spatialized" on the basis of our "objective" (physical) body, but on the basis of our "phenomenal" (experiential) body.

250. Cf. fn. 159. Italics ours. The "action *of* distance" should, of course, not be confused with the "action *in* distance" controversy of the rationalists.

251. Cf. p. 100.

252. Cf. p. 60.

253. Heidegger, *Being and Time*, p. 377.

254. *Ibid.*, p. 401.

255. *Ibid.* pp. 387 and 437. We use the word "out-standing" both in its etymological sense, and with all its connotations. The *"out-standing* movement of primordial dis-closure" is pro-jecting, ec-static, prominent, self-transcending, emerging and unsettled.

256. Note the spatio-temporal structure.

257. Heidegger, *Being and Time*, p. 469.

258. Henri Bergson, trans., *The Creative Mind*, New York, 1946, p. 178.

259. Cf. *Ibid.*

260. Cf. fn. 69.

261. Cf. Heidegger, *Being and Time*, Chap. VI, pp. 456–88.

262. Martin Heidegger, trans., *An Introduction to Metaphysics*, New Haven, 1959, p. 12.

263. E. N. 1094 a 17–21.

264. Cf. Viktor Frankl, trans., *The Doctor and the Soul*, New York, 1960, p. XI.

265. Cf. fn. 150.

266. Cf. pp. 121–123.

267. Cf. C. S. Lewis, *Studies in Words*, Cambridge, 1960, pp. 24–74.

268. Cf. pp. 142–145.

269. pp. 33–34.

270. Heidegger, *Introduction*, p. 14.

271. *Ibid.*, p. 101.

272. Lewis, *Words*, p. 37.

273. *Ibid.*, pp. 37–38.

274. Cf. Edgar De Bruyne, *Het Aesthetisch Beleven*, Antwerp, 1942, pp. 165–70.

275. We say, for instance, "at the officer's request he *produced* his driver's license."

276. We should be careful, therefore, not to understand the Aristotelian *poesis*, "the perfect making of something in matter," in its traditional restricted sense. When we have produced technically perfect equipment, we have not yet "produced" its fundamental potentiality or brought to light its essential meaning until we have related it to *physis*, until we have "pro-duced" its assignment to the human person. Fundamentally speaking, the distinction between technical and aesthetic arts is not an absolute one. A true "home" is the abode of *physis*, a "house" where our human spirit can flourish. "A great cathedral's beauty is in very large measure a matter of its being so *visibly* a house for the worshipper." (Jarrett, *Quest for Beauty*, p. 12) We, therefore, believe that the gradual beautification of equipment attending its increase in technical perfection is neither acci-

dental nor the result of embellishment, but inherent in the "nature" *(physis)* of things. The beauty of the modern jet is a far cry from the early flying cigar boxes.

277. Cf. Gabriel Marcel, trans., *Man against Mass Society,* Chicago, 1952, pp. 114–21.

278. *Ibid.,* p. 74.

279. *Ibid.,* p. 42.

280. Heidegger, *Introduction,* p. 175.

281. Cf. Bernard Boelen, *Eudaimonie en het Wezen der Ethiek,* Louvain, 1949, pp. 124–26.

282. Paul Häberlin, *Ethik im Grundriss,* Zürich, 1946, p. 37. Trans. ours.

283. It is precisely this *primordial* situation which is ignored by the so called "situation ethics." We will revert to this later on.

284. Cf. pp. 198–199.

285. We hyphenate the word "etho-logy" to indicate its fundamental meaning of "the *logos* of *ethos,*" and to differentiate it from traditional ethics as the "logic of *ethos*" on the one hand, and from "ethology" as the science of the formation of human character on the other.

286. Cf. Gabriel Marcel, trans., *The Mystery of Being,* Vol. I, London, 1950, p. 139.

287. For the accurate meaning of this term cf. pp. 59–61.

288. Cf. pp. 62–64.

289. Here the reader may be confronted with an embarrassing dilemma. Our discussion seems to imply that ethical life begins at a mature age. But who can deny that also children and adolescents have an ethical task in life? We have briefly touched upon this issue in a paper read to the ACPA. Cf. Bernard Boelen, "Human Development and Fixations in Moral Life," *Proceedings of the American Catholic Philosophical Association,* Vol. XXXV, 1961, pp. 204–16.

290. To be sure, this primordial de-cision implies the ambiguity of fundamental sym-bolism. It is "within" the unauthentic that the fundamental will de-cides to be authentic. This entails the *possibility* of a fundamental *option (optio fundamentalis)* between authentic and unauthentic existence. The fundamental option, therefore, is ontologically founded on the primordial de-cision, and not the other way around. The "primordial de-cision" de-cides upon our being ethical rather than *non*-ethical, whereas the "fundamental option" determines our being ethical or *un*ethical.

291. This will "in accordance with the *logos*" is the ethical "good will." In Kant's ethical formalism the "good will" is the autonomous will which acts from the motive of *duty* (Cf. his *Foundations of the Metaphysics of Morals,* and his *Critique of Practical Reason*). Elsewhere we had the opportunity to show not only the importance of Kant's doctrine, but also the fact that his formalistic conception of duty leaves the essence of ethical be-havior unthought. Or, more correctly, Kant encounters it near its vanishing point where the creativity of existential love coagulates into the stern "oughtness" of the categorical imperative in a last ditch fight against the temptations of immorality. (Cf. Boelen, *Eudaimonie,* pp. 127–28).

292. Martin Heidegger, trans., *An Introduction to Metaphysics,* New Haven, 1959, p. 21.

293. *Ibid.* We will further differentiate the ethical will in our discussion of the ethical will as existential love (Cf. pp. 239–63).

294. This should not be construed as an identification of the unauthentic and the evil. Having parted ways with the unauthentic makes the "fundamental option" possible.

295. Henri Bergson, trans., *The Creative Mind,* New York, 1946, p. 177.

296. *Ibid.*

297. William Luijpen, trans., *Existential Phenomenology,* Pittsburgh, 1960, p. 287.

298. According to Dorothy Lee *(Freedom and Culture,* New York, 1963, p. 43) the Wintu Indians did not even have a word for the English word "ruling." The English phrase: "the chief *ruled* the people," "is given in Wintu as: the chief *stood-with* the people."

299. Martin Heidegger, *On the Essence of Truth,* trans., in *Existence and Being,* ed. Werner Brock, Chicago, 1949, p. 333.

300. The unilateral authority of the *autocrat* mistakes the dis-obedience (multi-dimensional listening) of existential authority for unethical disobedience (non-listening).

301. Also *expert* authority belongs to the world of *functional* authority. For an expert is a "specialist," one who *controls* his special field of occupation.

302. Lee, *Freedom,* pp. 2–3.

303. Most of us are, unfortunately, familiar with the petrifying and suffocating atmosphere created in the classroom where the autocratic teacher has "things under perfect control." This is only possible by reducing the pupils to objects or "things." But "things" don't listen. Things are impenetrable, remain side by side, and are free from any germ of inspiration, enthusiasm or openness. Moreover, the closed and fixated self of this teacher leaves nothing to be "inter-ested in," or to "listen to."

304. Cf. fn. 244.

305. The most perverted form of hypocrisy, of course, is the false pretense of virtue as a cover up for intended evil.

306. Murderers of ethical life!

307. Cf. p. 105.

308. Erich Fromm, *The Art of Loving,* New York, 1956, p. 111.

309. It is as an attack upon this negativistic reduction to insensitivity that we should understand Nietzsche's diatribes against asceticism. During our discussion of existential love in the next chapter we will have an opportunity to deepen our insight into the very essence of authentic asceticism.

310. Erich Fromm, *The Art of Loving,* New York, 1956, p. 46. Italics Fromm's.

311. Ignace Lepp, trans., *The Psychology of Loving,* Baltimore, 1963, p. 188.

312. *Ibid.,* p. 200.

313, Fromm, *Art of Loving,* p. 103.

314. Cf. p. 212.

315. Cf. p. 214.

316. Cf. p. 212.

317. *"Caritas est forma omnium virtutum."* (II–II, q. 23, a. 8).

318. Paul Tillich, *Theology of Culture,* New York, 1959, p. 144.

319. Peter Bertocci, Richard Millard, *Personality and the Good,* New York, 1963, p. 403.

320. It is the task of the ethicist to work this out for each of the virtues.

321. Cf. fn. 292.

322. Erich Fromm, *Man for Himself,* New York, 1947, pp. 129–30.

323. The observant reader will recognize Heidegger's three existential modes of the "Being-in" of Being-in-the-world: *Befindlichkeit* (fundamental disposition, primordial mood); *Verstehen* (projecting understanding); *Rede* (discursiveness, *logos*).

324. Cf. Maurice Merleau-Ponty, trans., *Phenomenology of Perception*, New York, 1962, p. XIV.

325. This is not to say that love is "irrational," or that there are no "reasons" for loving. The role of particular reasons and motives in existential love will be discussed shortly.

326. As quoted by Abraham Maslow, *Motivation and Personality*, New York, 1954, p. 255. For "non-motivated" behavior cf. also *Ibid.* p. 76, and the chapters 11 and 15.

327. *Ibid.*, p. 296.

328. Cf. among others: Maslow, *Motivation*; Alan Watts, *Nature, Man and Woman*, New York, (Mentor Book), n.d.; Oswald Schwarz, *The Psychology of Sex*, Bungay, 1958 (Pelican Book).

329. William Luijpen, trans., *Existential Phenomenology*, Pittsburgh, 1960, p. 296.

330. "We thank people," says Gilbert K. Chesterton, "for birthday presents of cigars and slippers. Can I thank no one for the birthday present of birth?" ("The Ethics of Elfland" in *Orthodoxy*).

331. Martin Heidegger, trans., *An Introduction to Metaphysics*, New Haven, 1959, p. 145.

332. Cf. fn. 236.

333. Watts, *Nature, Man and Woman*, p. 26.

334. Cf. p. 183.

335. Cf. pp. 136–137.

336. Cf. pp. 160–161.

337. Fromm, *Art of Loving*, p. 90.

338. Cf. fn. 203.

339. Cf. p. 101.

340. The mysterious capacity of authentic lovers to penetrate into the very depth of one another's personality in a single perception has often been recognized. To our knowledge, however, it has never been viewed in the ontological perspective of the *logos*.

341. Schwarz, *Psychology of Sex,* p. 100: "That a woman possesses fair hair, a lovely voice, and a splendid figure, that she plays the piano well and is widely read, is very important, as one may rather crudely say, for her commercial value, but not for her lover; these attributes are not assets in the exclusive world of love."

342. Gabriel Marcel, trans., *Metaphysical Journal*, Chicago, 1952, p. 232.

343. Cf. Luypen, *Existential Phenomenology*, p. 216 and p. 223.

344. Cf. p. 157.

345. We will come to this point shortly.

346. Schwarz, *Psychology of Sex*, p. 102.

347. Cf. p. 237.

348. Cf. p. 134.

349. Cf. p. 118.

350. New York, 1956.

351. *Ibid.*, p. 4.

352. Cf. pp. 134–136.

353. Erotic love, therefore, is neither *genital* love (biological instinct) nor *existential* love *(differentiated* authentic love).

354. This unity of "sight" and "insight" is characteristic of "original" or "phenomenological" perception. Stephan Strasser, trans., *Phenomenology and the Human Sciences,* Pittsburgh, 1963, p. 253: "The intuition, spoken of by the phenomenologist encompasses both 'sight' and 'insight'."

355. Just as the "original perception" of primordial wonder is the *prephilosophical* source of philosophical thinking. The rationalistic moralist, of course, who identifies morality with perfect conformity to a static set of abstract rules, is unable to appreciate the ethical significance of immature stages of ethical development. Cf. Bernard Boelen, "Human Development and Fixations in Moral Life," *Proceedings of the American Catholic Philosophical Association,* Vol. XXXV, 1961, pp. 204–16.

356. Just as we did not accept a radical dichotomy between "pure" facts and philosophical insights, so we do not accept this dichotomy between "pure" facts and ethical values either. It is only "within" the context of existential thinking or ethical existence that facts are "originally" perceived and that they reveal their fundamental significance.

357. It is precisely this *spiritual* significance of erotic love which is denied by our rationalistic age. (Cf. L. Vander Kerken, *Menselijke Liefde en Vriendschap,* Bilthoven, 1962, p. 100) Rationalism mistakes "spirit" for "intelligence" or "reason," and fails to understand it as the "fundamental, knowing resolve toward the essence of being." (Heidegger, *Introduction,* p. 49).

358. Arthur Jersild, *The Psychology of Adolescence,* New York, 1963, pp. 280–81.

359. Fromm, *Art of Loving,* p. 53.

360. *Ibid.,* p. 4.

361. *Ibid.,* p. 56.

362. *Ibid.*

363. *Ibid.,* p. 55.

364. Maslow, *Motivation,* p. 252. An analogous dichotomy is found in the Christian tradition which regards Eros as antithetical to Agape *(caritas*—supernatural love). Unfortunately, there is no English equivalent for *caritas.* The word charity has lost its Christian and "charismatic" flavor. Charity has come to mean the giving of alms *(eleos*—pity), often to bolster one's own feeling of superiority. We agree with M. C. D'Arcy where he criticizes de Rougemont for allowing "for no kind of love in between the pagan passion of Eros and the Christian and supernatural love of charity." *(The Mind and Heart of Love,* Meridian Books, Cleveland, 1964, p. 48) It should be noted that existential love is both "graced" and "rooted in Eros."

365. Luijpen, *Existential Phenomenology,* p. 157.

366. *Ibid.*

367. Cf. Maslow, *Motivation,* p. 235; Schwarz, *Psychology of Sex,* p. 98; D'Arcy, *Mind and Heart of Love,* p. 250.

368. D'Arcy, *Ibid.*

369. Ludwig Binswanger, *Grundformen und Erkenntnis Menschlichen Daseins,* Zürich, 1953, pp. 565, 577, 582 and 664. By "objectivity" of love Binswanger means that genuine love is not a mere feeling, but an experiential "responsible act." *(Ibid.,* p. 565).

370. Martin Buber, trans., *Between Man and Man,* Boston, 1961, p. 105. Here we touch on the Being of "e-ducation." The creative understanding of the authentic personality's existential thinking and existential loving "pro-vokes" (calls forth) the self-project of the other's Being. The authentic personality *is* an "e-ducator" by being "creative understanding as co-Being" (*ex*—out; *ducere*—to lead). What our youth look for and need most (but seldom find in our technocratic age) is not words, techniques, systems or institutions, but the existential "pro-vocation" of authentic personalities.

371. Heidegger, *Introduction,* p. 145.

372. Schwarz, *Psychology of Sex,* p. 20.

373. Gabriel Marcel, trans., *The Mystery of Being,* Vol. I, London, 1950, p. 136: "Do not let us ever forget, that to admire is already, in a certain degree, to create."

374. The creative understanding of existential love is the *docta ignorantia* of the heart. Just as we found a twofold concealment of philosophical truth, so also the incommunicability of existential love due to the mystery of Being is further complicated by its "embodiment" in the beings of our everyday world, and in the realm of our psycho-somatic sub-structures.

375. The very antithesis of existential love's creative understanding is, of course, the Sartrean hateful *stare* which reduces the "beloved one" to an ob-ject, and which kills his authentic potentialities. Cf. Luypen's excellent discussion of the Sartrean stare in *Existential Phenomenology,* pp. 195–205.

376. Abraham Maslow, *Toward a Psychology of Being,* Princeton, 1962, p. 41.

377. This entails that love is truly "world-building" and, therefore, *historical* in the authentic sense of the term.

378. Martin Buber, trans., *Good and Evil,* New York, 1953, p. 129.

379. For existential thinking cf. p. 93; for existential loving cf. p. 218.

380. *Kritik der praktischen Vernunft,* trans. by T. K. Abbott in *Kant's Critique of Practical Reason and other Works on the Theory of Ethics,* London, 1909, p. 47.

381. Luijpen, *Existential Phenomenology,* p. 219.

382. "Love thy neighbor as thyself."

383. Fromm, *Art of Loving,* p. 60.

384. D'Arcy, *The Mind and Heart of Love,* p. 325.

385. Martin Heidegger, *Was ist Metaphysik?,* Frankfurt a.M., 1949, p. 42. Trans. ours.

INDEX

Behavior:
 authentic, 208–209
Being:
 and beings, 13
 as wonder, 26–27
 mystery of, 97–98
 primordial question of, 11
 see also primordial wonder,
Bergson, H., 15, 84, 87, 99, 103, 151,
 192, 193, 258
Bertocci, P., fn. 319
Binswanger, L., 254
Blindness of love, 254–256
Bliss, 183–184
Boelen, B., fn. 99, fn. 281, fn. 289, fn.
 355
Bohr, N., 78
Boredom, 31
Brunner, A., fn. 99
Buber, M., 254, 257
Bugbee, H., 157, 159
Bullough, E., 132, 133, 134, 187
Buytendijk, F., 18

Camus, A., 31–32
Causality, 6–7
Certainty, 63–64, 215–216
Charlesworth, M., fn. 230
Chesterton, G., 30, fn. 330
Circularity:
 of beginning of philosophy, 56–57
 of fundamental vs. straight thinking,
 25–26, 85–86, 94
Clarity:
 two kinds of, 99–100
Comic, 131
Common ground, 67–69
Conscience: 216–219, 259–260
 and *logos,* 217
 as creative, 218
 authoritative, 219
 definition, 216–217
 inadequate interpretations, 216–217
 no special faculty, 218
Consistency,
 and philosophical truth, 105
 ethical, 229–230
Creativity:

misconceptions, 59–61
 of existential thinking, 58–59
Cusa, N. of, fn. 31

D'Arcy, M.C., fn. 364, fn. 367, fn. 368,
 fn. 384
Datum:
 empirical, experimental and
 experiential, 89
 and original perception, 136
 see also Primary data,
Decision, 214–215
Decisiveness:
 as certainty, 63
 as criterion, 63
 as critical moment, 62, 179–180
 as existential decision, 62
 etymology, 62
 of the actual beginning, 62–64
De Bruyne, E., fn. 274
Deduction:
 and existential thinking, 85–88
 in logical thinking, 86
Definition:
 logical and ontological, 100–103
Depth, 91, 99–100, 186–188
Descartes, R., 172
De Vleeschauwer, H., fn. 170
De Waelhens, A., fn. 99
Dialectics:
 and existential discourse, 93
 and existential thinking, 92–95
 logical vs. ontological, 93–94
Distance,
 physical and phenomenological, 91
 psychical, 131
 see also Aesthetic distance,
Dondeyne, A., fn. 9, 18, fn. 21, fn. 55,
 61, 62, fn. 98, fn. 101
Dostoevsky, F., fn. 191
Dream-like consciousness, 160–161
Dufrenne, M., 123, fn. 174

Eastman, M., fn. 228
Ecstasy, 162
Edison, T., 157
Einstein, A., 78, 82
Enthusiasm: 42, 163